Volume 32   Number 2&3   2001

# Discourse Processes

A MULTIDISCIPLINARY JOURNAL

**Special Issue:
Argumentation in Psychology
Guest Editor:
James F. Voss**

## Contents

**Editor's Introduction**
Argumentation in Psychology: Background Comments . . . . . . . . . . . . . 89
  *James F. Voss and Julie A. Van Dyke*

The Origins and Nature of Arguments: Studies in
Conflict Understanding, Emotion, and Negotiation. . . . . . . . . . . . . . . 113
  *Nancy L. Stein and Elizabeth R. Albro*

The Development of Argumentive Discourse Style. . . . . . . . . . . . . . . . 135
  *Mark Felton and Deanna Kuhn*

Influence of Oral Discussion on Written Argument. . . . . . . . . . . . . . . 155
  *Alina Reznitskaya, Richard C. Anderson, Brian McNurlen, Kim Nguyen-Jahiel, Anthi Archodidou, and So-young Kim*

Changing Stances on Abortion During Case-Based Reasoning Tasks:
Who Changes and Under What Conditions . . . . . . . . . . . . . . . . . . . . 177
  *Ronan S. Bernas and Nancy L. Stein*

Science on the Web: Student Evaluations of Scientific Arguments . . . . . . . 191
  *Sarah K. Brem, Janet Russell, and Lisa Weems*

Narrative Structure, Information Certainty, Emotional Content, and
Gender as Factors in a Pseudo Jury Decision-Making Task . . . . . . . . . . 215
  *James F. Voss and Julie A. Van Dyke*

Acknowledgment of Reviewers for Volumes 31 and 32 . . . . . . . . . . . . . 245

# INTRODUCTION

# Argumentation in Psychology: Background Comments

### James F. Voss and Julie A. Van Dyke
*Learning Research and Development Center*
*University of Pittsburgh*

Argumentation constitutes 1 of the most common forms of human interaction. Yet despite its pervasiveness, relatively little psychological research has been conducted on the topic. This article serves as an introduction to this research and has 2 goals. One is to discuss a number of general issues relevant to the study of argumentation, including the definition, goals and functions, structure, evaluation of arguments and argumentation, and the relation of narrativity and argumentation. The 2nd goal is to describe some examples of the existing psychological research on argumentation, with emphasis on articles in this special issue. Topics include argumentation by children, argumentation skill, writing argumentative text, argumentation and case-based change, argumentation and critical thinking, and argumentation and narrativity in a legal context.

Argumentation constitutes one of the most common forms of human interaction. Yet despite its pervasiveness, relatively little psychological research has been conducted on the topic. This special issue of *Discourse Processes* addresses the topic of argumentation, with a number of articles illustrating how individuals employ argumentation in various contexts. This article serves as an introduction to these contributions and has two goals. One is to discuss a number of general issues relevant to the study of argumentation, and the other is to describe some examples of psychological research on argumentation, with emphasis on articles in this special issue.

---

Correspondence and requests for reprints should be sent to James F. Voss, 634 LRDC, University of Pittsburgh, 3939 O'Hara Street, Pittsburgh, PA 15260. E-mail: voss@pitt.edu

## ISSUES OF ARGUMENTATION

### What Is Argumentation?

Corbett (1986), in discussing the history of argumentation, noted that the nature of argumentation has been essentially constant over the centuries. Person A states an assertion and if it is not self-evident, he or she may provide support for it. Or, Person B may ask Person A to support it. After A provides the support, B may challenge A's argument by questioning the accuracy or acceptability of the support or by questioning whether the stated support really is supportive. Person B also may offer a counterargument and Person A may try to refute it. Other exchanges may occur that lead to an impasse or to a partial or full resolution, such as a compromise or a win-loss outcome. Scenarios similar to this occur in many situations, such as children arguing over a toy, family disagreements, political conflicts, classroom encounters, debates, board rooms, courtrooms, committee meetings, and controversies in professional literature. Indeed, the ubiquity of argumentation suggests that we are dealing with a type of discourse that not only permeates human thinking, but is fundamental to it.

The preceding account provides a definition of argumentation by example. More formal definitions have, of course, been stated. In one volume on argumentation theory, van Eemeren, Grootendorst, and Snoeck Henkemans (1996) presented the following: "Argumentation is a verbal and social activity of reason aimed at increasing (or decreasing) the acceptability of a controversial standpoint for the listener or reader, by putting forward a constellation of propositions intended to justify (or refute) the standpoint before a 'rational judge' " (p. 5). This definition has the problem of explicating the nature of a "rational judge."

From a somewhat different perspective, Zarefsky (1995) stated that a root concept for argumentation is "the practice of justifying decisions under conditions of uncertainty" (p. 43). He described this practice as a social activity, and used the term *justifying* as a contrast to *proving*, which cannot be done in argumentation. He also described making decisions as including consideration of choices and taking a position. Moreover, he noted that the decisions occur under conditions of uncertainty. This position may be contrasted with that of van Eemeren et al. (1996), who placed argumentation in the context of rationality and even possibly certainty.

Yet another definition, stated as a goal, is found in Perelman and Olbrechts-Tyteca (1958/1969): "The aim of argumentation is not to deduce consequences from given premises; it is rather to elicit or increase the adherence of the members of an audience to theses that are presented for their consent" (p. 9).

Thus, it appears that the question of what defines argumentation can be answered in multiple ways, depending on what the goals of the practice of argumentation are perceived to be. For some, its function is primarily one of social interaction aimed at conflict expression, possible resolution, and building consensus. For others the goal has an orientation emphasizing rationality and is aimed at justification and rebuttal of controversial positions. This multiplicity of definition has generated a rich body of scholarship, bridging the disciplines of philosophy, communication, literature, and psychology.

## The Goals and Functions of Argumentation

Historically, argumentation is at least as old as the *Iliad* and the Book of Job, and maybe as old as human interaction. The study of argumentation, however, became a serious matter of inquiry for early Greek and Roman scholars. Indeed, Corbett (1986) argued that many contemporary issues in the study of argumentation are largely restatements of the differences of Plato and Aristotle, adding that what has changed are the strategies employed. Of particular concern for our purposes are the goals of "seeking truth" in a sense of certainty and "seeking truth" under conditions of uncertainty and in social interaction as found in acts such as persuasion.

Plato, in his dialogues, provided accounts of Socrates seeking truth via the use of a dialectic procedure, reductio ad absurdum. Person A would state an assertion such as "Honesty is the best policy" and Person B then would ask Person A questions until Person A reached a contradiction of the assertion initially stated. A version of this procedure is found in today's courtrooms, in which it is assumed that truth may be obtained via questioning sworn witnesses.

Another attempt found in Plato to arrive at truth via inquiry is when Socrates, with appropriate questioning, was able to show that a slave could prove the Pythagorean theorem. However, as McCloskey (1985) pointed out, would this have been possible if Socrates had not already known the proof?

The truth and certainty that Plato was seeking generally was of an absolute nature, the ultimate reality. Later Descartes followed in the search for certainty, holding that if an assertion could not be demonstrated as true by logic or as a scientific fact (i.e., if there are doubts), it is worthless (Perelman & Olbrechts-Tyteca, 1958/1969). This tradition was a forerunner of positivism, which held that knowledge should consist of what can be logically demonstrated or what can be shown to be true in the context of general laws (see Govier, 1987). Probably the most ambitious attempt to develop this position in traditionally nonscientific domains was Hempel's (1942) Covering Law, which had as its objective bringing historical knowledge into the positivistic tradition.

The tradition of seeking certainty has been influential in the psychological study of reasoning. Aristotle developed the categorical syllogism, which provided certainty in the performance of logic-based tasks. Other logics have been developed, and over the last three quarters of the 20th century, the psychological study of reasoning primarily employed logic-based tasks. Such tasks are experimentally more tractable than tasks having uncertainty, and performance is relatively easy to evaluate in that it is logical or not logical; that is, the person either did or did not follow the rules of that logic. Use of such tasks has led to a number of important experimental and theoretical findings (e.g., Johnson-Laird, 1983). At the same time, deductivism and the use of logic-based tasks have been regarded as the "true" exemplars of the study of reasoning, and "good reasoners" or "rational thinkers" are those who can perform logic tasks according to logical rules. This viewpoint has been held even though the elements of such tasks are not found extensively outside the laboratory in which everyday and domain-related tasks are predominantly those involving uncertainty.

As an example of the concern of deduction, Anderson, Chinn, Chang, Waggoner, and Yi (1997) conducted a study with fourth-grade children that was aimed at determining whether students could verbalize the logical steps in solving a mathematics problem. The results indicated that there were large gaps in their reasoning process during which the students did not verbalize the steps. The authors noted that the unstated steps were often explicit in the textbook, however, so that the students apparently knew the steps even though they were not verbalized. It appears that these students applied deductively sound methods, a result that affords a certain amount of comfort.

The concern of argumentation is not with certain truth but with the probable truth that may be determined in the presence of uncertainty and with the social interaction that argumentation engenders. One goal of argumentation, considered with the seeking of truth under uncertainty, is that of justification. This concept is basic in argumentation because it indicates as a social norm that one person may ask another to provide some evidence for a particular assertion. That person is expected to answer, although he or she may not. In addition to justifying an assertion, argumentation also involves the undermining of the opponents' arguments, which can be viewed as the "flip side" of justification.

When a person engages in argumentation, the arguer has a commitment as well as a risk (Brockriede, 1986). The commitment is that the person felt the issue was of sufficient importance to enter the interaction; the risk is that an individual, by stating the argument, is setting it forth for examination and possible attack and even possible change of position. An interesting corollary of this idea is that if you are really sure of a belief or sure of something you want to do and you do not want it questioned, do not state any reason to support your assertion.

The second function of argumentation is pragmatic. This function refers to the goal or goals the arguer wants to achieve using argumentation. Primary among these is persuasion, which was discussed by Aristotle in his *Rhetoric* (trans. 1960). He identified three means of persuasion: appeal to the speaker's or writer's character (ethos), appeal to the emotions of the audience (pathos), and appeal to reason (logos). The offering of an argument then is a matter of logos, whereas persuasion is a matter of all three. Aristotle also provided extensive instruction on persuasion, discussing it in three contexts: courts (Greeks had to defend themselves), public forums, and special celebratory events. (See Pericles's funeral oration in Thucydides's History of the Peloponnesian War, trans. 1954, for a classic example of political rhetoric.) Aristotle also considered types of arguments to use, or *topoi*, and different types of reasons.

In recent times, the field of rhetoric has enjoyed and suffered changes in emphasis and status. At the time of the founding of the United States, rhetoric was an important academic topic. Debate became a major college activity that found students cheering for their school's teams. Subsequently, rhetoric lost status as an independent endeavor and was subsumed in other departments such as English or communication studies. Moreover, in the mid-20th century, rhetoric was regarded by many to emphasize expressiveness in language but not substance. "It is just rhetoric" was the perception. However, due in part to the publication of two books, Toulmin's (1958) *The Uses of Argument* and Perelman and Olbrechts-Tyteca's (1958/1969) *The New Rhetoric*, the field of rhetoric has enjoyed a resurgence. Each of these works argued for a jurisprudence model of argumentation rather than the traditional deductive-oriented model.

One aspect of this renewal has been the analysis of argumentation as found in a wide variety of subject matter domains, as for example, the rhetoric of science (Gross, 1990). Some of the rhetorical analyses also have occurred in a postmodern context that has been related to gender, race, and culture. Emphasized by some authors, such as Foucault (1969/1972), is the idea that people in power control the rhetoric being employed and therefore subordinate the rhetoric of minorities not in political control. Indeed, since ancient times, individuals ascending into power frequently have destroyed the symbols and writings of those removed from power. An interesting comment about the popularity of rhetoric is this:

> One fact that emerges from a study of the history of rhetoric is that there usually is a resurgence of rhetoric during periods of violent social upheaval. Whenever the older order is passing away and the new order is marching—or stumbling—in, a loud clear call goes up for the services of a man skilled with words. (Corbett, 1971, p. 32)

Argumentation is basic to rhetorical discourse and analysis. Indeed, rhetorical analysis in part consists of determining the "moves" made in argument development, what such moves were designed to accomplish, and what consequences they produced. Such analysis has the problem that alternative interpretations of the same material may be of equivalent acceptability. Furthermore, with few exceptions, rhetorical analysis has not been experimental, and this lack of a more psychological-like experimental–theoretical approach probably is one reason studies in rhetorical analysis have had little impact on psychological study. Moreover, the psychological research involving argumentation in a rhetorical context has occurred primarily in social psychology's study of persuasion or attitude change (Chaiken, 1980; Petty & Cacioppo, 1986), with relatively little study of rhetorical factors per se.

The goal of persuasion is found in different contexts. Speakers or writers attempt to persuade an audience, in which case it is important for the speaker or writer and the audience to have the same premises (Perelman & Olbrechts-Tyteca, 1958/1969; Tindale, 1992). Also, conflict situations involve attempts at persuasion, which becomes part of negotiation and conflict resolution. Stein and Bernas (1999) considered three outcomes—win–loss, compromise, and standoff—and emphasized the social interactions and goals of the participants. In one conflict resolution study, Allen and Burrell (1990) had college students, given premises of syllogisms, resolve disagreements regarding the syllogisms' conclusions. Arguing the merits of the case was the most frequent negotiation, but it yielded a relatively low percentage of correct responses. Looking at past precedents was the second most frequent negotiation, and it had a higher percentage of correct responses than arguing the case's merits. That the debate model of negotiation (i.e., defending and rebutting) is not effective in negotiation has been reported by Axelrod (1977). Three high-level political negotiations were studied, and it was concluded that the debate model did not hold. Instead, agreement evolved through a process of expressing new ideas that emerge from previous discussions, or are made from "outside"; that is, they do not follow directly from the debate.

The goal of argument justification is related to the pragmatic goal in the following way: Justification of an argument implicitly carries with it the idea that the argument is persuasive. In Perelman and Olbrechts-Tyteca's (1958/1969) terms, there is a universal audience that, although not a particular audience, does provide a sense that the argument is being justified as a social process. The relation of the pragmatic goal to the justification goal is that the argument to persuade may be adequately justified, but the goal of persuasion also may involve poorer justification. Just as the Sophists and some of today's advertisers and politicians, the persuading party may be trying to make weak reasons appear strong.

## The Structure of an Argument

The basic structure of an argument that is not an explicit deductive argument is, as termed by Aristotle, an *enthymeme*. This form of an argument consists of a claim supported by a reason (or conclusion supported by a premise). Support, of course, may consist of more than one supporting reason. Aristotle felt that the enthymeme was deductive in nature, essentially a syllogism with a premise missing. Although this has been a common interpretation of the enthymeme, Gerritsen (1999), in reviewing conceptual interpretations of the enthymeme, noted a pragmatic function, and this is of importance for present purposes. Also, rather than thinking of the enthymeme as a syllogism with a missing premise, Hitchcock (1995) argued that the enthymeme provides a self-contained argument. What is important about this interpretation is that the two-component argument is not sound deductively as it stands and the pragmatic function is regarded as primary to the logical function.

The pragmatic interpretation of the enthymeme brings up an important point, namely, the issue of the missing premise. Govier (1987) noted that an enthymeme can be made logically sound with the addition of one or more premises. Given this point, the logical validity of an enthymeme is essentially a given. It is instead its pragmatic function that is of importance to argumentation. "Abortion should be made illegal because it is the taking of a life" is an argument as it stands, and can be used as support or can be attacked.

Toulmin's model of argument structure is widely cited (Toulmin, 1958; Toulmin, Rieke, & Janik, 1979). The model consists of six components. The datum (D) or grounds and claim (C) constitute the basic argument. The datum and claim are connected by a warrant (W), which has the general form "If D, then C," and legitimizes the relation of D and C. Moreover, as Toulmin (1958) noted, the datum and claim are explicit, whereas warrants are usually implicit. So, for the argument "Capital punishment should be abolished because it constitutes cruel and inhuman treatment," "Capital punishment should be abolished" is the claim and "It (capital punishment) is cruel and inhuman treatment" is the datum. The warrant is "Punishment using cruel and inhuman treatment must be abolished," or "If cruel and inhuman treatment is used as punishment, it should be abolished." The argument typically is understood without statement of the warrant.

The three remaining components of the Toulmin model are backing, qualifier, and rebuttal. Backing provides support for the warrant. Thus, for the current example, the statement "Cruel and inhuman punishment is prohibited by the Constitution" would serve as backing. A qualifier, according to Toulmin, supplies any qualification in the statement of the strength of the warrant, as for this argument being "quite likely." Rebuttal offers the limitations of the argument, as "These are the conditions when the argument does not hold. . . ."

Toulmin's model has been targeted for a number of criticisms. One is that it pertains to only a single argument. However, Voss, Tyler, and Yengo (1983), by making three assumptions, generalized the Toulmin model to larger bodies of argument. The three assumptions were that a claim could be used as datum for another claim, backing could be an argument, and qualifiers and rebuttals could also be arguments. Although these additions provided for a more effective use of the model for larger bodies of argumentative text, the model did not capture the higher level problem-solving nature of the discourse.

A second criticism of the Toulmin model is that when attempting to analyze bigger bodies of text, it is sometimes difficult to classify particular components in terms of the Toulmin categories, as for example, distinguishing backing from datum or qualifier and rebuttal (see Stein & Albro, this issue). A third criticism (Perelman, 1984) is that Toulmin neglected the role of the audience; his model is one of structure and not of pragmatics.

## The Evaluation of Arguments

Nondeductive arguments classically have been evaluated in relation to two components, the acceptance of the support *qua* support, and the extent to which the support actually does provide support for the claim, sometimes termed *relevance*. Consider the previously stated argument, "Capital punishment should be abolished because it constitutes cruel and inhuman punishment." Evaluation on the basis of the acceptability of the supporting reason requires the evaluator to consider if capital punishment is cruel and inhuman. If the person does not agree with that statement, it is unlikely that the person thinks the statement provides good support for the claim. If the evaluator agrees with the statement, then the evaluator needs to judge whether that statement supports the claim that "capital punishment should be abolished."

A third criterion for argument evaluation is the taking into account of counterarguments (Angell, 1964). The assumption is that the strength of an argument is not independent of counterarguments and that, for example, an argument, although regarded as strong when standing alone, may be judged as less strong when a counterargument is offered. If the evaluation includes a counterargument, it suggests there is some type of argument integration function of the initial argument and the counterargument.

These evaluative criteria refer to judgments of the quality of the argument, but there is also another type of criterion, namely, effectiveness. If, for example, you are using an argument for persuasion, the effectiveness of the argument refers to whether it succeeded at the goal of persuasion. The suggestion of considering effectiveness in evaluation raises the concern that argument evaluation may vary across context (Santos & Santos, 1999; Tindale, 1992). One particularly important context is the audience. Consider the example of the same speech favoring gun control being given to a meeting of the National Rifle Association and to a meeting of parents who have lost children in drive-by shootings. Furthermore, consider the importance of the speaker and the audience being in agreement about the premises of the argument.

Context can also refer to different subject matter domains (e.g., Toulmin, 1992). It appears that although the general form of argumentation is highly similar across domains, what constitutes acceptable support varies considerably. Toulmin argued that sound arguments do not require deductive validity, and that the criteria for soundness varies from field to field, including subject matter disciplines and everyday contexts. In the context of his model, it is the nature of the warrants and backing acceptable within any domain that are able to produce soundness (cf. van Eemeren et al., 1996).

An important point about the evaluation of arguments is that although in many cases a premise may be evaluated on the basis of its truth value (e.g., Madison is the capitol of Wisconsin), it also may have a variable level of plausibility or acceptability. For example, consider the argument "There should be a tax cut because people need money." This argument may provoke a reaction such as "What people?" or "It seems some do and some do not." So, on a 1 (*low*) to 10 (*high*) acceptability scale, how would you rate the acceptability of that supportive statement and how would you rate the strength of the argument?

The inherent uncertainty of nondeductive evaluations, the lack of normative criteria, and the importance of the evaluator to the evaluation has led to a number of attempts to provide more certainty in evaluation, perhaps to establish a criterion for "good reasons." For example, the van Eemeren et al. (1996) definition mentioned earlier tried to provide some sense of certainty by hypothesizing a rational judge. Select groups of individuals also have been considered as candidates for evaluation. Perhaps experts in a given subject matter domain could provide some sense of certainty. Of course, experts in a given domain may and frequently do disagree, and when they do agree there generally is little or no argument.

There also is a cultural constraint on the consensus criterion. In Salem, Massachusetts, during the days of witch persecution, church leaders may readily have been able to provide arguments justifying the killing of witches, but that does not mean at some other time or place some other culture would have agreed with those arguments. Indeed, Van Knippenberg and Wilke (1992) experimentally demonstrated the proclivity of group members to maintain in-group norms. There even appears to be a total human in-group, cited by van Eemeren et al. (1996): "With mortals, gold outweighs a thousand arguments" (Euripides's *Medea*, trans. 1966).

### Argumentation and Narrativity

In the discussion of argumentation to this point, the arguments discussed largely have been of the enthymeme form. However, argumentation can take other forms. As shown by Felton and Kuhn (this issue), people use narratives to support their claims. McGuire (1990) suggested that there are three types of narratives: history, literary, and literary that are made to appear historical. McGuire further argued that "A rhetorically successful narrative, accordingly, must either be familiar to its audience (a sociological issue) or plausible for its audience as a typical story of how things are, and clearly comparable to the problematic uncertainty that it is intended to clarify" (p. 231). He also stated, "The idea of things as they might be accounts for the persuasive value of well-constructed narrative" (p. 231). The narrative thus stands as a means of supporting a given claim, when the premises are shared by the writer and reader, as McGuire suggested. Indeed, a relatively simple example is the narrative supporting the exposure of the killer in a mystery. Justification of political positions also has been accomplished via narratives, as well as positions of defendants and plaintiffs in legal contexts (see Voss & Van Dyke, this issue).

### Concluding Background Comments

A nonexhaustive number of argumentation-related topics have been surveyed in this review. As examples of issues not covered, there is the subject of fallacies and the development of the field of informal logic, which essentially is an effort to develop a logic-like analysis of the uncertain relations found in argumentation, and different types of arguments and their components, such as causal arguments, comparison of arguments, of explanations and reasons, and argumentation in science.

It should be apparent from this first section that argument and argumentation constitute a major share of everyday, as well as political and professional discourse. As such, it raises many questions, including whether a general theory of argumentation is possible and argumentation's relation to other discourse issues, such as the relation of argument and inference (Pinto, 1995). Finally, there is the question of why argumentation is important as a psychological phenomenon.

At least five reasons may be given for the study of argumentation. First, it is found in virtually all contexts and to see how it operates in each of these contexts is a more or less descriptive goal. This work would include the nature and criteria of justification across these domains, as well as the study of its effectiveness. Second, the study of argumentation is important for education. Results generally are not especially positive about the argumentation skills of the average person. Schools and media both can contribute to its improvement. People complain about the level of political discourse, but paraphrasing Demosthenes, if you want your politicians' speeches to be of high quality, enhance the quality of the audience. A third reason to study argumentation is that it affords a way to study social, cultural, and subject domain norms. Much is yet to be learned about justification and norms and how the norms were established. A fourth reason to study argumentation is that although it is found in many contexts, its ubiquity suggests it is a basic form of discourse that should have some commonalities across domains. Finally, a fifth reason is that the study of argumentation should help in developing epistemological understanding.

## ARGUMENTATION AND PSYCHOLOGICAL RESEARCH

### Children's Argumentation

One of the questions in argumentation research receiving considerable attention is at what age children demonstrate an ability to engage in argumentation and how their argumentation skills develop. Piaget (1959) suggested that children do not engage in genuine arguments until age 7 or 8, but a number of investigators have shown argumentation to occur in children age 3 or even younger. Such studies typically have involved observing children in a preschool classroom with the argumentation consisting of a dispute between two children (e.g., Boggs, 1978; Dawe, 1934; Eisenberg & Garvey, 1981; Genishi & DiPaolo, 1982). Some investigators have attempted to classify the verbal statements made in the dispute. Considering Eisenberg and Garvey's (1981) research as an example, these investigators assumed that an argument began when one person in a dyad stated an initial opposition. Nine strategies were defined as responses to the initial opposing statement. The most frequent response was insistence, with a polite firmness second, and an alternative proposal third. However, the most successful strategy in ending the dispute was compromise, followed by conditional ("I will do X, if you will do Y.") and an alternative proposal.

A number of other findings obtained in the studies just listed include the average duration of a dispute as 23 s (Dawe, 1934); that children use both simple and more complex argument forms (Boggs, 1978; Geneshi & DiPaolo, 1982); that the most frequent source of child disputes is possession (Geneshi & DiPaolo, 1982); and that children draw on their academic knowledge, but their social knowledge is of greater importance in dispute argumentation (Geneshi & DiPaolo, 1982). Regarding gender roles, boys argue more than girls (Dawe, 1934), and, following the ideas of Gilligan (1982), boys emphasize their own goals and control of the situation, whereas girls emphasize the relationship of the participants (Sheldon, 1990).

Stein and her colleagues conducted a series of argumentation studies with children, especially emphasizing the social goals of the participants. In one example of the role of social goals, as described by Stein and Bernas (1999), two 4-year-old boys, best friends, were asked to divide one large and two small dinosaurs. After the seventh conversational turn, one boy told the other that he (the other boy) could have them because there was no way to divide them. The boy continued by indicating that the other boy was to remember that the next time they had a fight, he (the boy who did not get the dinosaurs) would win (p. 99). A solution was reached, but at a cost, due to the need to maintain the social relationship on an equal basis.

Stein and Bernas (1999) also reported studies comparing adult arguments between spouses with arguments between children, concluding that both groups used essentially the same categories of responding when asked questions about a recent quarrel. Such questions included who initiated the argument, reasons for supporting or opposing a position, what verbal interchange occurred, the source of statements, and the outcomes and repercussions. In another comparison, 4-year-old children were able, similar to adolescents and adults, to support their own claims, state problems with their opponent's position, generate support for the opponent's position, and also find some problems with their own position. Although for older children and adolescents improvement occurred because of growth in knowledge and being better able to support their own position and see more problems in the opponent's position, the better arguers, according to Stein and Bernas, are those who are able to learn more about the strengths of the opposing position and weaknesses of their own.

Stein, Bernas, and Calicchia (1997) studied the outcomes of argumentation, based largely on the goal statements of the participants. Three dyad categories were defined: same gender for each gender and opposite gender. In this case, compromise strategies were the most frequent, followed by a win–loss strategy, followed by a standoff strategy. Also, dyads of the same gender, regardless of which gender, reached a compromise more quickly than mixed-gender dyads. Other studies often have found compromise to be a less frequent outcome (Hofer & Pikowsky, 1993; Stein & Bernas, 1999).

In their contribution to this journal issue, Stein and Albro address how argumentative skill is acquired, suggesting it develops first through family relationships and experience with conflict. Stein and Albro strongly emphasize the importance of the personal and social goals in argumentation, pointing out that during a period of argumentation, individuals make decisions about whether to continue in the argumentation based on the person's idea of what influence the argument will have on future social interactions with the other person. Related to this, Stein and Albro show that the particular emotional state evoked in the argumentation can influence the recall of the argument.

## Argument Skill

The preceding studies of argumentation in children have addressed argumentation in a social context, but another experimental paradigm for studying argument skill is argument generation. This research is usually carried out with an individual being asked to examine a statement or to answer a question about a particular topic and to take a position regarding the issue. The person is then asked to justify the position by providing reasons to support it, with the person usually being asked to provide opposing reasons as well. Other argument-related questions, such as whether the person's position would be maintained under all circumstances, may also be asked.

Using this paradigm, Kuhn (1991) studied argument generation in relation to age (teens, 20s, 40s, and 60s) and educational level (college or noncollege). Participants were asked three questions: (a) What causes prisoners to return to crime after they're released?, (b) What causes children to fail in school?, and (c) What causes unemployment? Kuhn was particularly interested in the theories (or hypotheses) people provided as answers and the nature of the evidence they provided.

With respect to causal theories, participants tended to provide theories with a single cause, with multiple causes presented in parallel, or with interactive multiple causes, as, for example, failing in school because of insufficient studying and excessive television watching. More individuals stated multiple parallel causes than single causes, with multiple interactive causes stated least.

With respect to evidence, although Kuhn (1991) defined genuine evidence broadly, including covariation and correlational evidence, the preponderance of stated evidence was what Kuhn called *pseudoevidence*. Genuine evidence involved presenting information that was differentiated from the theory and supported it. The genuine evidence also was often of narrative form. Pseudoevidence, on the other hand, was characterized by the lack of separation of the causal theory and evidence. In other words, the participants did not seem to know what was theory and what was evidence. Much of the pseudoevidence also was narrative in form and, along with genuine evidence, tended to be derived from personal experience. Participants in the 20s and 40s age groups tended to provide more genuine evidence than those in the teens or 60s age groups. A more pronounced effect was that college-educated individuals exceeded noncollege-educated individuals by a substantial margin in providing more genuine evidence than pseudoevidence. In addition, about half of the participants generated counterarguments, a relatively sophisticated move, with participants in their teens and 20s generating more than people in their 40s and 60s. The more educated also generated more counterarguments and rebuttals than the less educated participants.

Kuhn (1991) noted that many individuals felt with certainty that their theory was correct, although the evidence was minimal and of a personalized nature. For example, an individual might state that he or she knows a person who was in prison and when released, that person could not find a job. This person ultimately returned to prison after a conviction, and so the individual may conclude that people return to prison because they cannot find work. As Kuhn noted, this person's epistemology is uncritical. This case may be juxtaposed against another in which the person is aware of a certain case, but also has an awareness that he or she needs to be critical and look for more possible reasons. This difference was shown by the superior performance of the college-educated participants compared to the noncollege-educated participants. Such a difference has been underscored by Kuhn (1989) in indicating that in the sixth- to the ninth-grade period, she found a growth of argument skills in children. After that, educational level made the difference, with college-educated people performing better than ninth graders, but with people without a college education performing at a level between sixth and ninth graders (Kuhn, 1989).

Kuhn (2001) also investigated tasks in which a person is given a claim with two supporting statements, asking which is the better justification for the claim. With children 4 to 6 years old, pictures were given of a race with a cue for who won (boy holding trophy) and a cue for possible reason (shoe type). When asked who won the race, the children responded that the boy with the trophy won. When asked how they knew, however, they responded in an explanation-based manner, referring to the shoes (why he won) rather than the trophy (how you know he won). The 6-year-old children distinguished the difference more readily than 4-year-olds, who tended to merge the two justifications. Another similar study demonstrated that the development of the ability to distinguish explanation and evidence continues to improve through adolescence and college ages, with the level of beginning graduate students performing the best at these tasks. Brem and Rips (2000) pointed out how lack of available evidence may act to produce more explanation-based responses.

Kuhn (2001) argued that results such as these point to the importance of the development of epistemological distinctions, further noting that the metalevel of knowing how you know is quite important. Furthermore, the relatively low percentage of appropriate responses suggests that even at the level of beginning graduate students, performance shows that distinctions were not readily made. Kuhn suggested a three-stage development of epistemological understanding: absolutist, in which knowledge consists of facts; multiplist or relativist, in which knowledge is regarded as opinion; and evaluativist, in which claims and support are acknowledged.

Also asking questions to study argumentation, Means and Voss (1996) studied argument generation by children. In one experiment they asked children in Grades 5, 7, 9, and 11 questions such as, "What would you do if you saw your house was on fire?" In the second study, conducted with children in Grades 8, 10, and 12, students were asked questions about drug effects and drug use. Drug knowledge tests were also given. The factors under study were general mental ability as defined by Weschler questions, grade (age), and additionally in the second study, knowledge of drugs. The students provided oral protocols that were scored for argument measures such as number of reasons, qualifiers, counterarguments, and type of argument structure generated.

Argument use increased over low-, middle-, and high-ability students, and students with high drug knowledge performed better than children with low knowledge at each grade level for the high-ability students. Medium-ability-level students performed at about the same level across Grades 8 and 10 and a little higher at Grade 12, but knowledge within grade level did not produce differences. The students with the lowest mental ability yielded the lowest argument use, which was consistent over grade level. Knowledge also was not effective. That such lack of improvement could continue into adulthood for such students is suggested by findings of Voss, Blais, Means, Greene, and Ahwesh (1986). In addition, in the first study, 5th-grade high-ability students performed better than Grade 12 medium- and low-ability students. (The term *mental ability* is used here in strict operational terms as performance on the test employed.)

The research of Kuhn (1991) and Means and Voss (1996) suggested that argumentative skills as assessed by argument generation about particular topics and social issues became reasonably well developed for students with high mental ability and those who have a college education, two likely overlapping factors. Furthermore, these two factors likely facilitate both general and specific knowledge development. Nevertheless, the studies also found poorer performance in argument generation for many participants—a result also obtained by other investigators (Marttunen, 1994; Perkins, 1985; Perkins, Allen, & Hafner, 1983).

At first glance, the finding of relatively poor performance in argument generation for many individuals appears to be in conflict with the research reported in Stein and Bernas (1999), in that the latter found that children at young ages performed well, and the performance was similar for adolescents and adults in the types of arguments stated. This apparent disagreement can be resolved by noting the roles of two factors, the tasks and two types of knowledge, of subject matter and of argument-related verbal structures or schema. Young children have experience in conflict situations, and they become personally engaged in them. They have encountered peer and parent–child interpersonal conflict. When they enter into argumentation, their knowledge and experience in social relationships is activated with their related argument structures, even though in many cases the children probably could not verbalize the nature of such structures. However, what would happen if such a child were asked as an individual why people return to prison? The peer social interaction would be irrelevant, and the child might say because they committed a crime, or perhaps state some factor, but there would likely be less topic knowledge and experience available to the 3- or 4-year-old than to an adolescent or adult. Whether or not a person is able to perform reasonably in an argumentative situation depends on context, which includes the argument's contents.

Another comparison, however, is that of Kuhn's (2001) previously described results showing that some children as young as 4 to 6 years of age can distinguish evidence and explanation, with performance on such tasks increasing over age. As mentioned, the improved discrimination is attributed to metaknowing in epistemological development that provides for a change from an absolutist to an evaluativist. In contrast, the position of Stein and colleagues (e.g., Stein & Albro, this issue) is that the high similarity of performance categories over age in the social dispute situations does not require the operation of metalevel developmental change, but needs only differences in knowledge and perhaps schema-related activation over age. Stein's developmental position is based on relatively straightforward dispute situations in which social interaction is emphasized; the Kuhn research is based on individuals being able to make relatively difficult distinctions about the nature of support.

In the third article in this issue, Felton and Kuhn address the topic of strategy use in argumentation in adolescents and adults attending a community college. They report that adults were more aggressive in their development of counterarguments and rebuttals; were more likely to use strategies including event sequences that were designed to "set up" the opponent for a counterargument; and were more flexible at modifying their arguments, depending on whether the opponent's statement was supportive or oppositional. The teenagers seemed more intent on being sure the statements they made were argumentative. The findings thus support the idea of greater sophistication in argumentation for the older, college-attending participants.

## Writing Argumentative Discourse

Children are able to engage in argumentation at 3 years of age; but writing argumentative discourse is a more difficult task. Studies on the age at which children are able to write an acceptable argumentative text have produced conflicting results (see Piolat, Roussey, & Gombert, 1999, for a discussion of this issue). It appears that student familiarity and knowledge of the topic, as well as involvement, produce better argumentative texts (e.g., Golder, 1993). In one of a number of studies by Golder, Coirier, or both authors, two processes were delineated, one being the ability to state arguments that, the authors pointed out, may be done by young children. The second process is termed *negotiation*, which to Golder and Coirier (1994) essentially meant taking the audience into account. This process not only requires the use of writing skills, but includes the use of appropriate argumentative and rhetorical techniques. They noted that more sophisticated writers of arguments need to find common ground with their perceived audience, or as Perelman and Olbrechts-Tyteca (1958/1969) noted, the speaker's or writer's premises need to be the audience's for the speaker or writer to persuade the audience.

Golder and Coirier (1994) studied children ages 10 to 16 years of age in an argument-writing task that began with a 10-min classroom debate on pollution. Instructions to write a 15-line argumentative essay followed, in which the writer was to take and defend a position and acknowledge other positions. Golden and Coirier employed four markers of negotiation: the use of counterarguments; the use of moral or value judgment and obligation, as "one should not" or "that's good"; an expression of degrees of certainty as "surely" or "maybe"; and the speaker endorsement and accountability, as "I believe that." From ages 10 to 16, the percentage of children using each of the four measures increased. Counterargument use showed an especially substantial gain over ages 10 and 11 to 13 and 14, staying approximately at the same use for ages 15 and 16. Also, with increasing age, understanding of the relations of the components of the argument increased. Golder and Coirier also reported substantial individual differences in performance at each age level, which they attributed to knowledge differences and student differences in instruction.

Whereas Golder and Coirier (1994) used discussion of a controversial topic to furnish information for argumentative text writing, Reznitskaya et al. (this issue) report the results of a study with fourth and fifth graders in which they attempt to improve the quality of the student writing of argumentative text via a classroom discussion procedure termed *collaborative reasoning*. Studying and analyzing classroom conversation has become more frequent, due primarily to the Vygotskian view concerning the importance of social interaction to learning. An especially analytic study of argumentation in a classroom was carried out by Pontecorvo and Girardet (1993). Fourth-grade children, meeting in groups of five, discussed whether they agreed with a statement made by a 4th-century A.D. Italian historian. The discussion protocols were analyzed at three levels: frames, which were the broader topics of the discussion; discussion sequences, which occur within the frames; and idea units, which were expressed as a unit of argumentation and as an element in the historical discussion. Idea units were largely claims and justifications. To support their claims, children appealed to a number of different types of support: analogy, example cases, conditions, rules or principles, motives or goals, consequences, authority, times, sociocultural context, and spatial or temporal context.

The collaborative reasoning format of Reznitskaya et al. was designed not only to enhance angumentation in the classroom, but to instruct the students so that they could be tested on the goal of the study, namely, to teach argumentation so that it could be generalized to a new situation. The primary assumption of the procedure is that reasoning and argumentative skill develop via personal interaction. Reznitskaya et al. hypothesize that experience in collaborative reasoning for a 5-week period would lead to better argumentative essay writing compared with writings by students in a classroom that did not receive such experience. Golder and Coirier (1994) found discussion effective in a group situation, and other studies found that a dyad discussion of an issue involving argumentation produced improvement in writing an essay (e.g., Kuhn, Shaw, & Felton, 1997).

The collaborative reasoning condition allowed students to discuss without raising their hands, and the teacher acted to probe and to model argumentative moves for the students. Reznitskaya et al. note that this procedure is aimed specifically at using the skills of argumentation, as opposed to less focused classroom discussion or a focus emphasizing another issue.

Students experiencing the collaborative procedure produced essays that contained more arguments, counterarguments, rebuttals, and other argumentative components than did the essays of the control condition students. Collaborative reasoning, therefore, not only produced more argumentation-related comments in the classroom than found in a control classroom, it also transferred to the writing of a persuasive essay about a new topic.

## Argumentation and Case-Based Change

Bernas and Stein (this issue) are concerned with how being exposed to specific cases about a controversial topic may change a person's position regarding that topic. The procedure used consisted of determining people's position and the strength of their attitude toward abortion and subsequently presenting specific cases that agreed or disagreed with the person's viewpoint. The question then is how the position changed.

There are at least two bodies of literature that are related to this issue—one being simply what type of performance is obtained when you ask individuals to generate reasons supporting and opposing your position. In one study, Zammuner (1987) measured the attitudes of different women toward abortion, asking them to write essays that were either favorable on unfavorable to the topic. The study was conducted in Italy, which has cultural norms opposing abortion. The data supported the idea that women advocating a prochoice position had to be more careful and thorough in writing their argumentative essay than anti-abortion women because prochoice women were starting from a different cultural baseline than the women with anti-abortion positions. Thus, the beliefs and values of the women in the Zammuner study may readily have been a factor.

The possible role of values in argument was addressed by Perelman and Olbrechts-Tyteca (1958/1969). As previously mentioned, there is a need for a speaker or writer to have the same premises as the audience if the speaker or writer wants the audience to agree. However, Perelman and Olbrechts-Tyteca also delineated two classes of premises, one being the real, consisting of facts, truths, and presumptions about which there is usually assumed to be consensus. The other is the preferable, including premises consisting of values and value hierarchies. With value-related premises, it is the sharing of values and their hierarchies that provides the speaker with the opportunity to have a conclusion accepted, provided the audience has the same values. Moreover, the idea that values are likely activated in the course of considering a controversial argument that does not explicitly state a value was supported by the results of Voss, Fincher-Kiefer, Wiley, and Silfies (1993).

Within the Perelman and Olbrechts-Tyteca (1958/1969) theory, the audience may disagree with a speaker about the premises when the audience wants the speaker to provide more evidence about the truth of a premise. The audience also may disagree if the speaker assumes a value hierarchy dissimilar to that held by the audience, or when the speaker considers premises that the audience does not consider relevant. Similarly, an audience may adopt a changed position if the speaker provides new information that modifies the audience's premises, if the speaker is able to show why a change in the value hierarchy of the audience is important, and if the speaker shows something to be relevant that the audience had previously considered irrelevant. In the Bernas and Stein article, it appears that premises were changed with novel cases (new information), especially when the premises were not strongly held.

Returning to the question of what happens when a person is asked to generate arguments for and against his or her own position, typically more reasons are stated supporting your own side (Perkins et al., 1983; Stein & Bernas, 1999), individuals usually state relatively few reasons—three or four—even though they in all likelihood know of more (Hoch, 1984), and in unpublished results we have found that what reasons are regarded as strong or weak are generally agreed on by people on each side. The difference is in weighting, with "my side" strong reasons receiving a higher rating than the other side's strong reasons. Similarly, "my side" weak arguments are rated low, but the other side's are rated lower.

A second body of literature that the Bernas and Stein article in this issue is related to is attitude change. The reader is referred to Eagly and Chaiken (1993) for a discussion of this work. From the communication side, Arnold (1986) wrote a paper relating rhetoric to social-psychological theory.

### Argumentation and Critical Thinking

For some time, argumentation has been linked to critical thinking (Ennis, 1962; Nickerson, Perkins, & Smith, 1985). Kuhn (1993) endeavored to show how informal reasoning is much like scientific reasoning, both making up critical thinking. However, although argumentation skills are related to and part of critical thinking, they are not the same thing. To examine this issue, we delineate between argument generation and argument evaluation. In the former, as pointed out by Govier (1989), the statement of an argument most frequently is the product of reasoning and critical thinking. Moreover, much of the reasoning that occurred in the development of the argument is likely not to be stated in the argument. There is not much information available on the thinking that goes into argument development, but one of the most intensive protocol studies on the issue was conducted by Stratman (1994).

Stratman (1994) was concerned with the mental representation an attorney had of a case when the attorney was working on that case to take to an appellate court. Stratman also was interested in comparing the attorney's representation to that of the appellate court clerk who read the brief written by the attorney. Thus, the work serves as an example of how protocol studies may be used to develop an idea of the thinking that goes into the development and criticism of arguments.

Stratman (1994) was especially interested in which of two strategies of argument presentation may be employed: an *adversarial strategy*, in which an attorney presented only his or her own side of an argument, and a *scholarly strategy*, in which the attorney presented both sides of an argument. In the latter, concessions usually were made on specific points, there were explicit statements of rebuttals, insinuations were avoided, and there were citations to adverse precedents. The adversarial strategy was the opposite in these characteristics. The adversarial strategy attempted to present one side of the argument, whereas the scholarly strategy endeavored to show a sense of fairness.

Analyses indicated that attorneys presenting their case to the appellate court usually used the adversarial strategy, perhaps because of time limitations to prepare, or to encourage the other side to use the scholarly strategy, which may be more easily attacked. The clerks who read the briefs tended to analyze them in terms of a scholarly strategy. The protocols revealed thoughts of the attorneys thinking about, for example, narrowing down what to present, as well as thoughts of the clerks when, for example, they thought of an opposing citation that an adversarial attorney should have cited.

Argument evaluation is important to critical thinking, the primary reason being that an individual, when presented with a text or speech, should be able to state the argument (i.e., the claim and the support) as well as any other argument characteristics of the discourse. To go beyond simply describing the argument, the evaluator needs to have sufficient knowledge of the argument's subject matter to make appropriate judgments.

The use of computers for initiation and evaluation of argumentation has raised questions about how they may or may not facilitate argumentation skills. Marttunen (1992), for example, found online interaction facilitated learning argumentation skills, but traditional interaction yielded better subject matter learning. Brem, Russell, and Weems (this issue) consider the view of evaluation when the student is faced with analyzing scientific information found on a Web site. As the authors note, relatively poor evaluations may result because of a student's failure to analyze sufficiently.

### Argumentation and Narrativity in the Legal Context

One way in which argumentation and narrativity are related, as previously noted, is when the narrative is used to support a claim. These two components have been brought together in a series of studies by Pennington and Hastie (e.g., Pennington & Hastie, 1993) involving jury decision making. These authors found that jurors frequently construct a narrative of the events of a crime, as they are able to determine from the witnesses, documents, and their own experiences. At the conclusion of the courtroom hearing, the judge typically charges the jury, defining the verdicts the jury may consider. Among their findings, Pennington and Hastie (1993) found that the type of narrative generated is related to the verdict that is selected.

Schum (1993) argued that although temporally related narrative arguments are found in jury decision making, juries also represent a case in a relational or hierarchical manner, much like the solving of an ill-structured problem. The narrative and the relational representations appear to be inconsistent with each other, but a study in which people were asked to indicate why the Soviet Union collapsed revealed that a number of participants wrote a narrative protocol, but within the narrative were expository-like statements that described or elaborated on people or events of the narrative (Voss, Carretero, Kennet, & Silfies, 1994).

In the final article in this issue, Voss and Van Dyke also are concerned with the use of narrative discourse in a legal setting, but the discourse involved is a hypothetical summary statement by a prosecuting attorney. Three experiments are reported in which individual "jurors" are asked to judge the accused on a guilt–innocence scale and also to rate the goodness of the prosecuting attorney's narrative. Such judgments were made in relation to the discourse coherence and evidence quality in one experiment, and in relation to information certainty or the lack thereof and the presence or absence in the prosecutor's summary of emotional statements. In addition, gender was orthogonal to the other variables in all experiments. The general finding across all three studies is that narrative characteristics of the prosecuting attorney's summary can influence the juror's decisions.

### CONCLUDING COMMENTS

Should I or should I not read the articles in this issue of *Discourse Processes*? These suggestions support a positive answer: They appear to be interesting. I would like to learn about at least some of this work on argumentation. It seems to be an old yet developing field. On the other hand, here are some suggestions in support of a negative answer: I am really busy. I may have other things to read with higher priority. The work is not directly related to my research. Although these reasons may evoke uncertainty in the reader, and although the articles will not provide any absolute truth or certainty, they do provide justified claims and persuasive arguments.

## REFERENCES

Allen, M., & Burrell, N. A. (1990). Resolving arguments accurately. *Argumentation, 4,* 213–221.
Anderson, R. C., Chinn, C., Chang, J., Waggoner, M., & Yi, H. (1997). On the logical integrity of children's arguments. *Cognition and Instruction, 15,* 135–167.
Angell, R. B. (1964). *Reasoning and logic.* New York: Appleton-Century-Crofts.
Arnold, C. C. (1986). Implications of Perelman's theory of argumentation for theory of persuasion. In J. L. Golden & J. J. Polotta (Eds.), *Practical reasoning in human affairs* (pp. 37–52). Boston: D. Reidel.
Axelrod, R. (1977). Argumentation in foreign policy settings. *Journal of Conflict Resolution, 21,* 727–744.
Boggs, S. T. (1978). The development of verbal disputing in part-Hawaiian children. *Language in Society, 7,* 325–344.
Brem, S. K., & Rips, L. J. (2000). Explanation and evidence in formal argument. *Cognitive Science, 24*(4), 573–604.
Brockriede, W. (1986). Arguing: The art of being human. In J. L. Golden & J. J. Pilotta (Eds.), *Practical reasoning in human affairs* (pp. 53–68). Norwell, MA: Kluwer.
Chaiken, S. (1980). Heuristic versus systematic information processing and the use of source versus message cues in persuasion. *Journal of Personality and Social Psychology, 39,* 752–766.
Corbett, E. P. J. (1971). *Classical rhetoric for the modern student* (2nd ed.). New York: Oxford University Press.
Corbett, E. P. J. (1986). The changing strategies of argumentation from ancient to modern times. In J. L. Golden & J. J. Pilotta (Eds.), *Practical reasoning in human affairs* (pp. 21–36). Norwell, MA: Kluwer.
Dawe, H. C. (1934). An analysis of 200 quarrels of preschool children. *Child Development, 5,* 139–157.
Eagly, A. H., & Chaiken, S. (1993). *The psychology of attitudes.* New York: Harcourt Brace Jovanovich.
Eisenberg, A. R., & Garvey, C. (1981). Children's use of verbal strategies in resolving conflicts. *Discourse Processes, 4,* 149–170.
Ennis, R. (1962). A concept of critical thinking. *Harvard Educational Review, 32,* 81–111.
Foucault, M. (Ed.). (1972). *The archeology of knowledge* (A. M. Sheridan Smith, Trans.). New York: Pantheon. (Original work published 1969)
Genishi, C., & DiPaolo, M. (1982). Learning through argument in a preschool. In L. C. Wilkinson (Ed.), *Communicating in the classroom* (pp. 49–68). New York: Academic.
Gerritsen, S. (1999). The history of the enthymeme. In F. H. van Eemeren, R. Grootendorst, J. A. Blair, & C. A. Willard (Eds.), *Proceedings of the Fourth International Conference of the International Society for the Study of Argumentation* (pp. 228–230). Amsterdam: Sic Sat.
Gilligan, C. (1982). *In a different voice: Psychological theory and women's development.* Cambridge, MA: Harvard University Press.
Golder, C. (1993). Framed writing of argumentative monologues by sixteen and seventeen-year-old students. *Argumentation, 7,* 343–358.
Golder, C., & Coirier, P. (1994). Argumentative text writing: Developmental trends. *Discourse Processes, 18,* 187–210.

Govier, T. (1987). *Problems in argument analysis and evaluation.* Providence, RI: Foris.
Govier, T. (1989). Critical thinking as argument analysis? *Argumentation, 3,* 115–126.
Gross, A. G. (1990). *The rhetoric of science.* Cambridge, MA: Harvard University Press.
Hempel, C. G. (1942). The function of general laws in history. *The Journal of Philosophy, 39,* 40–52.
Hitchcock, D. (1995). Does the traditional treatment of enthymemes rest on a mistake? In F. H. van Eemeren, R. Grootendorst, J. A. Blair, & C. A. Willard (Eds.), *Analysis and evaluation: Proceedings of the Third ISSA Conference on Argumentation* (Vol. II, pp. 113–129). Amsterdam: Sic Sat.
Hoch, S. J. (1984). Availability and interference in predictive judgment. *Journal of Experimental Psychology: Learning, Memory, and Cognition, 10,* 649–662.
Hofer, M., & Pikowsky, B. (1993). Validation of a category system for arguments in conflict discourse. *Argumentation, 7,* 135–148.
Johnson-Laird, P. N. (1983). *Mental models.* Cambridge, MA: Harvard University Press.
Kuhn, D. (1989). Children and adults as intuitive scientists. *Psychological Review, 96,* 674–689.
Kuhn, D. (1991). *The skills of argument.* Cambridge, England: Cambridge University Press.
Kuhn, D. (1993). Connecting scientific and informal reasoning. *Merrill-Palmer Quarterly, 39*(1), 74–103.
Kuhn, D. (2001). How do people know? *Psychological Sciences, 12*(1), 1–8.
Kuhn, D., Shaw, V., & Felton, M. (1997). Effects of dyadic interaction on argumentative reasoning. *Cognition and Instruction, 15,* 287–315.
Marttunen, M. (1992). Commenting on written arguments as a part of argumentation skills—Comparison between students engaged in traditional vs. on-line study. *Scandinavian Journal of Educational Research, 36*(4), 289–302.
Marttunen, M. (1994). Assessing argumentation skills among Finnish university students. *Learning and Instruction, 4,* 175–191.
McCloskey, D. N. (1985). *The rhetoric of economics.* Madison: University of Wisconsin Press.
McGuire, M. (1990). The rhetoric of narrative: A hermeneutic critical theory. In B. K. Britton & A. D. Pellegrini (Eds.), *Narrative thought and narrative language* (pp. 219–236). Hillsdale, NJ: Lawrence Erlbaum Associates, Inc.
Means, M. L., & Voss, J. F. (1996). Who reasons well? Two studies of informal reasoning among children of different grade, ability, and knowledge levels. *Cognition and Instruction, 14,* 139–178.
Nickerson, R. S., Perkins, D. N., & Smith, E. E. (1985). *The teaching of thinking.* Hillsdale, NJ: Lawrence Erlbaum Associates, Inc.
Pennington, N., & Hastie, R. (1993). The story model for juror decision making. In R. Hastie (Ed.), *Inside the juror* (pp. 192–221). Cambridge, England: Cambridge University Press.
Perelman, C. (1984). The new rhetoric and the rhetoricians: Remembrances and comments. *The Quarterly Journal of Speech, 70,* 188–196.
Perelman, C., & Olbrechts-Tyteca, L. (Eds.). (1969). *The new rhetoric: A treatise on argumentation* (J. Wilkinson & P. Weaver, Trans.). Notre Dame, IN: University of Notre Dame Press. (Original work published 1958)
Perkins, D. N. (1985). Postprimary education has little impact on informal reasoning. *Journal of Educational Psychology, 77,* 562–571.
Perkins, D. N., Allen, R., & Hafner, J. (1983). Difficulties in everyday reasoning. In W. Maxwell (Ed.), *Thinking: The expanding frontier* (pp. 177–189). Philadelphia: Franklin Institute Press.
Petty, R. E., & Cacioppo, J. T. (1986). *Communication and persuasion: Central and peripheral routes to attitude change.* New York: Springer-Verlag.
Piaget, J. (1959). *The language and thought of the child* (3rd ed.). London: Routledge & Kegan Paul.
Pinto, R. C. (1995). The relation of argument to inference. In F. H. van Eemeren, R. Grootendorst, J. A. Blair, & C. A. Willard (Eds.), *Perspectives and approaches: Proceedings of the Third International Conference on Argumentation* (Vol. 1, pp. 271–286). Amsterdam: Sic Sat.
Piolat, A., Roussey, J. Y., & Gombert, A. (1999). The development of argumentative schema in writing. In J. Andriessen & P. Courier (Eds.), *Foundations of argumentative text processing* (Vol. 5, pp. 117–135). Amsterdam: Amsterdam University Press.

Pontecorvo, C., & Girardet, H. (1993). Arguing and reasoning in understanding historical topics. *Cognition and Instruction, 1,* 365–395.
Santos, C. M. M., & Santos, S. L. (1999). Good argument, content and contextual dimensions. In G. Rijlaarsdam & E. Espéret (Series Eds.) & J. Andriessen & P. Coirier (Vol. Eds.), *Studies in writing: Vol. 5. Foundations of argumentative text processing* (pp. 75–95). Amsterdam: Amsterdam University Press.
Schum, D. A. (1993). Argument structuring and evidence evaluation. In R. Hastie (Ed.), *Inside the juror* (pp. 175–191). Cambridge, England: Cambridge University Press.
Sheldon, A. (1990). Pickle fights: Gendered talk in preschool disputes. *Discourse Processes, 13,* 5–31.
Stein, N. L., & Bernas, R. (1999). The early emergence of argumentative knowledge and skill. In G. Rijlaarsdam & E. Espéret (Series Eds.) & J. Andriessen & P. Coirier (Vol. Eds.), *Studies in writing: Vol. 5. Foundations of argumentative text processing* (pp. 97–116). Amsterdam: Amsterdam University Press.
Stein, N. L., Bernas, R. S., & Calicchia, D. J. (1997). Conflict talk: Understanding and resolving arguments. In T. Givon (Ed.), *Conversation: Cognitive, communicative and social perspectives* (pp. 233–267). Amsterdam: John Benjamins.
Stratman, J. F. (1994). Investigating persuasive processes in legal discourse in real time: Cognitive biases and rhetorical strategy in appeal court briefs. *Discourse Processes, 17,* 1–57.
Tindale, C. W. (1992). Audiences, relevance, and cognitive environments. *Argumentation, 6,* 177–188.
Toulmin, S. (1958). *The uses of argument.* New York: Cambridge University Press.
Toulmin, S. (1992). Logic, rhetoric, and reason: Redressing the balance. In F. H. van Eemeren, R. Grootendorst, J. A. Blair, & C. A. Willard (Eds.), *Argumentation illuminated* (pp. 3–11). Amsterdam: Sic Sat.
Toulmin, S., Rieke, R., & Janik, A. (1979). *An introduction to reasoning.* New York: Macmillan.
van Eemeren, F. H., Grootendorst, R., & Snoeck Henkemans, F. S. (1996). *Fundamentals of argumentation theory.* Mahwah, NJ: Lawrence Erlbaum Associates, Inc.
Van Knippenberg, D., & Wilke, H. (1992). Prototypicality of arguments and conformity to group norms. *European Journal of Social Psychology, 22,* 141–155.
Voss, J. F., Blais, J., Means, M. L., Greene, T. R., & Ahwesh, E. (1986). Informal reasoning and subject matter knowledge in the solving of economics problems by naive and novice individuals. *Cognition and Instruction, 3,* 269–302.
Voss, J. F., Carretero, M., Kennet, J., & Silfies, L. N. (1994). The collapse of the Soviet Union: A case study in causal reasoning. In M. Carretero & J. F. Voss (Eds.), *Cognitive and instructional processes in history and social sciences* (pp. 403–429). Hillsdale, NJ: Lawrence Erlbaum Associates, Inc.
Voss, J. F., Fincher-Kiefer, R., Wiley, J., & Silfies, L. N. (1993). On the processing of arguments. *Argumentation, 7,* 165–181.
Voss, J. F., Tyler, S. W., & Yengo, L. A. (1983). Individual differences in the solving of social science problems. In R. F. Dillon & R. R. Schmeck (Eds.), *Individual differences in cognition* (pp. 205–232). New York: Academic.
Zammuner, V. L. (1987). For or against: The expression of attitudes in discourse. *Text, 7,* 411–434.
Zarefsky, D. (1995). Argumentation in the tradition of speech communication studies. In F. H. van Eemeren, R. Grootendorst, J. A. Blair, & C. A. Willard (Eds.), *Perspectives and approaches: Proceedings of the Third International Conference on Argumentation* (Vol. 1, pp. 32–52). Amsterdam: Sic Sat.

# The Origins and Nature of Arguments: Studies in Conflict Understanding, Emotion, and Negotiation

Nancy L. Stein
*Department of Psychology*
*University of Chicago*

Elizabeth R. Albro
*Department of Psychology*
*Wheaton College*

The emergence and development of argumentation skills in interpersonal conflict situations are the focus of this study. The mental structures used to understand arguments are related to those used to understand social conflict and goal-directed action. The desire to maintain or dissolve a relationship, to persuade, and to understand a position operate throughout interpersonal arguments. Decisions made about whether a relationship should be maintained influence the reasoning and thinking during negotiation, the negotiation strategies, and the outcome of an argument. Because social goals are crucial to understanding argument, negotiations and memory for an argument may be affected as to bias and accuracy.

The ability to understand an argument is claimed to emerge early in development. By 3 years of age, children understand and generate the principle components of an argument, either in face-to-face interaction or individual interviews. The ability to construct detailed, coherent rationales in defense of a favored position improves with age. This development, however, does not guarantee a deeper understanding of one's opponents. The conditions that prevent greater understanding of the opposition from developing are discussed. The ways in which biases and limited understanding can be overcome are also considered.

In this article, we focus on the social origins and nature of argument. Our analysis describes how children and adults represent, evaluate, and resolve arguments. We have, in our research (Albro & Stein, 2000; Stein, Bernas, & Calicchia, 1997;

---

Correspondence and requests for reprints should be sent to Nancy L. Stein, Department of Psychology, The University of Chicago, 5848 University Avenue, Chicago, IL 60637. E-mail: n-stein@uchicago.edu

Stein, Bernas, Calicchia, & Wright, 1996; Stein & Miller, 1990, 1993a, 1993b), focused on oral argument skill and its development in real-world contexts. In our studies, children and adults are asked to remember past conflicts with significant others, to negotiate and resolve conflicts using different strategies, and to remember the nature and content of face-to-face interaction that occurred during a negotiation. We have found that young children have complex knowledge of argument in social situations that are personally significant.

Our interactive approach contrasts with studies of written or oral argument skill, in which participants are assigned a topic that may or may not involve personally significant issues. We hope to increase the psychological validity of argument research by understanding how individuals participate in everyday arguments that are personally significant. We believe that the study of personally significant situations reveals knowledge and strategies not found when people are asked to respond to arguments that carry little personal significance.

Our theory assumes that human goals are important in regulation of the structure and content of an argument. Argument knowledge, as in narrative and emotional understanding (Stein & Albro, 1996; Stein & Glenn, 1979; Stein & Trabasso, 1982, 1989; Trabasso & Stein, 1994, 1997), is acquired through coping with challenges to personally meaningful goals.

Goals may regulate arguments in several ways. Arguments focus on two (or more) persons' views about the worth of accomplishing incompatible goals. Both parties, to begin an argument, must recognize that they have a goal conflict and that both of their goals cannot be attained at the same time. If either party is unaware of the conflict, an argument cannot begin. If mutual recognition occurs and the two parties seek to resolve their conflict by defending and advancing a position, then an argument can be pursued. Arguers almost always enter a negotiation with the goal of persuading their opponent of the worth of their stance, especially at the beginning of a negotiation. They believe that their position is better and more valid than their opponent's position. Consequently, the frequency of overt justification and explanation of goals and stances is high in arguments.

The evaluation and regulation of social relationships is always present in arguments. An arguer may believe that maintaining a relationship with an opponent is more important than his or her own stance. If so, the arguer may discontinue or abort the argument. When the reverse is true and the relationship is less important than the stance, the arguer may disregard the logic or rationale of anything that is said during an interchange with the opponent (Fisher & Brown, 1988; Fisher & Ury, 1981; Stein et al., 1997; Stein et al., 1996; Stein & Miller, 1990, 1993a, 1993b; Ury, 1991). In many situations, two people enter into an argument not to see who will win, but to determine who will be the more dominant person in a relationship. Maynard (1985), in a sociolinguistic analysis, described how young, elementary school children in reading groups form temporary alliances against individuals with whom they disagree to gain power and control. Goals of dominance and control may guide much of the seemingly irrational behavior that occurs in arguments.

In this article we discuss the importance of *relationship goals* and the role that emotion plays in the resolution of interpersonal conflict. In many arguments, individuals are sometimes so highly invested in attaining personal goals that they choose to dissolve a relationship with their partner (Fisher & Brown, 1988; Fisher & Ury, 1981). Omission of the role of relationship goals in the development of argument skill may lead to a misrepresentation and an underestimation of an arguer's ability to negotiate and reason logically. Children, in fact, first learn to argue with others in the context of family and social relationships (Dunn & Munn, 1987; Hay & Ross, 1982; Shantz & Hobart, 1989). They argue with the purpose of achieving personally significant goals such as possession or ownership (Hay & Ross, 1982). Assessing children's arguments under different feeling states and social contexts can result in a broader, more representative understanding of argument skill. This claim extends itself to adult arguments. Our focus, then, is on young children and their understanding of conflicts experienced with their parents and peers. We also examine the similarities and differences of younger children with older children and adults in argument knowledge and behaviors.

## SOCIAL ORIGINS OF ARGUMENT SKILL

### Parent–Child Conflict

Conflict talk among children and parents emerges early in childhood (Duncan & Farley, 1990; Hay & Ross, 1982). By 2 years of age, children are highly familiar with conflict interchanges, and by the age of 4, they are veteran observers of, and participants in, family conflicts. Preschool children learn how to raise opposition to dominant, older members of the family. As they acquire more language, cognitive skills, and social knowledge about rules and rights (Ross, Filyer, Lollis, Perlman, & Martin, 1994; Tesla & Dunn, 1992), they become more successful at negotiating. They may even prevail, at times, in disputes with parents or older siblings (Eisenberg, 1992; Kuczynski, Kochanska, Radke-Yarrow, & Girnius-Brown, 1987; Perlman & Ross, 1997a, 1997b).

The ways in which children and parents learn to resolve conflict influence their thinking and problem-solving skills and their skills at participating in psychologically constructive social interchanges. Acquiring the concept of mutual regard and understanding for other people is considered to be the core issue in children's early understanding of conflict. Erikson (1963), Piaget (1932), and Sullivan (1953) all argued that children's early conflict experiences have a profound effect on the development of knowledge about social rules, relationships, family processes, and the self. Shantz (1993) and her colleagues (Shantz & Hartup, 1992; Shantz & Hobart, 1989) credit experience with interpersonal conflict as seminal in promoting the development of young children's cognitive skill. Acquiring negotiation skill is also important in children's developing ability to differentiate themselves from others (e.g., the apprehension of another person's vs. one's own goals) and in preserving relationships with others (e.g., the desire to reconcile or resolve conflicts and differences of opinion).

The types of goals that children adopt in family relationships vary within, as well as between, families. Children have different sets of feelings for each of their parents and their siblings. The nature of their social relationships as well as their feelings for each family member are reflected in and affected by the types of interactions children have with each family member. All families experience a moderate degree of goal conflict, but the ways in which family members chose to resolve their differences vary within families as well as between families. Children have been observed to be very sensitive to the changing contexts of arguing, especially when their personal goals are at stake. In one situation, they may appear to be irrational and incapable of the complex language and thinking skills needed to carry out an argument. In another situation, the same children can be observed to be highly rational, carrying out negotiations that reflect a great deal of understanding about the issues at hand, as well as the nature of the relationship at stake.

Smetana (1989); Vuchinich (1987); and Vuchinich, Vuchinich, and Coughlin (1992) showed that adolescents who participate in negotiations with their parents use less complex reasoning in the throes of an ongoing argument when compared to their recall and evaluation of an earlier argument. The decline in skill expression during face-to-face family conflicts is due partially to the fact that different goals operate in face-to-face interactions than in individual interviews. During an interaction, old arguments may be rekindled, causing two arguers to engage in an intense emotion exchange rather than in a discussion about the pros and cons of each position. The missing logic during face-to-face interaction is often expressed in an elaborated fashion during individual interviews.

## Peer Conflict

Children's ability to articulate their positions and reasons is also evident in studies carried out on peer conflicts. Some researchers have claimed that young children are unable to negotiate effectively because of their inability to appreciate the goals of their opponent or take the perspective of the other (Berkowitz, Oser, & Althof, 1987; Selman, 1980). Other research (Levine, Stein, & Liwag, 1999; Ross, Ross, Wilson, & Smith, 1999; Stein & Trabasso, 1982), however, has demonstrated that young children are quite capable of understanding and using the goals of their opponents during an argument. Indeed, observers of young children engaged in conflict note that although many children follow a "simple" pattern of insistence on the maintenance of their own goals (Corsaro & Rizzo, 1990; Genishi & DiPaolo, 1982; Phinney, 1985), a significant proportion of young children argue in a complex fashion.

Any response that adds new information to the ongoing argument, in favor of or against a position, is considered to be an elaborated move, or a *complex strat-*

*egy* (Phinney, 1985). Typical examples of a complex strategy include the provision of a self-referenced reason for holding a position, a statement of the benefits the opponent will accrue by supporting the speaker's point of view, and a citation of the harms that will accrue if a person upholds the opposition. Indeed, providing reasons for one's own actions is the second most frequent strategy used by young children after insistence on maintaining their position (Eisenberg & Garvey, 1981; Levine et al., 1999). Citing problems with the opposition's position is also a frequent strategy used by young children (Stein & Miller, 1993a, 1993b).

Gottman and his colleagues also have provided an extensive discussions of elaborated strategies, which they call *conflict management behaviors* (Gottman, 1983; Katz, Kramer, & Gottman, 1992). They list six behaviors that function to de-escalate a conflict and help the dyad move back into friendly interaction. The six behaviors are: "a) referring to a rule to resolve the argument; b) giving a reason for the disagreement; c) making an offer or a compromise; d) exploring the feelings of the child who was upset; e) using a weakened form of the demand that permits face-saving; f) making a humorous or self-deprecating remark" (Katz et al., 1992, p. 137). The ability of at least one participant to carry out these behaviors is correlated with the dyad's ability to begin or maintain a friendship. To sustain interactive play, the main goal of preschool children is to figure out positive ways to get beyond a conflict and to return to friendly interaction (Corsaro, 1985; Gottman & Mettetal, 1986). Thus, in the case of friendship, young children explicitly manage and coordinate two types of goals: those specific to the topic of the argument and those specific to the friendship.

## DEFINING A GOOD ARGUMENT

One reason researchers disagree on the emergence and expression of argumentative skill is that they differ on what dimensions they believe need to be included in the construction of a good argument. Criteria for judging the goodness of an argument often are based on models of formal argumentation, such as those advocated by Toulmin (1958), Kneupper (1978), Ramage and Bean (1992), and Rottenberg (1994). In formal argumentation models, opponents attempt to establish the validity of each of the two positions, seeking, if you will, "the truth." In presenting evidence that supports a point of view, formally, arguers are constrained by the rules of logic and must provide supporting and opposing reasons for both positions. Toulmin and other researchers used these principles of formal logic rather than principles of reasoning based on psychological explanation, justification, and coherence (see Stein & Bernas, 1999, for an extended discussion of this issue).

Fulkerson (1996), however, raised several criticisms regarding the use of Toulmin's model as a standard for argument generation. He contended that the model is primarily an analytic tool (i.e., a framework for analyzing argumentative texts). Even when the model is used for analysis, argument scholars themselves have difficulty identifying warrants in a text. Furthermore, the only empirical study that has tested the effectiveness of Toulmin's model does not present positive results (McCleary, 1979). Thus, although philosophical principles of argumentation are interesting, they often have little bearing on ways in which arguments are organized, understood, and produced in everyday settings.

The difficulty with using a formal argument model is apparent in evaluating everyday arguments. Whereas formal arguments are regulated by the intellectual goal of validating the truth value and logic of evidence, everyday arguments are regulated by interpersonal goals. Depending on the goals of two arguers, especially when both arguers seek to maintain their relationship, compromising is a more productive resolution, in which the goals of both persons are used to construct a new solution to the problem. During the process of compromising, the focus is on identifying a goal that both parties can support, with specific types of conditions attached to the goal. The conversation between two compromisers involves determining the positive and negative consequences that will ensue for each condition attached to the maintenance of a particular goal.

A discourse analysis of compromise (Stein et al., 1997) shows that statements similar to those that Toulmin (1958) described as being essential to a good argument (e.g., claim, evidence, warrant, backing, counterargument, and qualifier) do occur in natural face-to-face negotiation. However, it takes two people to generate the entire argument structure, and many components are missing. Furthermore, the reasons given to support the maintenance of a goal are often based on personal preferences and values. Standards of logic and formal definitions of acceptability are not used. Finally, one participant may delete components of an argument because the other participant can easily infer them or because one participant does not want the other one to have access to certain information.

The use of a win strategy in negotiation is more likely to result in the reasoning and language that conforms to Toulmin's (1958) definition of a good argument. Even in win situations, however, each arguer relies on the other to generate central components of the argument. When arguers decide to go for a win, the six functional categories of Toulmin's argument form are more likely to be included. However, Toulmin did not speak to the importance of the interaction in regulating both the content and sequence of the argument. We (Stein & Bernas, 1999) found that winners in arguments are more likely to include evidence, warrants, and counterarguments in their talk, but only as a function of responding to the point of view of the other person.

Even when winners do include a coherent analysis of the evidence supporting their position, they make systematic errors in remembering accurately the counterevidence that has been raised against their own position. They also make overgeneralization errors in citing qualifications and counterarguments to their opponent's position. Finally, winners rarely cite any of the positive elements in the opposition's argument. Thus, our difficulty in using Toulmin's (1958) model lies in its failure to consider the fundamental importance of interaction. Three components of interaction are important. The interleaving of conversation controls how and which components of arguments are generated, the criteria that are used for generating valid reasons, and the importance of winning the argument rather than providing evidence that results in the best possible logical structure of argumentation.

We present an example next, in which we illustrate both the relevance and shortcomings of Toulmin's (1958) formal analysis. Previously, we (Stein & Miller, 1993a) showed just how Toulmin's functional categories can be mapped onto the functional categories that occur in an interactive argument. As an example, a conflict arises between two siblings, a 9-year-old boy, Ariel, and his 6-year-old brother, David. These boys share a bedroom, and their parents recently bought them a bunk bed. As soon as the bed was installed, an intense dispute erupted as to who would sleep on the top bed. After a heated interchange, the boys agreed that they would switch beds each night. At this time, both agreed to uphold the terms of their contract and to check on each other to make sure that the agreement was being kept.

Two weeks passed, and one night, as Ariel (A) and David (D) got ready for bed, a conflict erupted that turned into an argument:

A: Well, tonight it's my turn to sleep on the top. I get the top.
D: No way. It's my turn tonight. I get the top. I get the top. You slept on top last night and tonight it's my turn. You're breaking our promise. You can't do that. It's mine, mine!! You have to wait 'til tomorrow night. You made a promise.
A: David, you're dumb. You forgot. I let you sleep on top three nights in a row. You were really scared a spider would bite you. So we traded places for three nights. Now I get to make up the nights I didn't get to sleep on top.
D: Yeh, but you slept on top last night.
A: So what. I missed two nights. When you make a promise you're gonna get to sleep on top the same number of nights as the other person, you have to keep your promise.
D: Yea, but we have to trade every night.
A: No, not when you got to sleep there three nights. We only have to trade if we each got the same number of nights, David. That's what we promised.
D: How do you know how many nights I slept there?
A: 'Cause I counted. The whole point of taking turns is so we get the same number of nights.

The discussion continued as Ariel showed David just how many nights each of them had slept on top. The argument was concluded when David agreed that Ariel would sleep on top.

The first component of an argument is a *claim*. According to Toulmin (1958), a claim is an assertion that the arguer believes to be true. A claim is the stance taken at the beginning of an argument. In Ariel and David's argument, each claimed that he should be the one to sleep on the top bed. From our standpoint, both children had goals. Each stated his desire as such. Each felt that he would enhance his well-being by attaining his goal, and each decided that achieving that outcome was important. Thus, a claim contains a statement about the desire to advance or maintain certain beliefs, outcomes, or actions that the arguer considers valuable (Stein & Miller, 1990).

The second component of an argument includes the *reasons* given to support a claim. Reasons consist of evidence or data used to justify a claim. Data can consist of several types of information: single observations, data gathered over periods of time, testimony by other people (usually authorities) affirming the validity of a claim (by reason of their knowledge and observations), or another claim that supports the original claim.

In David and Ariel's argument, each gave reasons for his claim. David's reasons were (a) the boys had promised that they would take turns sleeping on the top bed, (b) tonight was David's turn because Ariel had slept on top the night before, and (c) they had agreed that they would switch bunks every night. Thus, David's first reason consisted of a reminder of the principle stipulating how the bed should be shared. He then provided data in the form of his observation that Ariel had a turn the previous night. According to the principle of nightly turn taking, it was David's turn. Given these data, David's claim should prevail.

A *warrant* is the third part of an argument. Warrants often remain unstated, and are thus difficult to identify, even in contexts in which arguers understand the necessity of providing clear evidence. Generally, warrants are beliefs and assumptions that guide an arguer's choice of the kind of evidence that must be offered in support of his or her claim. Warrants provide the information that allows evidence to assume meaning in relationship to a claim. In David and Ariel's argument, many of the warrants were implied because the rules and assumptions about sharing the bed were explicitly stated in the conversation that led to their initial agreement.

For example, both boys believed that contracts and agreements are valuable to settling disputes. They also believed that, because both had agreed to uphold the contract, they were bound to honor the tenets of the agreement. In the argument, David nearly provided an explicit warrant in his reminder to Ariel that they both made a promise and that Ariel was breaking the promise. Ariel's statement that when you make a promise you are obliged to keep it corresponded more closely to our conception of an actual warrant.

The *backing* for a warrant is the fourth part of an argument. Backing provides additional data about the warrant's validity. In many arguments, backing is included when someone challenges the validity of the warrant. In the case of the boys' argument, no backing appeared because the warrant was not challenged. However, if one of the boys had challenged the warrant by saying that promises are not a good way to settle disputes and that one does not have to abide by a promise, the other might have cited instances and data in which promises have been used to resolve and regulate social conflict. Moreover, a backing could have been provided as a reminder that both parties viewed the promise as valid at the time of agreement. Further backing could then have been provided that spoke to the consequences of not abiding by a promise (see Toulmin, 1958, pp. 103–104).

*Qualifiers* and *counterarguments* are the fifth and sixth parts of an argument. We introduce them together because they often occur in close temporal proximity and share certain features. Theoretically, the person who advances the position should introduce qualifiers and counterarguments against a position. In an analysis of different types of social interactive arguments, however, the person opposed to a position generally introduces qualifiers and counterarguments. In David and Ariel's argument, this was in fact the case (Stein & Miller, 1993a).

A qualifier is a piece of information that limits the conditions under which a claim is valid. A counterargument is evidence that challenges the validity of the claim. When counterarguments are introduced, they serve as reasons for not supporting a claim. The difficulty in making distinctions between these two components of an argument is that they both limit the applicability of a claim. However, a counterargument challenges the validity of the claim as well. We can see the distinction between the two in Ariel's reply to David's claim.

Ariel first introduced a counterargument to David's position by reminding David that for three nights in a row, they had not switched beds; therefore, Ariel should be allowed to even the count, implying that the principle on which they had agreed was equality through alternation and not simple alternation. Because equality had been violated, alternation should stop until equality was restored. Thus, alternation was no longer valid, and David's claim was false.

When Ariel recognized that David did not understand the true nature of their promise, however, he then introduced qualifications to David's conception of the promise. Ariel asserted that alternating the sleeping arrangements was valid only when each of the boys had slept on top an equal number of times. Thus, he limited the conditions under which the alternation principle applied. As soon as the qualifier was introduced, Ariel reasserted his initial counterargument against David's claim, thereby winning the argument with David.

Taking both boys' statements into consideration, five of Toulmin's six categories were explicitly used: claims, reasons for the claim, warrants, qualifiers, and counterarguments. Taken individually, the two arguments differ. David provided a less elaborated argument than did Ariel: David stated a clear claim (i.e., gets the top bed). He gave his reasons (i.e., Ariel got to sleep on top last night, and by the terms of their agreement, it was now David's turn) and stated a partial warrant (i.e., promises are not to be broken).

Ariel's statements included five categories: a claim, reasons for the claim, a warrant, a qualifier, and a counterargument. However, the qualifier and counterargument introduced by Ariel did not qualify or invalidate his own claim. Rather, they served to constrain and invalidate David's claim. As we stated, it is generally the opponent who supplies the qualifiers and counterarguments against an arguer's claim. In David and Ariel's argument, this was exactly what happened.

The problem with a formal analysis of argument is that it does not include a method for coding compromise solutions, which are considered the most constructive type of social solution that two individuals could adopt. Furthermore, formal theories of argument do not consider the seminal role that the topic of an argument plays in influencing the complexity of the argument discourse between two children.

## A Goal-Based Model of Argument

To define a good argument, one must take into account the goals and relationships of the arguers. Corsaro and Rizzo (1990) and Phinney (1985) studied children who argued over the possession of objects. In their studies, the children repeatedly insisted that the disputed object was theirs. Insistence strategies focus on goal objects and leave out other critical categories of argument. Formal analysis marks this kind of strategy as an impoverished form of argument because it includes only statements of the arguer's claims. The insistence strategy is only one indicator, is likely restricted to arguments over valued objects between siblings or peers, and is likely to underestimate young children's skill at argument. It should be noted that when Corsaro and Rizzo did further analysis, they found that children drew on complex and elaborated forms of argument strategies during disputes over access to play, with references to reasons, qualifiers, warrants, and counterarguments.

Complexity of an argument depends on who wins and who loses. Stein and Liwag (1999) found that winning was associated with complexity of argumentation in both children and parents. When the outcome of the argument was one in which the parent won, it was the parent who provided the most complex form of argumentation. When the child won the argument, it was the child who provided the most complex form of arguing. Stein et al. (1997) replicated this finding on arguments between adolescents. In their study, the winner evidenced a more complex form of argument than did the loser.

Stein et al. (1997) also showed that winners generated more complex arguments and that they had more knowledge about their own position than their opponent did before the argument began. They also showed, however, that despite the winners' greater knowledge about their own position, winners had less knowledge about the reasons for their opponent's position than opponents had about the winner's position. This asymmetry in mutual understanding favored the winners. Winners had less accurate memory than did the losers for what was said in face-to-face negotiation. Stein and Liwag (1999) replicated this finding in parent–child argumentation.

Adults, preschool children, and elementary children have acquired a rich knowledge base about the nature of argument in social interaction, the goals and reasons of participants, and the consequences of these interactions. Children recognize, understand, and act on the goals of their opponent (Levine & Stein, 2001; Levine et al., 1999; Stein & Albro, 1997). They also respond in a contingent fashion to their opponent's behavior and adjust their actions and words to take into account the actions and words of their opponents (Eisenberg & Garvey, 1981; Lein & Brenneis, 1978; O'Keefe & Benoit, 1982; Phinney, 1985; Slomkowski & Dunn, 1992).

Clark and Delia (1976) found that by 7 years of age, children recognize and report that others have different agendas and that they try to coordinate their requests and actions accordingly. Levine et al. (1999) found that 3- to 5-year-old children know that their goals can stand in direct opposition to their parents' goals. Thus, even when children appear to be generating a simple argument form, insisting on their own point of view, they do respond to the goals and concerns of others, whether they are in competitive or cooperative situations.

Children also know how to use each other to build a more complex and coherent form of argument (Lein & Brenneis, 1978). In fact, they come to depend on the oral interactive form of argument. This may be one reason children (and adults) often have difficulty formulating and writing arguments. The automatic schema they develop is one in which they learn to depend on their antagonist to supply knowledge about the opposition as well as knowledge about problems with their own position.

Adults have the same reliance on face-to-face negotiation. The oral rather than written form of argument dominates legal proceedings, especially during a trial. Lawyers who write legal briefs are usually not the ones who develop into expert trial lawyers. The two types of legal discourse (oral argumentation and brief writing) have different structures and different requirements. Therefore, the specific type of argument discourse required and the demands of the situation must be considered before we draw any conclusions about the lack of ability in either children or adults.

## REASONING AND THINKING IN PARENT–CHILD ARGUMENT

The development of argument skill can easily be observed in parent–child attempts to cope with everyday problems, conflicts, and disputes. Stein and Albro (1997) studied preschool children and parents' talk about conflicts. Their data are part of a larger study that involved 180 families (Liwag & Stein, 1995; Stein & Albro, 1997; Stein & Liwag, 1997, 1999). Parents were asked to nominate and talk about a series of events that made their children experience different types of emotions (e.g., happiness, sadness, anger, and fear). Thirty parents were asked to talk further about two recent conflicts that they had with their children, one in which they had observed their child express anger and one in which they had observed their child express sadness. After the parents nominated and narrated each of the two events, the children were also asked to remember and recount the same conflicts.

Stein and Albro (1997) chose to pursue the importance of conflict in parent–child relationships because they found that 67% of all parent-nominated events that provoked anger in their children were focused on recent conflicts (Liwag & Stein, 1995; Stein & Liwag, 1997). Levine et al. (1999) also noted that although parents reported their children feeling angry during conflict, more than 60% of the children disagreed with their parents and said that they felt sad during the conflict. Because prior work illustrated that anger events were understood differently than sad events, it is necessary to understand whether different emotional responses to a conflict influence the negotiation strategies and types of outcomes that result from negotiation.

In the Stein and Albro (1997) study, parent conflict nominations were classified into eight different categories, as listed in Table 1. Although the types of conflict that provoked anger overlapped with those that provoked sadness, two types of conflict were more associated with anger than with sadness, and two were more associated with sadness than anger. The conflicts that aroused anger in children most frequently were those in which parents took children's possessions away from them (23%) and those in which parents' and children's goals for pursuing a future course of action were in conflict (20%).

The conflicts that resulted in sadness in children most frequently were those in which the child was denied affection or interaction (27%) or when the child was punished (18%). Note that parents had more difficulty reporting a prior conflict that elicited sadness rather than anger in their children. When children were presented with the topic of their parents' nominations, they were more likely to recall parent-nominated anger conflicts (98%) than parent-nominated sad conflicts (77%). Thus, the conflicts in which children expressed anger, from parents' points of view, were more memorable to both children and parents.

Table 2 shows that outcomes of parent–child conflict can be predicted by the jointly reported emotions of parents and children. Over the 48 reported conflicts, in which children and parents agreed on the outcome, 58% ended with parents

TABLE 1
Types of Parent-Nominated Conflicts
(Stein & Albro, 1997)

| Event Categories[a] | Child Anger[b] | Child Sadness[c] |
|---|---|---|
| Child has possessions taken away | .23* | .14 |
| Child's goal conflicts with parent's goal | .20** | .00 |
| Child is forced to do something | .13 | .18 |
| Child is intruded on | .13 | .09 |
| Child is punished | .10 | .18** |
| Child is denied desirable object | .10 | .05 |
| Child is denied affection or interaction | .06 | .27** |
| Child stopped from engaging in desired activity | .06 | .09 |

[a]Number of parents generating event. [b]$n = 30$. [c]$n = 22$.
*$p < .05$. **$p < .01$.

TABLE 2
Concordance Between Children's Reported Emotion,
Parent's Reported Emotion, and the Outcome of Conflict

| Emotions Reported | No. of Dyads | Parent Wins | Other Outcomes |
|---|---|---|---|
| Both express anger | 6 | 1 parent win | 5 standoffs |
| Both express sadness | 8 | 3 parent wins | 5 compromises |
| Child-sadness/Parent-anger | 17 | 14 parent wins | 3 standoffs |
| Child-happiness/Parent-anger | 10 | 4 parent wins | 6 child wins |
| Child-happiness/Parent-sadness | 5 | 2 parent wins | 3 child wins |

winning, 19% ended with children winning, 12% ended in a standoff, and 9% ended in compromise.

When parents and children both reported reacting with anger, the most frequent outcome was a standoff. Parents and children were unable to negotiate and come to a resolution. They focused on their own goals and ways that each of them functioned as an obstacle to the attainment of the other's goal. When both parents and children expressed sadness, parental wins and parent–child compromises occurred. It should be noted that compromise occurred only when both expressed sadness; that is, parents and children constructed a solution that took into consideration some of both of their needs. The experience of sadness provoked a joint consideration of what they could do to recover a positive thrust in their relationship. Their conversations were much like those described by Katz et al. (1992).

These results clearly indicate that emotion is related to both the strategies and the outcomes of conflict. Furthermore, the conjoint interactive expression of emotion is important in predicting the outcome. When anger was expressed during a conflict, parents and children were unable to come to a resolution. This outcome occurs, we believe, because experiencing anger leads both disputants to believe that the only way to resolve the conflict is for their opponent to change their position and adopt the self's claims and beliefs. Under these conditions, neither party is willing to change or attempt to adopt some of the other person's perspective. However, sadness enabled compromise, and this suggests a focus on the future. The emotion of sadness may be linked to a goal of maintaining the relationship. Thus, parents and children shift the focus of the dispute away from blame and what has happened in the past to creation of a resolution that enables a continued positive relationship.

## CONFLICT WITH LIKED AND DISLIKED OPPONENTS

The degree of liking and caring that two people express toward each other predicts the topic of the dispute and the nature of the conflict resolution. Albro (1996) asked 4-year-old children to remember and spontaneously report both good times and conflicts with their best friend and their most disliked peer. Children were also questioned about the particular conflicts and good times. In a second study, Stein and Liwag (1999) asked parents and children to recall parent–child conflicts and good times. Children and parents were also asked about how well they got along with each other and how much they liked being with each other.

The data from both studies were explored as a function of liking in the dyadic relationship. In both studies, the degree of liking did not influence recalling the conflict. In the Albro (1996) study, 67% of the children recalled conflicts with their best friend and 64% recalled conflicts with the peer they disliked. Similarly, in the Stein and Liwag (1999) study, children who liked being with their mothers recalled 63% of their conflicts; those who disliked being with their mothers recalled 54% of their conflicts. The degree of liking, however, did influence the recall of good times. For the children recalling good times with peers, 88% recalled good times with their liked peers. On the other hand, only 24% of the children could remember good times with peers they disliked. Similarly, in the Stein and Liwag study, 87% of the children who liked being with their mothers remembered good times. For children who did not like being with their mothers, approximately 50% could recall a good time.

The degree of liking thus has a pervasive effect on the frequency and quality of remembering good times. Children who expressed some type of dislike for peers often spontaneously reported that there were no good times to be had with the disliked peer because they tried to put the disliked peer at a physical distance from themselves.

Albro (1996) further showed that liking affected what kind of conflict was recalled. The most frequent conflict with good friends focused on object possession (41%), whereas the most frequent conflict with disliked peers focused on physical harm (54%). Similar findings were discovered in the Stein and Liwag (1999) children's recall of parent–child conflicts. When children did not enjoy being with their mothers, the most frequent conflicts focused on failing to comply with parental regulations, physical aggression (especially toward a sibling), and physically intrusive events (62%). Children who liked being with their parents focused on bedtime disagreements, being forced to join in a family activity, and being forced to eat distasteful foods (51%).

The degree of liking in a relationship influences outcomes of conflicts. When arguing with a parent, the prototypic resolution was that of a win–loss. Seventy-three percent of those conflicts end in a win–loss scenario (54% and 19% were parental or child wins, respectively). In peer interaction, disputes with liked peers also ended frequently in win–loss scenarios, whereas conflicts with disliked peers ended in standoffs or required the intervention of a third party. Compromises were infrequent in parent–child conflicts and liked peer conflicts, and never occurred in conflicts with disliked peers. These data are illustrated in Table 3.

TABLE 3
Conflict Outcomes in Preschool Children's Recall

| Outcome | Parent–Child | Liked Peer | Disliked Peer |
|---|---|---|---|
| Win–loss | .73 | .64 | .23 |
| Standoff | .17 | .23 | .36 |
| Third-party intervention | .00 | .09 | .32 |
| Compromise | .09 | .04 | .00 |

## THE STRUCTURE AND ORGANIZATION OF RECALL OF ORAL ARGUMENTS

When children report their conflicts with peers or with parents, they use particular structural and functional organizations in their reports. Table 4 compares preschool children's recall of arguments they had with either a parent or a peer with categories found in married couples' arguments. The majority of the children recalled the same definition categories of adults, regardless of whether the dispute was with a parent or a peer. More than 90% of the children recalled the topic of the conflict, their reasons for supporting or opposing a position, who initiated the conflict, what the outcome of the conflict was regardless of who their opponent was, and the repercussions that the argument had for them. Preschool children clearly use the same argument structures as do adults.

TABLE 4
Proportion of Participants Who Recalled Each Argument Category

| Argument Category | Stein and Albro (1997) | Albro and Stein (2000) | | Stein and Ross (1996) |
|---|---|---|---|---|
| | | Liked Peer | Disliked Peer | Adult Married Couples |
| Topic | 100%* | 100%* | 100%* | 100% |
| Recognition of conflict | 100%* | 64% | 68% | 94% |
| Reasons for supporting or opposing a position | 92%* | 91%* | 91%* | 92% |
| Who initiated the event that led to the conflict | 92%* | 86%* | 95%* | 94% |
| Verbal interchange in resolving the conflict | 90%* | 68% | 77%* | 82% |
| Outcomes | 98%* | 100%* | 100%* | 92% |
| Repercussions | 90%* | 68% | 54% | 78% |

*$p < .05$.

The actual verbal interchange that occurred during negotiation depended on the type of conflict reported. Children reported verbal interchanges with their parents more often than they did in arguments with their peers. This difference was expected because parents use verbal negotiation techniques more than peers during conflicts. Parents also point out the consequences of their children failing to cooperate. Children were also more likely to mention repercussions or consequences of an argument with a parent than with a peer. These findings may reflect the differential in power status of parental relationships versus peer relationships.

## DEVELOPING ARGUMENT SKILL AND LEARNING HOW TO COMPROMISE

As children move from preschool to elementary school they are able to generate longer arguments. Older children give more reasons for supporting their own position than younger children do, and older children find more problems with their opponents' position than younger children. Older children are also more adept at winning their arguments than are younger children. Despite these differences, young preschool children generate all the parts of an oral argument, they recognize their opponent's goals, they respond to these goals in talk and action, and they adjust their strategies of argumentation to the responses of their adversaries.

Despite being able to better defend their own position, older children and adults do not necessarily demonstrate an increase in knowledge about the positive aspects of their opponent's position or problems with their own position. Children's skill at argument improves primarily in the reasons (causes or explanations) that they generate to support their own position and the problems they find with their opponent's position.

Stein et al.'s (1997) study on adolescents found individual differences in knowledge about the respective positions before an argument. This knowledge of each position predicted the types of outcomes in the ensuing negotiations. Arguers who were able to effect a compromise had more prior knowledge about both positions than did either winners or losers. Winners had high knowledge about their own position but low knowledge about the other's position. Losers had the lowest relative prior knowledge of both positions. Stein et al. also assessed memory of the negotiation between adolescents. The two types assessed were source memory and memory for the content of what was said. *Source memory* refers to the accuracy of recalling who uttered a particular statement during the negotiation. *Content memory* refers to what was said.

Figure 1 displays data on the types of memory shown by those who compromise, win, or lose. Figure 1 indicates that losers evidenced the best memory for who said something. Losers tied those who compromised for remembering accurately what was said. Thus, during a negotiation, losers acquire knowledge about the problems with their own position and the strengths of their opponent's position. This information came from the oral arguments by the winner.

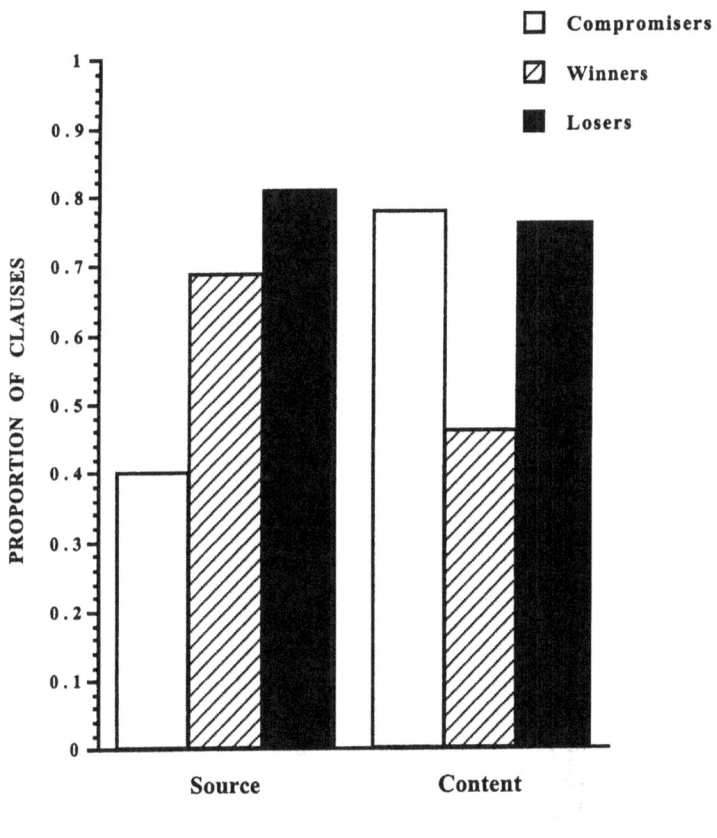

FIGURE 1   Memory for negotiation conversation.

Winners, in Figure 1, remembered accurately the source. They offered the most challenges and qualifications to their opponents and this helped their subsequent memory of who said what. However, they made significantly more errors in remembering accurately what their opponent said, either against their own position or in favor of their opponent's position, consistent with their prior knowledge of the positions. Furthermore, winners almost always misrepresented a loser's initial reasons for adhering to a particular position. Although the winners recalled well the loser's statements of the benefits for his or her own side, the winners were poor at remembering the reasons losers gave for these benefits.

Those who compromised were the best at remembering the content of what each person said in support of a position. Basically, they focused their negotiation on the construction of new goal plans to resolve the problem. These plans incorporated goals and beliefs of both positions, necessary for compromise. Thus, those who compromised were better at attending to and understanding both sides of an argument in resolving the conflict.

Those who compromised had difficulty identifying accurately the person who gave suggestions for the new solution. Both thought that they had made the majority of suggestions for the compromise solution. Arguers who compromised successfully shared equally in devising each component of the solution. They could not, however, identify what they or what their partner had suggested.

## CONCLUSIONS

Argument skill emerges early, especially in parent–child or peer–child conflicts. The relationship goals and affective responses of the participants influence the quality of argument. Arguers of all age levels, from preschool to adulthood, generate all the central parts of an argument. Arguers exhibit similar biases in their understanding and memory for a conflict, independent of their age. The development of argument skill does not necessarily lead to compromise solutions and adaptive or constructive social relationships.

Constructing more complex and logically cohesive arguments may result in winning more disputes, but this skill does not lead to an accurate or deeper understanding of the other person's position. A conflict may exist between displaying good argument skills and participating in morally and socially responsible negotiations. This potential conflict should be explored in future studies. Is it the case that successful arguers have less knowledge about, and poorer social relationships with, their opponents? Learning to communicate logically and coherently is essential to the creation of an argument, but so is the ability to understand and appreciate the other's point of view. The latter is important to resolutions that are mutually beneficial to both parties and to better social relationships. The question, then, is how to teach skill in negotiation that leads to personal and interpersonal success rather than to personal success at the expense of another.

## ACKNOWLEDGMENTS

This research was funded by National Institute of Child Health and Human Development Grants HD38895 to Nancy L. Stein and HD 25742 to Tom Trabasso and Nancy L. Stein, by a Provost's Grant to Nancy L. Stein and Tom Trabasso, by a Social Sciences Grant to Nancy L. Stein and Tom Trabasso, and by a Smart Grant to Nancy L. Stein. We thank Tom Trabasso for his conceptual and insightful editorial comments; Kristen Mercado for her conceptual comments; and Ronan Bernas, Jennifer Wiley, and Shaifali Sandhya for their helpful commentaries.

## REFERENCES

Albro, E. R. (1996). *The role of liking in children's memories and appraisals of peer conflict.* Unpublished doctoral dissertation, University of Chicago.
Albro, E. R., & Stein, N. L. (2000). *How liking affects children's memory of their peers.* Unpublished manuscript, Wheaton College, Wheaton, IL.
Berkowitz, M. W., Oser, F., & Althof, W. (1987). The development of socio-moral discourse. In W. K. Kurtines & J. L. Gewirtz (Eds.), *Moral development through social interaction* (pp. 322–352). New York: Wiley.
Clark, R. A., & Delia, J. G. (1976). The development of functional persuasive skills in childhood and early adolescence. *Child Development, 47,* 1008–1014.
Corsaro, W. A. (1985). *Friendship and peer culture in the early years.* Norwood, NJ: Ablex.
Corsaro, W. A., & Rizzo, T. A. (1990). Disputes in the peer culture of American and Italian nursery-school children. In A. Grimshaw (Ed.), *Conflict talk: Sociolinguistic investigations of arguments in conversations* (pp. 21–66). Cambridge, England: Cambridge University Press.
Duncan, S., & Farley, A. (1990). Achieving parent–child co-ordination through convention: Fixed- and variable-sequence conventions. *Child Development, 61,* 742–753.
Dunn, J., & Munn, P. (1987). Development of justification in disputes with mother and sibling. *Developmental Psychology, 23,* 791–798.
Eisenberg, A. R. (1992). Conflicts between mothers and their young children. *Merrill-Palmer Quarterly, 38,* 21–43.
Eisenberg, A. R., & Garvey, C. (1981). Children's use of verbal strategies in resolving conflicts. *Discourse Processes, 4,* 149–170.
Erikson, E. (1963). *Childhood and society.* New York: Norton.
Fisher, R., & Brown, S. (1988). *Getting together: Building a relationship that gets to yes.* Boston: Houghton Mifflin.
Fisher, R., & Ury, W. (1981). *Getting to yes: Negotiating agreement without giving in.* New York: Penguin.
Fulkerson, R. (1996). The Toulmin model of argument and the teaching of composition. In B. Emmel, P. Rosch, & D. Tanney (Eds.), *Argument revisited; argument redefined: Negotiating meaning in the composition classroom* (pp. 45–72). London: Sage.
Genishi, C., & DiPaolo, M. (1982). Learning through argument in a preschool. In L. C. Wilkinson (Ed.), *Communicating in the classroom* (pp. 49–68). New York: Academic.
Gottman, J. M. (1983). How children become friends. *Monographs of the Society for Research in Child Development, 48*(3, Serial No. 201).
Gottman, J. M., & Mettetal, G. (1986). Speculations about social and affective development: Friendship and acquaintanceship through adolescence. In J. M. Gottman & J. G. Parker (Eds.), *Conversations of friends: Speculations on affective development* (pp. 192–240). Cambridge, England: Cambridge University Press.
Hay, D. F., & Ross, H. S. (1982). The social nature of early conflict. *Child Development, 53,* 105–113.
Katz, L. F., Kramer, L., & Gottman, J. M. (1992). Conflict and emotions. In C. U. Shantz & W. L. Hartup (Eds.), *Conflict in child and adolescent development* (pp. 122–149). Cambridge, England: Cambridge University Press.
Kneupper, C. W. (1978). Teaching argument: An introduction to the Toulmin model. *College Composition and Communication, 29,* 237–241.
Kuczynski, L., Kochanska, G., Radke-Yarrow, M., & Girnius-Brown, O. (1987). A developmental interpretation of young children's noncompliance. *Developmental Psychology, 23,* 799–806.
Lein, L., & Brenneis, D. (1978). Children's disputes in three speech communities. *Language and Society, 7,* 299–323.
Levine, L., & Stein, N. L. (2001). Children's understanding of emotional experience in the self and other. *Child Development.* Manuscript submitted for publication.

Levine, L., Stein, N. L., & Liwag, M. (1999). Remembering children's emotions: Sources of concordant and discordant accounts between parents and children. *Developmental Psychology, 5,* 210–230.

Liwag, M. D., & Stein, N. L. (1995). Children's memory for emotional events: The importance of emotion-related retrieval cues. *Journal of Experimental Child Psychology, 60,* 2–31.

Maynard, D. W. (1985). On the functions of social conflict among children. *American Sociology Review, 50,* 207–223.

McCleary, W. J. (1979). *Teaching deductive logic: A test of the Toulmin and Aristotelian models for critical thinking and college composition.* Unpublished doctoral dissertation, University of Texas, Austin.

O'Keefe, B. J., & Benoit, P. J. (1982). Children's arguments. In J. R. Cox & C. A. Willard (Eds.), *Advances in argumentation theory and research* (pp. 154–183). Carbondale: Southern Illinois University Press.

Perlman, M., & Ross, H. S. (1997a). The benefits of parent intervention in children's disputes: An examination of concurrent changes in children's fighting styles. *Child Development, 68,* 690–700.

Perlman, M., & Ross, H. S. (1997b). Who's the boss? Parents' failed attempts to influence the outcome of conflicts between their children. *Journal of Social and Personal Relationships, 14,* 463–480.

Phinney, J. S. (1985). The structure of 5-year-olds' verbal quarrels with peers and siblings. *Journal of Genetic Psychology, 147,* 47–60.

Piaget, J. (1932). *The moral judgment of the child.* New York: Free Press.

Ramage, J. D., & Bean, J. C. (1992). *Writing arguments* (2nd ed.). New York: Macmillan.

Ross, H. S., Filyer, R. E., Lollis, S. P., Perlman, M., & Martin, J. (1994). Administering justice in the family. *Journal of Family Psychology, 8,* 254–273.

Ross, H., Ross, M., Wilson, A., & Smith, M. (1999). The dandelion war. In S. R. Goldman, A. C. Graesser, & P. Van den Broek (Eds.), *Narrative comprehension, causality, and coherence: Essays in honor of Tom Trabasso.* Mahwah, NJ: Lawrence Erlbaum Associates, Inc.

Rottenberg, A. T. (1994). *Elements of argument: A textured reader* (4th ed.). Boston: St. Martin's.

Selman, R. L. (1980). *The growth of interpersonal understanding: Developmental and clinical analyses.* New York: Academic.

Shantz, C. U. (1993). Children's conflicts: Representations and lessons learned. In R. R. Cocking & K. A. Renninger (Eds.), *The development and meaning of psychological distance* (pp. 185–202). Hillsdale, NJ: Lawrence Erlbaum Associates, Inc.

Shantz, C. U., & Hartup, W. W. (Eds.). (1992). *Conflict in child and adolescent development.* Cambridge, England: Cambridge University Press.

Shantz, C. U., & Hobart, C. J. (1989). Social conflict and development: Peers and siblings. In T. J. Berndt & G. W. Ladd (Eds.), *Peer relationships and child development* (pp. 71–94). New York: Wiley.

Slomkowski, C., & Dunn, J. (1992). Arguments and relationships within the family: Differences in young children's disputes with mothers and siblings. *Developmental Psychology, 28,* 919–924.

Smetana, J. (1989). Adolescents' and parents' reasoning about everyday conflict. *Child Development, 60,* 1052–1067.

Stein, N. L., & Albro, E. R. (1996). Building complexity and coherence: Children's use of goal-structured knowledge in telling good stories. In M. Bamberg (Ed.), *Learning how to narrate: New directions in child development* (pp. 5–44). Mahwah, NJ: Lawrence Erlbaum Associates, Inc.

Stein, N. L., & Albro, E. R. (1997, April). *Children's and parents' understanding of conflict: Evidence from past memories.* Paper presented at the biennial meeting of the Society for Research in Child Development, Washington, DC.

Stein, N. L., & Bernas, R. S. (1999). The early emergence of argumentative knowledge and skill. In P. Coirier & J. Andriessen (Eds.), *Foundations of argumentative text processing* (pp. 113–136). Amsterdam: Amsterdam University Press.

Stein, N. L., Bernas, R. S., & Calicchia, D. J. (1997). Conflict talk: Understanding and resolving arguments. In T. Givon (Ed.), *Conversation: Cognitive, communicative and social perspectives: Typological studies in language* (Vol. 34, pp. 233-267). Amsterdam: John Benjamins.
Stein, N. L., Bernas, R. S., Calicchia, D. J., & Wright, A. (1996). Understanding and resolving arguments: The dynamics of negotiation. In B. Britton & A. G. Graesser (Eds.), *Models of understanding* (pp. 257-287). Hillsdale, NJ: Lawrence Erlbaum Associates, Inc.
Stein, N. L., & Glenn, C. G. (1979). An analysis of story comprehension in elementary school children. In R. O. Freedle (Ed.), *New directions in discourse processing* (pp. 255-282). Norwood, NJ: Ablex.
Stein, N. L., & Liwag, M. D. (1997). A goal-appraisal process approach to understanding and remembering emotional events. In P. van den Broek, P. Bauer, & T. Bourg (Eds.), *Developmental spans in event comprehension and representation* (pp. 199-236). Hillsdale, NJ: Lawrence Erlbaum Associates, Inc.
Stein, N. L., & Liwag, M. D. (1999, April). *Affective and cognitive factors that regulate the process and success of parent–child negotiation.* Paper presented at the biennial meeting of the Society for Research in Child Development, Albuquerque, NM.
Stein, N. L., & Miller, C. A. (1990). I win–you lose: The development of argumentative thinking. In J. Voss, D. Perkins, & J. Segal (Eds.), *Informal reasoning and education* (pp. 265-290). Hillsdale, NJ: Lawrence Erlbaum Associates, Inc.
Stein, N. L., & Miller, C. A. (1993a). The development of memory and reasoning skill in argumentative contexts: Evaluating, explaining, and generating evidence. In R. Glaser (Ed.), *Advances in instructional psychology* (Vol. 4, pp. 285-335). Hillsdale, NJ: Lawrence Erlbaum Associates, Inc.
Stein, N. L., & Miller, C. A. (1993b). A theory of argumentative understanding: Relationships among position preference, judgments of goodness, memory, and reasoning. *Argumentation, 7,* 183-204.
Stein, N. L., & Ross, M. (1996, November). *Discussing conflicts: Similarities and differences in husband's and wife's description of the same conflicts.* Paper presented at the meeting of the Psychonomic Society, Chicago.
Stein, N. L., & Trabasso, T. (1982). Children's understanding of stories: A basis for moral judgment and dilemma resolution. In C. Brainerd & M. Pressley (Eds.), *Verbal processes in children: Progress in cognitive development research* (pp. 212-267). New York: Springer-Verlag.
Stein, N. L., & Trabasso, T. (1989). Children's understanding of changing emotional states. In C. Saarni & P. L. Harris (Eds.), *Children's understanding of emotion* (pp. 50-77). Cambridge, England: Cambridge University Press.
Sullivan, H. S. (1953). *The interpersonal theory of psychology.* New York: Norton.
Tesla, C., & Dunn, J. (1992). Getting along or getting your own way: The development of young children's use of argument in conflicts with mother and sibling. *Social Development, 1,* 107-121.
Toulmin, S. E. (1958). *The uses of argument.* Cambridge, England: Cambridge University Press.
Trabasso, T., & Stein, N. L. (1994). Using goal-plan knowledge to merge the past with the present and the future in narrating events on line. In M. Haith, J. Benson, R. Roberts, Jr., & B. Pennington (Eds.), *The development of future-oriented processes* (pp. 323-349). Chicago: University of Chicago Press.
Trabasso, T., & Stein, N. L. (1997). Narrating, representing, and remembering event sequences. In P. van den Broek, P. Bauer, & T. Bourk (Eds.), *Developmental spans in event comprehension and representation* (pp. 237-270). Hillsdale, NJ: Lawrence Erlbaum Associates, Inc.
Ury, W. L. (1991). *Getting past no: Negotiating with difficult people.* New York: Bantam.
Vuchinich, S. (1987). Starting and stopping spontaneous family conflicts. *Journal of Marriage & the Family, 49,* 591-601.
Vuchinich, S., Vuchinich, R. A., & Coughlin, C. (1992). Family talk and parent–child relationships: Toward integrating deductive and inductive paradigms. *Merrill-Palmer Quarterly, 38,* 69-93.

# The Development of Argumentive Discourse Skill

Mark Felton
*Department of Education*
*San Jose State University*

Deanna Kuhn
*Teachers College*
*Columbia University*

The skills involved in argument as a social discourse activity presumably develop during the childhood and adolescent years, but little is known about the course of that development. As an initial step in examining this development, a coding system was developed for the purpose of analyzing multiple dialogues between peers on the topic of capital punishment. A comparison of the dialogues of young adolescents and those of young adults showed the teens to be more preoccupied with producing the dialogue and less able to behave strategically with respect to the goals of argumentive discourse. Teens also did not exhibit the strategic skill that adults did of adapting discourse to the requirements of particular argumentive contexts (agreeing vs. disagreeing dialogues).

Contemporary research in argumentation theory has led to revisions in the normative models of argument. Compelling models have been developed in informal logic (Walton, 1995), communication theory (Jacobs & Jackson, 1982), and pragma-dialectics (van Eemeren & Grootendorst, 1992). A common thread running through these approaches has been the examination of argument in the context of natural conversation (Gilbert, 1997). Argumentation is viewed as a social activity in which two or more people advance, defend, and compare arguments in support of opposing positions (Willard, 1983). Largely absent are the mathematical models of formal logic that divorce arguments from the contexts in which they arise. Instead, normative models are based on the social construction of argument.

---

Correspondence and requests for reprints should be sent to Mark Felton, Department of Education, San Jose State University, 1 Washington Square, San José, CA 95112–3613. E-mail: mfelton2@yahoo.com

They examine how individuals construct arguments in relation to the advances, questions, challenges, and critiques of conversational partners.

This trend is of particular interest to us as developmental psychologists studying argumentation. First, it grounds theory in empirical data on how people engage in argument. Psychologists have a long history of studying argument empirically and developmental psychologists, specifically, have produced a substantial literature on the development of individual children's reasoning abilities. Second, this new trend defines argument as an activity that a person engages in with others rather than a product generated by an isolated individual. This latter approach is relatively new to the field of psychology and scant psychological research exists on argument in social contexts.

The hypothesis pursued in the research we describe here is that the skills of argumentive discourse develop. This developmental hypothesis seems a tenable one given that complex cognitive capabilities are clearly invoked in argumentive activity, and the most plausible way to explain their presence is that they are an outcome of a gradual process of development. Little evidence exists, however, to address this hypothesis. Although there is substantial data on development in argumentive reasoning, we know very little about development in the ability to navigate and direct argumentative discourse with others. The conceptual and empirical work described in this article is devoted to identifying salient features of the development of argumentive discourse skills.

## ARGUMENT AS PRAGMATIC

The advantage of a discourse-based model is that it acknowledges the role of social interaction in the construction of argument. Only in very formal settings, such as courtroom proceedings or political debates, are arguments presented outside of a conversational context. Most often, arguments arise from disagreements people have with one another. Arguments are likely to be initially incomplete and to grow as the speaker addresses the challenges presented by a conversational partner. Henle (1962) supported this claim by showing that arguments may be logically sound even if they are incomplete by the standards of formal logic; that is, an argument may be valid even though its underlying premises remain implicit. Furthermore, individuals may not elaborate arguments unless they recognize the need to clarify themselves or convince their audience. Grice's (1975) maxim of quantity holds that a speaker will provide only as much information as necessary for an audience to construct meaning. Thus, discourse is integral to the construction of an argument. If this is the case, then the best way to examine the development of argumentive competence is to examine the process by which individuals construct arguments in the context of discourse.

## ARGUMENT AS STRATEGIC

Walton (1989) developed a useful model for examining argumentive discourse. In *critical dialogue*, each speaker elicits a set of commitments from a partner. A *commitment* is a presumptive or inconclusive premise that the partner is willing to concede. The goal of critical dialogue is to draw one's own conclusion from a partner's commitments; that is, each participant in the dialogue must get the partner to accept certain premises. Once these are granted, the individual can construct an argument based on these concessions. Thus, according to Walton, each participant has two goals in a critical dialogue. The first is to secure commitments from the partner that can be used to support one's own claims. The second is to undermine the partner's position by identifying and challenging unwarranted premises. If one's assertion is presumptive, a commitment must be secured from the opponent that concedes this premise. If an opponent's assertion is presumptive, the individual must challenge the assertion. The strategies entailed in argumentive discourse function to direct argumentive discourse to address these goals.

## A DEVELOPMENTAL MODEL OF STRATEGIC ARGUMENTIVE DISCOURSE

Activity theory (Leont'ev, 1981) offers a useful framework for conceptualizing the development of strategy in argumentive discourse. According to Leont'ev, an activity is composed of goal-directed behaviors known as actions. The development of an activity proceeds as we adapt our behavior to fit more and more advanced goals. Thus, development occurs on two fronts. First, activity develops as the individual produces more sophisticated behaviors in pursuit of a goal. Second, activity develops as the individual refines the goals being pursued. The former involves the development of goal-directed strategies, whereas the latter entails development of the goals themselves.

Thus, if we regard argumentive discourse as an activity in the process of development, two forms of development can be identified. One is enhanced skill in directing the course of critical dialogue to meet the activity's objectives. The other is enhanced understanding of the goals of argumentive discourse. These two forms of development, we predict, reinforce one another. In other words, progress in strategic performance is propelled in part by a better understanding of the goals of discourse. At the same time, exercise of these strategies in discourse activity promotes more refined understanding of the goals of the activity. More generally, as has been proposed in other areas of strategic cognitive development, metalevel understanding both directs and is informed by strategic performance (Kuhn, 2001b).

As the first step toward understanding discourse strategies in this developmental framework, this article reports the development of an analytic scheme for identifying the strategies that appear in simple argumentive discourse, that is, the argumentive discourse of individuals not explicitly trained in these respects. We then employ the scheme to compare the argumentive discourse strategies exhibited by a group of young adolescents to those exhibited by a group of adults.

## METHOD

The empirical data reported here are based on transcriptions of a series of dyadic discussions on the topic of capital punishment (CP). Participants were drawn from two populations: One was a group of young adolescents and the other was a group of young adults. Prior and subsequent to the series of dialogues with 5 different peers, participants were asked to indicate and justify their own individual positions regarding CP. These pre- and posttest assessments were the basis of an earlier study of the effects of cognitive engagement on argumentive reasoning (Kuhn, Shaw, & Felton, 1997). The intervening dialogues provided the data for the work presented here.

### Participants

Both samples were from the same inner-city population of low socioeconomic status. The adults were 31 students at a vocationally oriented community college, and the adolescents were 33 seventh- and eighth-grade students attending a small, alternative, public junior high school. Roughly equal numbers of males and females participated in both groups, and adolescent participants met in same-sex dyads.

### Procedure

*Assigning participants to dyads.* At the start of the study, participants identified their positions on CP using a 13-point opinion scale. This scale, adopted from Kuhn and Lao (1996), presents 13 statements of position from which participants may choose. The middle position on the scale reads, "I have mixed or undecided opinions about capital punishment." Each position above and below the middle point is slightly more extreme in favor of or against CP than the one before. Altogether, the scale provides six pro positions, six con positions, and one neutral position from which to choose. Reports on the opinion scale were used to assign participants to agreeing, disagreeing, and neutral dyads. Over the course of five dialogues, each with a unique partner, every participant was assigned to at least one of each kind of dyad.

*Dialogues.* The five dialogues took place over an interval of 5 to 6 weeks, with an average interval of 1 week between dialogues. Each dialogue began with a brief set of instructions in which participants were asked to share their opinions on CP. If the dyad members agreed with each other, they were asked to find all of the reasons they agreed. If they disagreed, they were asked to try to resolve their differences of opinion and reach a consensus. If the participants had difficulty maintaining the dialogue during the prescribed time, the investigator repeated the instructions to prompt further dialogue. Dialogues lasted an average of 10 min among adolescents and 15 min among adults (see Kuhn et al., 1997). All of the verbal dialogue data were recorded on audiotape and later transcribed for coding and analysis.

Analytic Scheme

The purpose of the analytic scheme developed for use in this research is to categorize each utterance in a dialogue based on its function relative to the preceding utterance. This functional objective predominates over characterization of conversational content. (The completed scheme is available in manual form from Mark Felton.) It includes for each code a definition, examples, and contrasting cases. The scheme comprises three broad categories: transactive questions, transactive statements, and nontransactive statements. An utterance is defined as transactive if it attempts to engage the partner in discourse either by referring to the partner's preceding utterance or by prompting a response from the partner.

*Development of the analytic scheme.* Two pools of dialogue, each representing roughly one quarter of the total data set, were randomly selected. One pool was used to develop the scheme. The second was used for the purpose of cross-validation and calculation of interrater reliability. The first stage of development of the scheme involved reading transcripts from the first pool and the drafting of a provisional set of codes. This phase of the work was conducted by a four-person group that included ourselves and two graduate research assistants. When the scheme was completed, the provisional codes were applied to the remainder of the data in the first pool independently by members of the research group. The members then came together to ascertain reliability and identify new codes for any utterances that were not classifiable in the provisional system. As this process was reiterated, the need for revisions or additions to the scheme diminished, and satisfactory interrater reliability was achieved.

*Reliability.* Two raters, blind to the treatment, time, and identity of the dialogue participants, established interrater reliability by coding the second pool of dialogues reserved for this purpose. For each conversational turn in a dialogue, raters applied the code, checked their agreement, and tallied reliability. Depending on the number of speech acts produced, as many as three codes could be assigned to a single conversational turn. Therefore, when raters disagreed on the number of codes to apply, the higher number was added to the total number of codes and the disagreement was added to the tally. Raters then resolved any disagreements by discussion before moving on to the next conversational turn. Percentage agreement between the raters was 87% (Cohen's $\kappa = .85$). Once the reliability had been tallied, the remaining dialogues from the data set were divided equally between the raters and coded.

*Summary of scheme.* The codes included in the scheme are summarized in Table 1. Transactive questions are utterances that request a response from the partner. They often take the grammatical form of a question (e.g., What do you mean? or Why do you prefer capital punishment over life in jail?). When transactive questions are not in the form of a question they are either commands for the partner to say something (e.g., Now tell me why you say that) or implied requests (e.g., Say it was your mother who was sentenced to death [would you still be in favor of the death penalty?]). In either case, the function of the utterance is to elicit a response from the partner. These codes fall under the category of directives in Searle's (1979) taxonomy of speech acts.

Transactive statements do not directly request a response from the partner. Instead, they are expressions of the speaker's thoughts offered in response to the partner. They are transactive because they connect directly to the partner's preceding utterance. These codes include both assertives and commissives from Searle's (1979) taxonomy.

Nontransactive statements are utterances that fail to connect to the partner's preceding utterance; that is, they neither address the partner's previous utterance nor prompt the partner to respond. "Continue" is used when the speaker ignores the partner's preceding utterance and continues his or her own train of thought. In such cases, the speaker is connecting to his or her own last utterance rather than to the partner's. "Unconnected" is used when the speaker fails to connect to either the partner's or his or her own last utterance. In such cases, the speaker is breaking from the preceding conversation and introducing a new argument or train of thought.

In the exchange illustrated in Table 2, Speaker A opens with a transactive question. She asks her partner to clarify his position (Clarify-?). Speaker B responds with a transactive statement of clarification (Clarify) and Speaker A retorts with a critique (Counter-C). Each utterance serves a specific function in the conversational exchange.

# RESULTS

The primary objective of our empirical analysis is to identify differences between adolescents and adults in the use of the utterance types in Table 1. For this purpose, we confined ourselves to those dialogues in which there existed unambigu-

TABLE 1
Summary of Utterance Types in the Analytic
Scheme for Coding Argumentive Dialogue

| | |
|---|---|
| Transactive questions | |
| Agree-? | A question that asks whether the partner will accept or agree with the speaker's claim |
| Case-? | A request for the partner to take a position on a particular case or scenario |
| Clarify-? | A request for the partner to clarify his or her preceding utterance |
| Justify-? | A request for the partner to support his or her preceding claim with evidence or further argument |
| Meta-? | A question regarding the dialogue itself (vs. its content) |
| Position-? | A request for the partner to state his or her position on an issue |
| Question-? | A simple informational question that does not refer back to the partner's preceding utterance |
| Respond-? | A request for the partner to react to the speaker's utterance |
| Transactive statements | |
| Add | An extension or elaboration of the partner's preceding utterance |
| Advance | An extension or elaboration that advances the partner's preceding argument |
| Agree | A statement of agreement with the partner's preceding utterance |
| Aside | A comment that does not extend or elaborate the partner's preceding utterance |
| Clarify | A clarification of speaker's own argument in response to the partner's preceding utterance |
| Coopt | An assertion that the partner's immediately preceding utterance serves the speaker's opposing argument |
| Counter-A | A disagreement with the partner's preceding utterance, accompanied by an alternate argument |
| Counter-C | A disagreement with the partner's preceding utterance, accompanied by a critique |
| Disagree | A simple disagreement without further argument or elaboration |
| Dismiss | An assertion that the partner's immediately preceding utterance is irrelevant to the speaker's position |
| Interpret | A paraphrase of the partner's preceding utterance with or without further elaboration |
| Meta | An utterance regarding the dialogue itself (vs. its content) |
| Null | An unintelligible or off-task utterance |
| Refuse | An explicit refusal to respond to the partner's preceding question |
| Substantiate | A utterance offered in support of the partner's preceding utterance |
| Nontransactive statements | |
| Continue | A continuation or elaboration of the speaker's own last utterance that ignores the partner's immediately preceding utterance |
| Unconnected | An utterance having no apparent connection to the preceding utterances of either partner or speaker |

ous contrast in the positions of the 2 participants (disagreeing dialogues). Participants who indicated a neutral position (middle point on the 13-point scale) at the outset of the study (4 adults and 9 adolescents) are therefore excluded from the analysis. The remaining participants who initially indicated nonneutral positions sometimes changed their positions across the sequence of dialogues. Hence, it was necessary to examine the positions expressed by each participant at the begin-

TABLE 2
An Example of the Coding Scheme Applied to an Excerpt of Adult Dialogue

| Code | Speaker/Utterance |
|---|---|
| Clarify-? | A: Do you mean to say society must be protected? |
| Clarify | B: Yes, they must. |
| Counter-C | A: I agree, but if it is the only way to safeguard us from those murders, then [the murderers] must be killed. |
| Disagree | B: No, but you see— |
| Continue | A: —But, you see, the person who poses a threat to the life of others must lose his whole right to live. |

ning of a dialogue. Only if the positions expressed at this point represented opposing (pro vs. con) positions was the dialogue included in the data set as a disagreeing dialogue. The number of participants included in this set, which forms the basis for the analysis presented here, was 26 adults and 24 adolescents. There were 51 dialogues produced by the adults and 55 dialogues produced by the adolescents.

## Age Differences in Argumentive Dialogues in Disagreeing Dyads

Frequency of use within a participant's discourse was calculated for each of the utterance codes in Table 1. Those codes that represented more than 1% of the total dialogue for each group were examined for differences between the two age groups. The mean percentage of total dialogue for each code in each group is presented in Table 3. Statistically significant differences between adolescents and adults in disagreeing dyads appeared with respect to six utterance codes (see Table 3).

We begin with discussion of the codes that were more prevalent in adolescent discourse than in adult discourse: Case-?, Position-? and Clarify. *Case-?* is defined as a request for the partner to make a decision regarding a particular case or scenario that the speaker poses. Typically, the speaker introduces either a hypothetical or a real situation and asks the partner to indicate whether CP should be applied. If successful as an argumentative strategy, the request leaves the partner to defend an unappealing stance, take a position that contradicts his or her CP position, or heavily qualify his or her position. Table 4 presents an example from the adolescents' discourse.

Clearly, case-based questions are intended to pursue argumentive ends. However, rather than directly dismantling a partner's argument, they seek to challenge the partner's position in extreme cases in which the position is most difficult to defend. In Table 4, Speaker A is trying to get Speaker B to qualify or soften her position on CP. In fact, Speaker B concedes that the justice system should be

TABLE 3
Mean Percentage Use of Each Utterance Type in Disagreeing Dialogues

|  | Adult | | Adolescent | | |
| --- | --- | --- | --- | --- | --- |
| Code | M | SD | M | SD | p |
| Case-? | 3.08 | 3.27 | 8.32 | 8.74 | *** |
| Clarify-? | 9.84 | 6.56 | 7.94 | 5.14 | * |
| Justify-? | 1.54 | 1.59 | 1.24 | 1.52 | |
| Position-? | 1.12 | 1.25 | 2.92 | 1.91 | **** |
| Add | 12.66 | 9.54 | 13.01 | 8.44 | |
| Agree | 8.34 | 7.74 | 9.20 | 8.98 | |
| Aside | 3.12 | 2.98 | 3.45 | 4.76 | |
| Clarify | 23.19 | 12.64 | 29.55 | 11.70 | ** |
| Counter-A | 1.78 | 3.24 | 1.14 | 1.76 | |
| Counter-C | 20.42 | 8.08 | 8.51 | 5.74 | **** |
| Disagree | 2.08 | 4.00 | 1.79 | 2.80 | |
| Interpret | 3.43 | 5.70 | 1.11 | 2.04 | ** |
| Meta | 4.33 | 5.01 | 4.27 | 4.43 | |

*$p < .10$. **$p < .05$. ***$p < .01$. ****$p < .001$.

TABLE 4
Example of Case-?

| Code | Speaker/Utterance |
| --- | --- |
| Case-? | A: Say [a guy] was robbing someone—he was like robbing a store and he was trying to get away. The people across the street getting into their car got shot accidentally. Should he get [the death penalty] for that? |
| Clarify | B: Yeah. |
| Case-? | A: What if he was sorry that he did it? |
| Clarify | B: I dunno. He should like go to jail for a long time instead [of getting the death penalty]. |

more lenient on a remorseful criminal. Both speakers end up focused on the conditions for applying CP rather than on any argument for or against CP. Thus, although case-based questions may succeed in challenging an opponent's position on an issue, they often leave that opponent's arguments intact. Hence, they represent a relatively weak argumentive strategy. They may serve the function of eliciting a partner's commitment—consistent with the goals of strategic discourse—but they do not represent an attempt to direct the course of that argument, per se.

A second utterance type found significantly more often in adolescent discourse is *Position-?*. This utterance requests the partner to take a stand on CP. In adult discourse, this code generally appears at the start of a dialogue as the partners establish their position. In adolescent discourse, in contrast, it arose throughout the dialogues. Adolescents were likely to use the question to prompt their partner to advance an argument. This action may serve the function of eliciting a partner's commitment, consistent with the goals of argumentive discourse. However, it does not attempt to direct the course of that argument. Hence, it is strategic in only a very weak sense.

The final utterance type found more often in adolescent discourse is *Clarify*. This code is defined as a statement produced by the speaker in response to the partner's preceding utterance. It occurred most commonly as the response to a question. The age difference, then, may simply be epiphenomenal to the finding that adolescents produced more Case-? and Position-? questions, which require a response from the partner, than did adults.

The three remaining utterance types for which adult and adolescent use differed—Interpret, Counter-C, and Clarify-?—occurred more commonly in adult than in adolescent discourse. Significantly, each of these reflects an effective argumentation strategy, clearly more effective than the weak strategies just considered for which adolescent use surpassed that of adults. Interpret, Counter-C and Clarify-? all address the partner's argument and undertake to weaken it, directly in the case of Counter-C and indirectly in the case of Interpret and Clarify-? Table 5 presents an adult exchange from our database in which all three of these types appear.

In Table 5, Speaker B asks Speaker A to clarify her argument ("Do you really think jail is making them suffer?"). There is a specific purpose to this question. Speaker B wants to elicit what she sees as a weak argument from Speaker A. The strategic role of requests for clarification is that they elicit a commitment from the partner. This commitment may constitute a concession to an argument being advanced by the speaker, or as in this case, it may elicit a commitment to an argument that the speaker is prepared to critique. Next, we see that Speaker A accepts this argument, so Speaker B interprets this argument in its weakest form ("Sitting in jail is the same as dying . . ."). In this way she undermines Speaker A's position. However, Speaker A retorts with a counterargument to Speaker B's argument ("The chair isn't the same as being murdered, either"), thus undermining the opponent's claim. In this exchange, both speakers engage in strategic, goal-

TABLE 5
Examples of Interpret, Counter-C, and Clarify-?

| Code | Speaker/Utterance |
|---|---|
| Clarify | A: Let [murderers] go to jail, make them think about what they done [. . .] Let them rot there. |
| Clarify-? | B: Do you really think jail is making them suffer? |
| Clarify | A: Uh huh. |
| Interpret Clarify | B: So, by sending them to jail, we make them suffer the same way they made their victim suffer. Sitting in jail is the same as dying at the hands of some crazed killer. I say they should just kill him and let him feel what it's like. |
| Counter-C | A: The chair isn't the same as getting murdered either. It's painless. At least in jail he's got no rights, no freedom. That's worse. |

directed discourse. They each attempt to gain the upper hand by dismantling the opponent's position.

All three strategies employed in Table 5 represent powerful forms of argumentive discourse because they explicitly pursue argumentive goals. Clarify-? elicits a commitment from the partner, Interpret undermines the strength of the partner's argument, and Counter-C dismantles the partner's argument through critique. In contrast to case-based questions, these strategies directly address arguments the partner has advanced.

It is important to note, however, that Interpret and Clarify-? need not always reflect argumentive strategies. In the course of dialogue, individuals could produce these utterances without argumentive goals in mind. However, in a context of disagreeing dialogue, and as illustrated here, they represent an orientation toward directing and defining the opponent's argument with the intention of weakening it.

## Strategic Sequences

The preceding illustration highlights the fact that argumentive strategies may extend across multiple utterances to achieve their intended goal. After the coding of individual utterances in our database was completed, we reexamined all dialogues in search of patterns of utterances that might represent an attempt to advance or preempt an extended argumentive strategy. We identified three such sequences that appeared with some frequency in the dialogues of multiple participants. Each of the three clearly reflects argumentive discourse goals. Moreover, empirical analysis of the database shows that each of the three occurred more frequently in the adult dialogues than in the adolescent dialogues. The first of the three we term a *corner sequence*. It is defined as either a Clarify-? or Interpret by the speaker, a response by the partner, and then a Counter-C by the speaker. In such sequences, it is clear that the speaker's goal in advancing the initial Clarify-? or Interpret is to elicit a commitment from the partner that the speaker is prepared to critique. Thus, the speaker corners the partner in an untenable or weak position. In Table 6, for example, Speaker A questions his partner for the purpose of establishing an inconsistency in the partner's position, which Speaker A is then able to criticize.

A second strategic sequence we identified is *rebuttal*, defined as any Counter-C that follows a Counter-C or Counter-A produced by the partner. Its intent is to eliminate or reduce the force of a partner's counterargument by critiquing it, thereby restoring force to one's own argument. As we see in Table 7, Speaker A offers the critique that CP does not bring back the dead (Counter-C). Speaker B rebuts by arguing that CP does prevent further murders from occurring (Counter-C).

The sequence in Table 7 demonstrates strategic behavior in that it addresses an attempt to dismantle the speaker's argument. It is an essentially defensive move, but one that demonstrates an awareness of the goals of argumentive discourse.

TABLE 6
Example of a Corner Sequence

| Code | Speaker/Utterance |
| --- | --- |
| Clarify-? | A: So, you think we should give him two or three chances and that's it? |
| Clarify | B: No. That's two or three [more] dead people. Two or three! They might kill your mother. They might kill my mother second. No, no, no. Don't give them opportunities to keep killing. |
| Clarify-? | A: So, you said that we should only kill repeat offenders. How are you gonna determine which are repeat offenders if you don't give them a chance to kill again? |
| Clarify | B: Well, I'm not saying [...] I'm saying wait until they commit a few serious crimes. |
| Counter-C | A: But the way you explain it, that's the only way to do it, because you're saying we should only kill repeat offenders [...] or those who need help and can't be fixed [...] the only way to figure that out is to sit back and wait and see what happens. |

TABLE 7
Example of a Rebuttal

| Code | Speaker/Utterance |
| --- | --- |
| Clarify | B: I'm not saying that everyone who commits a crime should be put to death. I mean if it's a situation where you know the crime was committed [by the accused] or where [the accused] admits to it and it's like a situation where he says he just doesn't care, then why shouldn't that person be put to death? |
| Counter-C | A: OK, what if you put that person to death, has that solved the problem? It still don't bring that person back. |
| Counter-C | B: It doesn't bring the dead person back, but it prevents that person who killed from killing again. |

A third strategic sequence we identified is the *block*. Like rebuttals, blocks represent a defensive move on the part of the speaker. Blocking occurs when the speaker rejects or counterargues the premise of a leading question posed by the partner. In so doing, the speaker avoids being forced to undermine his or her position. For example, in Table 8, Speaker A advances a leading question in asking whether Speaker B would favor the death penalty in the case of manslaughter. In refusing to accept her partner's premise, Speaker B presumably anticipates the damaging intent of the assertion. Otherwise, she would have little reason not to go along with her partner's hypothetical scenario. In this sense, then, Speaker B's speech reflects an attempt to preempt a strategic sequence because it anticipates a partner's later utterance.

Each of the three sequences identified—corner, rebuttal, and block—occurred more frequently in adult dialogues than they did in adolescent dialogues. In the case of corners and rebuttals, we found significant between-group differences. In the case of block, we found only marginally significant between-group differ-

TABLE 8
Example of a Block

| Code | Speaker/Utterance |
|---|---|
| Case-? | A: Okay, let's say somebody gets hit by a car and they say it's manslaughter. And he was running across the street and the guy's just driving and he couldn't hit the brakes in time. And witnesses say it's true, it's true he did it for real. [Should the driver get] the death penalty? |
| Counter-C | B: You can't get the death penalty for that. The most that they give you is probably—I don't know what they'll give you. |

TABLE 9
Mean Frequency of Each Sequence Type in Disagreeing Dialogues

| | Adult | | Adolescent | | |
|---|---|---|---|---|---|
| Sequence | M | SD | M | SD | p |
| Corner | 1.27 | 1.39 | 0.21 | 0.62 | ** |
| Rebuttal | 5.02 | 4.47 | 1.07 | 1.54 | ** |
| Block | 0.25 | 0.56 | 0.08 | 0.29 | * |
| Case-?  Counter-C | 0.21 | 0.46 | 0.14 | 0.51 | |

*$p < .10$. **$p < .001$.

ences. Our findings with respect to blocking remain tentative because our results were only marginally significant and both groups generated the sequence rather infrequently.

A fourth sequence we identified, one for which adolescents and adults did not show differential use, is worth noting. It is a variant of the corner sequence defined by Clarify-? followed by Counter-C. Instead of Clarify-?, the opening statement is Case-?. Adults and adolescents produced roughly equal numbers of Case-?/Counter-C sequences (see Table 9). Similar to the Clarify-?/Counter-C sequence, case-based sequences reflect offensive attempts to direct the partner's argument. Table 10 presents an example of a Case-?/Counter-C sequence.

Speaker A in Table 10 leads Speaker B with a line of reasoning. He presents a case-based question about the death penalty, elicits a response, and then points out that Speaker B is inconsistent. He has shown that Speaker B will not maintain his position under certain circumstances. Similar to the simple Case-? utterance code on which they are based, case-based sequences aim to challenge the partner. However, similar to Case-?, case-based sequences fail to address arguments, focusing instead on the partner's position (see earlier discussion of Case-?). In this respect, they lack the strategic power corner sequences possess. Interestingly, then, whereas adolescents produced significantly more case-based questions than adults, adults and adolescents produced roughly equal numbers of case-based sequences. This finding suggests that when adults do resort to using a case-based

TABLE 10
Example of a Case-?/Counter-C Sequence

| Code | Speaker/Utterance |
|---|---|
| Case-? | A: Let's say somebody got killed and [...] they were close to you. Would you want [the killer] to get the death penalty, yes or no? |
| Clarify | B: At that moment, I would, at that moment. |
| Counter-C | A: So then you agree with me. But if it was like somebody else that you don't know, you wouldn't agree. |

strategy, they at least use it to their argumentive advantage; that is, it culminates in an effective Counter-C offensive against the partner's argument. Based on the far greater number of case-based questions than case-based sequences in adolescent discourse, it would appear that adolescents, once they have initiated a Case-? utterance, are less able to follow the Case-? strategy through to an effective conclusion.

### Argumentive Strategy in Agreeing Dialogues

The preceding analysis portrays a picture of young adolescents as less adept strategically than young adults in pursuing the goals of argumentive discourse in disagreeing dialogues. Another respect in which the strategic nature of argumentive discourse might be assessed is by examining the extent to which strategies are adapted to fit particular argumentive contexts. We do this here by comparing participants' argumentive discourse in dyads in which both partners held the same pro or con position on CP, which we termed agreeing dyads (see criteria presented earlier for categorizing dyad types). The number of participants engaged in agreeing dialogues was 27 adults and 18 adolescents.[1] There were 65 dialogues produced by the adults and 23 dialogues produced by the adolescents.

Paralleling Table 3, Table 11 presents mean percentage use of utterance types for agreeing dialogues with two additions. Means for the codes Advance and Substantiate did not appear in Table 3 because each utterance type represented less than 1% of participants' disagreeing dialogues. Adolescents, Table 11 shows, exceed adults in the frequency of use of the same three categories in which they exceed adults in disagreeing dialogues—Case-?, Position-?, and Clarify—in addition to a fourth category, Clarify-?, in which adolescents now exceed adults. In this respect, adolescents' discourse is fairly stable across the two types of dialogues.

A similar picture emerges when we compare adolescents' frequency of use of each utterance type across the two dialogue types. This comparison yields only

---

[1] Adolescents were more likely to change positions and to centrate than adults in the study (see Kuhn, Shaw, & Felton, 1997). Thus, the disparity in the number of agreeing dialogues between groups was due to the greater degree of fluctuation in the opinions of adolescents in the study.

TABLE 11
Mean Percentage Use of Utterance Types in Agreeing Dialogues

|  | Adult | | Adolescent | | |
| --- | --- | --- | --- | --- | --- |
| Code | M | SD | M | SD | p |
| Case-? | 1.60 | 1.55 | 7.51 | 8.27 | ** |
| Clarify-? | 6.13 | 4.75 | 12.08 | 8.10 | ** |
| Justify-? | 1.15 | 1.54 | 1.79 | 3.01 | |
| Position-? | 0.96 | 1.37 | 2.22 | 2.13 | * |
| Add | 28.85 | 14.98 | 9.72 | 6.91 | *** |
| Advance | 4.16 | 3.58 | 0.78 | 1.52 | *** |
| Agree | 16.94 | 8.50 | 3.78 | 4.42 | *** |
| Aside | 4.34 | 4.06 | 5.65 | 6.98 | |
| Clarify | 13.94 | 7.89 | 34.56 | 12.61 | *** |
| Counter-A | 0.75 | 0.97 | 0.79 | 1.39 | |
| Counter-C | 5.97 | 5.26 | 8.43 | 8.01 | |
| Disagree | 0.88 | 1.79 | 1.40 | 2.23 | |
| Interpret | 1.81 | 2.77 | 0.29 | 0.84 | ** |
| Meta | 4.57 | 4.52 | 5.09 | 7.41 | |
| Substantiate | 2.07 | 1.77 | 0.91 | 1.41 | ** |

*$p < .05$. **$p < .01$. ***$p < .001$.

TABLE 12
Example of Add

| Code | Speaker/Utterance |
| --- | --- |
| Add | A: What they're [promoting] is an eye for an eye, a tooth for a tooth. |
| Agree | B: Exactly. |
| Continue | A: That's wrong because what they're really teaching is [...] well this guy killed people so the government can come and kill him. So if my friend hits me, I'm gonna hit him right back because that's what I'm feeling. |
| Add | B: You know, it defeats itself [...] The idea of society is to teach other people that to take a life is wrong [...] it defeats itself because what it actually tells people is that it's okay to kill. |

three categories in which adolescents' use deviates more than 1 percentage point across the two dialogue types. These are Clarify-?, which, as just noted, becomes more prevalent when adolescents are conversing with agreeing partners, and Clarify, which is even more prevalent in agreeing dialogues than it was in disagreeing dialogues—most likely reflecting the increased responding to the increased frequency of Clarify-?. A third change, in which the prevalence of Agree decreases in agreeing dialogues, is not readily explainable.

Adults in agreeing dialogues, in contrast, show a marked departure from the discourse patterns they exhibited in disagreeing dialogues, as observed by comparison of Tables 3 and 12. In agreeing dialogues, adults reduce the prevalence of six different utterance types and increase the prevalence of five others. Disagree, unsurprisingly, becomes less prevalent, but so do the utterance codes that we identified in our earlier analyses as reflecting strategic discourse in disagreeing dialogues: Counter-C, Interpret, Clarify-?, and Case-? (the sixth, Clarify, is the only nonstrategic type and decreases, most likely, as a secondary effect of its association with Clarify-? and Case-?).

At the same time, five utterance types increase in prevalence when adults move from disagreeing to agreeing dialogues: Agree, Add, Advance, Substantiate, and Aside. In comparisons between adults and adolescents in frequencies of utterance types in agreeing dialogues, Agree, Add, Advance, and Substantiate are now all more common in adult dialogues than they are in adolescent dialogues, as is Interpret (which was also more common among adults than adolescents in disagreeing dialogues). In each of these cases, the adult participant in discourse establishes agreement with the partner, but then (in using any of the remaining codes) endeavors to build on the partner's argument. Add, for example, is defined as an extension or elaboration of the partner's immediately preceding utterance. Table 12 presents an example of Add.

## DISCUSSION

In educational literature, one finds repeated reference to critical thinking as a central goal of education. In definitions of critical thinking, the effective use and comprehension of argument invariably figure prominently. The realization of these goals in educational practice, however, has been constrained by the very limited empirical evidence that exists regarding what needs to develop cognitively during childhood and adolescence to enable students to engage in effective argumentive discourse (Kuhn, 1999).

In developmental psychology, the empirical data related to argument largely address individuals' ability to support a claim, or, more commonly, to draw correct inferences from information that has been presented (Moshman, 1998). As noted earlier, the growing emphasis in argumentation theory on argumentive discourse as a social phenomenon offers a framework for empirical investigation of the relevant cognitive skills and how they may develop. In particular, we have drawn on Walton's (1989) ideas regarding the dual goals of argumentive discourse—to secure commitments from the partner that can be used to support one's own claims and to undermine the partner's claims. Also key to our analysis is the idea of argumentive strategies, by means of which these goals are pursued. Leont'ev's (1981) writings are useful here in conceptualizing development as occurring along dual fronts, one in continuing refinement of one's understanding of the goals and the other in development and refinement of strategies that meet those goals. These two trajectories we conceptualize as mutually reinforcing: Exercise of strategies enhances goal understanding, which in turn directs strategy use (Kuhn, in press-b). The strategic differences we observed across age groups, then, may in part reflect differences in understanding of discourse goals.

Our results, we believe, indicate a number of respects in which adults behave more strategically in argumentive discourse than do young teens. Adults use the directly offensive strategy of counterargument more than twice as often as teens. Moreover, in other conversational moves, such as Interpret and Clarify-?, adults are preparing the way for counterargument by directing and defining the partner's argument with the intent of weakening it. Such sequences, extending over multiple conversational moves, are less frequent among teens. Also less frequent among teens are defensive strategic sequences—notably, the key strategy of rebuttal.

The other key way in which adults can be seen to behave more strategically than young teens is in their adaptation of strategies to the requirements of discourse context. Teens, strikingly, showed minimal modification of discourse behavior when moving from disagreeing to agreeing partners. Counterargument, most notably, remained at about the same level of frequency when a difference in position did not exist as when it did. Adults, in contrast, in discourse with a partner who shared their position, diminished use of strategies directed toward weakening the partner's argument and increased use of strategies that might enhance and strengthen their own position (Add, Advance, and Substantiate).

Until they are replicated in other populations and argumentive contexts, the developmental differences we have identified are only tentative. Still, they are suggestive of what the developmental challenges may be as children and young adolescents begin to develop more sophisticated discourse skills. Young adolescents appear more preoccupied with merely producing argumentive discourse—that is, with generating the form of dialogue that they understand to be required in argumentive discourse. Speakers must take turns, must address the topic, and should try to articulate their views adequately. We have evidence that teens embrace and achieve these goals. Frequencies of unconnected or off-topic utterances are low. Moreover, teens (as well as adults) undertake to express their own views clearly. In disagreeing dialogues (Table 3), teens make clarifying statements regarding their own position almost four times as frequently as they seek clarification of the partner's position and four times as frequently as they critique the partner's position. Although they do show some use of counterargument, it is not clear to what extent teens understand the goal of undermining the partner's argument—a goal that needs to be distinguished from the goal of undermining the partner's position. The latter goal could be understood as attainable by a superior presentation of one's own position. A favored discourse mode of teens, we saw, is Case-?, although teens are less likely to use it with the strategic intent that is observed on the part of adults. Instead, to the extent the earlier mentioned discourse requirements (of articulating positions) are perceived as having been met, the adolescent may see posing scenarios as a way of keeping the discourse going, with an implicit goal of furthering the articulation of positions.

Our evidence regarding the strategic adaptation of argumentive discourse to fit discourse type or context highlights the importance of strategic flexibility, a performance factor, as well as strategic understanding, a competence factor (Kuhn,

2001a). Adolescents, perhaps due to a combination of social and cognitive constraints, show less flexibility in their argumentive discourse than do adults. Our data suggest that we should pay more attention to the role of discourse strategy as a source of developmental differences in argumentation. This approach may be especially fruitful in light of research that has claimed that many of the apparent differences between adult and child argumentation result from differences in knowledge base rather than reasoning (Stein & Miller, 1991). The study reported here provides new avenues for examining developmental differences in argumentation that may extend beyond knowledge of content or an understanding of argument structure.

Our data also highlight the fact that not all argumentive discourse is disagreeing. Agreeing discourse may be fully as strategic as disagreeing discourse, although its goals differ. In articulating, supporting, and enriching a position, it may be very productive, as Gilbert (1997) argued on philosophical grounds. Recent empirical research (Keefer, Zeitz, & Resnick, 2000; Kuhn et al., 1997; Lao, 1999) has supported this view.

Indeed, an adequate taxonomy of argumentive discourse contexts is likely to contain many more than two types (Gilbert, 1997; Keefer et al., 2000). Empirical delineation of such a taxonomy will be important to further research on the development of argumentive discourse skills, especially to the extent that strategic flexibility in adapting discourse to context proves to be a salient dimension of this development. Also, as mentioned earlier, there is a need to examine other populations, including those with argumentive expertise, to verify the developmental trends identified here. In this same vein, and the objective of a forthcoming paper (Felton, 1999), there is the need to document in experimental research that the discourse skills of young participants are amenable to advancement along the developmental paths that have been suggested by this research.

## REFERENCES

Felton, M. (1999). *Metacognitive reflection and strategy development in argumentive discourse.* Unpublished doctoral dissertation, Teachers College, Columbia University, New York.

Gilbert, M. A. (1997). *Coalescent argument.* Mahwah, NJ: Lawrence Erlbaum Associates, Inc.

Grice, H. P. (1975). Logic and conversation. In P. Cole & J. L. Morgan (Eds.), *Syntax and semantics: Vol. 3. Speech acts* (pp. 41–58). New York: Academic.

Henle, M. (1962). On the relation between logic and thinking. *Psychological Review, 69,* 366–378.

Jacobs, S., & Jackson, S. (1982). Conversational argument: A discourse analytic approach. In J. R. Cox & C. A. Willard (Eds.), *Advances in argumentation theory and research* (pp. 205–237). Carbondale: Southern Illinois University Press.

Keefer, M., Zeitz, C., & Resnick, L. (2000). Judging the quality of peer-led student dialogues. *Cognition and Instruction, 18,* 53–82.

Kuhn, D. (1999). A developmental model of critical thinking. *Educational Researcher, 28,* 16–25.

Kuhn, D. (2001a). How do people know? *Psychological Science, 12*(1), 1–8.

Kuhn, D. (2001b). Why development does (and doesn't) occur: Evidence from the domain of inductive reasoning. In R. Siegler & J. McClelland (Eds.), *Mechanisms of cognitive development: Neural and behavioral perspectives.* Mahwah, NJ: Lawrence Erlbaum Associates, Inc.

Kuhn, D., & Lao, J. (1996). Effects of evidence on attitudes: Is polarization the norm? *Psychological Science, 7,* 115–120.

Kuhn, D., Shaw, V., & Felton, M. (1997). Effects of dyadic interaction on argumentive reasoning. *Cognition and Instruction, 15,* 287–315.

Lao, J. (1999). *Cognitive engagement and attitude development.* Unpublished doctoral dissertation, Teachers College, Columbia University, New York.

Leontev, A. N. (1981). The problem of activity in psychology. In J. V. Wertsch (Ed.), *The concept of activity in Soviet psychology* (pp. 37–61). New York: M. E. Sharpe, Inc.

Moshman, D. (1998). Cognitive development beyond childhood. In W. Damon (Series Ed.), D. Kuhn & R. Siegler (Vol. Eds.), *Handbook of child psychology: Vol. II. Cognition, perception, and language* (pp. 947–978). New York: Wiley.

Searle, J. R. (1979). *Expression and meaning: Studies in the theory of speech acts.* Cambridge, England: Cambridge University Press.

Stein, N. L., & Miller, C. A. (1991). I win—you lose: The development of argumentive thinking. In J. F. Voss, D. N. Perkins, & J. W. Segal (Eds.), *Informal reasoning and education* (pp. 265–290). Hillsdale, NJ: Lawrence Erlbaum Associates, Inc.

van Eemeren, F. H., & Grootendorst, R. (1992). *Argumentation, communication and fallacies: A pragma-dialectic perspective.* Hillsdale, NJ: Lawrence Erlbaum Associates, Inc.

Walton, D. N. (1989). Dialogue theory for critical thinking. *Argumentation, 3,* 169–184.

Walton, D. N. (1995). *A pragmatic theory of fallacy.* Tuscaloosa: University of Alabama Press.

Willard, C. A. (1983). *Argumentation and the social grounds of knowledge.* Tuscaloosa: University of Alabama Press.

# Influence of Oral Discussion on Written Argument

Alina Reznitskaya and Richard C. Anderson
*Center for the Study of Reading*
*University of Illinois at Urbana-Champaign*

Brian McNurlen
*Office of Instructional Resources*
*University of Illinois at Urbana-Champaign*

Kim Nguyen-Jahiel, Anthi Archodidou, and So-young Kim
*Center for the Study of Reading*
*University of Illinois at Urbana-Champaign*

This article examines the effects of participation in oral argumentation on the development of individual reasoning as expressed in persuasive essays. Engagement in oral argumentation is the essential feature of a classroom discussion method called collaborative reasoning. A premise of this method is that reasoning is fundamentally dialogical and, hence, the development of reasoning is best nurtured in supportive dialogical settings such as group discussion. Students from 3 classrooms participated in collaborative reasoning discussions for a period of 5 weeks. Then, these students and students from 3 comparable classrooms who had not engaged in collaborative reasoning wrote persuasive essays. The essays of collaborative reasoning students contained a significantly greater number of relevant arguments, counterarguments, rebuttals, formal argument devices, and uses of text information.

The development of reasoning has been a historic ambition of American schools. In the words of Thomas Jefferson, general education should "enable every man to judge for himself what will secure or endanger his freedom" (Jefferson, as cited in Karp, 1985, p. 70). Today, the development of reasoning remains a pressing national educational goal. Unfortunately, nationwide assessments (e.g., Applebee, Langer, Mullis, Latham, & Gentile, 1994; Langer et al., 1995) have documented

---

Correspondence and requests for reprints should be sent to Alina Reznitskaya, Center for the Study of Reading, 165 Children's Research Center, 51 Gerty Drive, Champaign, IL 61820. E-mail: reznitsk@uiuc.edu

that the majority of American students do not have a firm grasp of argumentative discourse. People have difficulty writing a well-developed persuasive essay; comprehending a written argument; differentiating between theory and evidence; and generating genuine evidence, alternative theories, counterarguments, and rebuttals (e.g., Crowhurst, 1990; Kirsch, Jungeblut, Jenkins, & Kolstad, 1993; Kuhn, 1991; McCann, 1989; Means & Voss, 1996).

One explanation to account for inferior performance on argumentative tasks is that students lack a well-developed schema for this type of discourse (Crowhurst, 1988; Erftmier, as cited in Knudson, 1992; Hidi & Hildyard, 1983; Scardamalia & Bereiter, 1986). According to Govier (1987), insight into an argument is

> something quite elementary and yet illusive to many not encouraged to think about reasoning, argumentation, and the justification of claims. It is the sense that reasoning is going on, that there is an inference made from some propositions to others, and that this inference can be critically scrutinized. (p. 233)

Today it is widely believed that social interaction is the primary means for promoting individual reasoning (e.g., Cazden, 1988; Commeyras, 1994; Kuhn, 1992; Lipman, 1997; Onosko, 1990; Paul, 1986; Waggoner, Chinn, Yi, & Anderson, 1995). The idea that group interaction offers a good context for the development of reasoning can be traced back to Vygotsky (1981), who asserted that "the higher functions of child thought first appear in the collective life of children in the form of argumentation and only then develop into reflection for the individual child" (p. 157).

According to Kuhn (1992), the educational implication of Vygotsky's thesis is that "social dialogue offers us a way to externalize the internal thinking strategies we would like to foster within the individual" (p. 174). Discussions can expose children to alternative perspectives, stimulate children to formulate and make public their own ideas, and create situations in which these ideas will be challenged by their peers. Social interaction can lead to appropriation of cognitive and social competencies that can later be used by an individual in different contexts and with no external support. "Children need to experience dialogical thinking because such thinking is essential for rationally approaching the most significant and pervasive everyday human problems" (Paul, 1986, p. 137).

Considering the widespread belief in the efficacy of discussions in promoting the development of reasoning, there have been surprisingly few studies that have put this idea to an empirical test. Studies evaluating educational programs concerned with improvement of reasoning (e.g., Lipman's [1987] philosophy for children) are not uncommon. However, evaluation studies are designed to form an opinion regarding overall program effectiveness, rather than to understand the underlying mechanisms of cognition. Such studies typically employ pre–post test designs, assessing the program as a whole, often with the use of a battery of standardized tests (e.g., Burnes, 1981; Higa, 1980; Nickerson, Perkins, & Smith,

1985; Simon, 1975). Therefore, these studies provide little information about particular components of the intervention and their relative contribution to the acquisition of intended skills.

Kuhn, Shaw, and Felton (1997) tried to address the specific effects of participation in a discussion on the quality of argumentative reasoning by comparing individuals' written arguments about an ill-structured problem before and after their participation in a two-person discussion. Several qualitative improvements in reasoning abilities of participants were noted, including an increased range of arguments, the propensity to consider counterarguments, and metacognitive awareness of alternative perspectives. However, as Kuhn et al. acknowledged, generalizability of reasoning skills was not established by the study because the analysis was largely descriptive. Also, both the oral discussions and the writing task were on the topic of capital punishment. Thus, it is unclear whether participants were generating arguments or merely recalling points brought up in their discussions.

We are aware of at least one study that did not show improved written argumentation following oral interaction. Knudson (1992) investigated the effects of adding oral interaction to an instructional intervention designed to improve the persuasive writing of elementary school students, but she found no significant gains in students' written argumentation. Knudson suggested that this "very disappointing result" was, perhaps, due to the type of the oral interaction employed in her study, which involved teacher-led discussions and highly structured problem-solving tasks rather than debates among students.

To recapitulate, there is a recognized need for students to improve their reasoning. It is widely believed that social interaction is a primary means for promoting individual reasoning. This theoretical proposition, however, has not been extensively investigated and the empirical case for the proposition is weak. This study aims to provide evidence about the effects of discussions in which children engage in oral argumentation on the reasoning that the children then exhibit in persuasive essays. The study employs an approach to discussion, called *collaborative reasoning* (CR), that has undergone an extensive period of development and field testing (Anderson, Chinn, Waggoner, & Nguyen, 1998; Anderson et al., 2001; Chinn, Anderson, & Waggoner, 2000). This should enable the study to escape the ambiguity experienced by investigators who are not able to distinguish a failure due to deficiencies in an ad hoc intervention from a more fundamental problem with the theory that social interaction is the major avenue for growth of individual reasoning.

CR is an approach to discussion that aims to provide elementary school children with an opportunity to become skilled in the discourse of reasoned argumentation. During CR, students participate in small group discussions of controversial issues raised by texts they have read. Texts are chosen to embody themes that are engaging for young students and that can stimulate thoughtful and lively dialog. A distinctive feature of CR discussions is open participation. This means that students do not have to raise their hands and can communicate freely without being nominated by the teacher. The rationale for open participation is that "higher levels of productive student behavior are probable if there is a balance between the interactional rights of the teacher and children" (Au & Mason, 1981, p. 150).

Students in CR discussions decide when to talk and what to discuss. The teacher's role is to promote reflective thinking and collaboration among the students (Anderson et al., 1998). Characteristic teaching strategies include: (a) prompting students for their positions and reasoning, (b) demonstrating reasoning processes by thinking aloud, (c) challenging students with countering ideas, (d) acknowledging good reasoning, (e) summing up what students have said, and (f) using the vocabulary of critical and reflective thinking. Specific teacher moves hinge on the degree of control students currently have over thinking strategies, the dynamics of the group, and the direction that the discussion has taken. The emphasis in CR discussions is not on reaching a consensus on the issue, but rather on having students experience the process of reflective judgment. The ultimate goal of CR includes "inculcating the values and habits of mind to use reasoned discourse as means for choosing among competing ideas" (Anderson et al., 1998, p. 172). "Collaborative reasoning discussions offer students opportunities to expand their repertoire of responses to literature by learning to think in a reasoned manner and to explore diverse views prompted by what they read" (Waggoner et al., 1995, p. 583).

CR tries to help students develop an overall sense of an argument, or *argument schema*. According to our theory, an argument schema is an abstract knowledge structure that represents extended stretches of argumentative discourse. Generalizing from research on other schemas or discourse structures (Anderson & Pearson, 1984; Goldman & Rakestraw, 2000), we hypothesize that an argument schema enables organization and retrieval of argument-relevant information, facilitates argument construction and repair, and provides the basis for anticipating objections and for finding flaws in one's own arguments and the arguments of others. An important feature of an argument schema is that it is abstract and therefore enables transfer among situations. Operationally, an indication that students possess an argument schema is their ability to use argument skills in varied contexts and communicative modes.

Another key assumption of our theory is that the development of argumentative knowledge is best fostered in a group setting. Following Vygotsky (1981) and Bakhtin (1981, 1986), we believe that "reasoning is fundamentally dialogical. Thinkers must hear several voices within their own heads representing different perspectives on the issue. The ability and disposition to take more than one perspective arises from participating in discussions with others who hold different perspectives" (Anderson et al., 2001).

Empirical studies suggest that CR affects the discourse of classroom discussions in the intended way. Most student utterances during CR discussions consist of arguments, challenges to the arguments of other participants, and rebuttals

(Anderson, Chinn, Chang, Waggoner, & Yi, 1997; Anderson et al., 1998; Chinn & Anderson, 1998). This is quite different from the conventional discussion approach of recitation in which students respond to the teacher's questions with specific story information and "almost never express arguments about an issue raised in the story" (Anderson et al., 1998, p. 185).

Chinn et al. (2000) confirmed that, as compared to baseline discussions in the same classrooms, during CR discussions, children more frequently provide explanations, elaborate ideas by linking them to prior knowledge, draw inferences that connect different parts of texts they have read, support ideas with evidence, build on each others' knowledge to coconstruct ideas, and critique each others' ideas. A body of research indicates that the foregoing discourse features are associated with better learning, problem solving, and transfer (e.g., Chi, de Leeuw, Chiu, & LaVancher, 1994; Chinn, O'Donnell, & Jinks, in press; King, Staffieri, & Adelgais, 1998; O'Donnell, 1999; Okada & Simon, 1997; Teasley, 1995). Hence, these discourse features serve as proximal indicators of the educational value of CR discussions.

A recent study has demonstrated that children participating in CR discussions acquire functional rhetorical moves, or argument stratagems, introduced by innovative group members. For example, one argument stratagem identified by Anderson et al. (2001) was used in situations in which the speaker wants to personalize and extend the story world to invite the discussion participants to experience the dilemma faced by the protagonist. The stratagem has a general form of "Places classmate in [SCENARIO]" and is exemplified by the following statement from one of CR discussions: "Allen, what if you fell in the ice and Trent said, I don't want to save you." Anderson et al. analyzed occurrences of 13 different argument stratagems during 48 CR discussions, concluding that "once an argument stratagem emerges in a discussion, it tends to spread to other children and occur with increasing frequency" (p. 41). Children seem to appropriate an argument stratagem when they judge that the stratagem would be a useful tool for advancing understanding or adding to the persuasive force of an argument. Hence, there is evidence that CR discussions promote children's acquisition of skills of argument.

The question remains, however, whether CR students will exhibit improved argumentation in a context other than the one in which the skill was originally practiced. In fact, a fundamental concern of any educational initiative is transfer of learning. This study focuses on exactly this issue. It examines whether oral discussions can help students acquire "portable" knowledge of argumentation. The study compares persuasive essays of students from three classrooms that participated in CR with students from three comparable classrooms that did not. The goal of the study is to determine whether the CR classrooms exhibit better skills of argument. The approach was to code students' essays into categories reflecting aspects of argumentation and test the differences between CR and contrast classrooms.

## METHOD

### Sample

Students and teachers from four public schools in central Illinois participated in the study. Two same-grade classrooms were selected in each of two schools (School A and School B), one of which participated in CR discussions, and the other served as contrast. In the third school (School C), the contrast classroom was not selected from the same school because the teacher in the corresponding classroom had previously worked with CR and had incorporated CR into her instruction. The CR classroom in School C was matched with a contrast classroom from the fourth school (School D). School D was selected because it served the same population of students in terms of the ethnic and socioeconomic composition. Students from contrast classrooms received regular language arts instruction and did not participate in CR.

School A was a rural public school with students from primarily European American families. School B was a small-city public school serving mainly middle-income families. Schools C and D were small-city public schools serving mainly low-income families. The latter two schools had a large percentage of African American students. Students in Schools A, C, and D were fifth graders. In School B, students in both the CR and the contrast classrooms were fourth graders.

The total number of student participants was 115. There were 27 boys and 26 girls in CR classrooms, and 33 boys and 29 girls in contrast classrooms.

The six teachers were volunteers. Teachers who were to implement CR in their classrooms attended a workshop to familiarize them with the CR model. In addition, CR teachers received continuous coaching and support throughout the project from members of the research team.

### Procedure

Students in CR and contrast classrooms completed a vocabulary test, indicating the words they knew from a list of 88 words and nonwords. Tests of this type have been shown to be reliable and valid measures of vocabulary knowledge (Anderson & Freebody, 1983).

During the 5-week period of the intervention, students from CR classrooms met twice a week in small groups (6 to 8 participants) to discuss controversial issues. The discussions typically lasted 15 to 20 min. The stories that provided the basis for discussions were identical across the classrooms. As previously explained, students were supposed to take positions on each issue and provide supporting reasons and evidence for their opinions. With coaching from the teacher, students were supposed to challenge each other's viewpoints, offer counterarguments, respond to counterarguments with rebuttals, and ask for clarification as needed. Children were prompted to use the story information as the basis for their claims.

Students were exposed to the specific formal argument devices that promote the development of reasoned discourse. For example, a teacher would model, prompt, or encourage students to explicitly reference information as coming from the story by saying: "In the story it said, [EVIDENCE]?" or "Where does it say that [EVIDENCE]?" Another formal argument device frequently advanced in CR discussions is "Other people might say [COUNTERARGUMENT]" or "Some people may disagree because [COUNTERARGUMENT]." The latter form is used to prompt students to think of alternative perspectives and, possibly, reconcile their own positions with the positions of others. As implemented in this study, the CR method did not include any direct teaching of argument concepts or strategies, and there were no planned opportunities for students to reflect on the strengths and weaknesses of their discussions.

In addition to oral discussions, twice per week students engaged in 15-min CR discussions with the other participating classrooms via Web forums. Each forum, consisting of 6 to 8 participants, was moderated by one of the teachers or a research assistant who provided support for children's acquisition of reasoning skills.

At the end of the 5-week period, students from CR and contrast classrooms were asked to write a persuasive essay based on a story about a boy named Thomas. Thomas wins the school Pinewood Derby race, but he breaks the rules by not making his model car by himself. He confides to his classmate, Jack, that he has received help in making his car. Jack is faced with the dilemma of whether he should tell on Thomas. Jack feels sorry for Thomas, who has never won a race before and is not liked by many students, and Jack does not want to be a tattle-tale. On the other hand, Jack worked very hard on his own car and really wanted to win. Plus, Jack feels that cheating in the car race is not right. Students were asked to write an essay answering the question of whether Jack should tell on Thomas, and they were given 40 min to complete the task. A writing prompt for the essay read as follows:

In the next few pages, write whether or not you think Jack should tell on Thomas. Remember:
- Use good reasons and evidence to support your writing.
- Some people might disagree with you. Think about what these people might say to you and how you would respond to them.
- Do your best and write as much as you can. You can go back and reread the story if you like.

*Essay scoring.* A coding system was devised to provide a low-inference, quantitative measure of students' reasoning. The objective of the coding system is to measure students' ability to consider a variety of relevant arguments, counterarguments, and rebuttals. It is also designed to assess students' disposition to use textual information as evidence and to employ certain formal argument devices. It should be emphasized that the coding system does not assess quality of writing as reflected by spelling, grammar, organization, or niceties of expression.

Essays were coded in five steps. During the first step, essays were divided into idea units that represent the distinct parts of a claim. Generally, an idea unit is defined as a sentence or a clause that contains a verb or a participle and expresses one action. For example, the following sentence contains four idea units:

All the other kids *worked* on their own cars (1) and *missed* their favorite TV shows (2), while Thomas *was watching* TV (3), or *doing* something fun (4).

Second, each unit is classified into one of the following categories:

1. *Coded*. This category includes idea units that are clear and relevant to the main question. It also contains the formal argument devices described earlier.
2. *Not coded*. This category includes idea units that are unclear (i.e., unintelligible or illegible), irrelevant (i.e., claims that do not pertain to the issue under consideration), or supplementary (i.e., additional statements that are not arguments, such as restatements of a taken position and phrases like "The End" or "That's all, folks!").

Third, only coded units are further classified into one of the following subcategories, with the restriction that an idea unit can appear in only one subcategory:

1. *Position*. Identifies the student's position on the main issue. The position is categorized as positive (yes), negative (no), or undecided. The coding is assigned after reading the whole essay.
2. *Argument*. Represents a relevant idea unit that supports the taken position.
3. *Counterargument*. Designates a relevant idea unit that opposes the taken position.
4. *Rebuttal*. Stands for a relevant idea unit that responds to the opposing position.
5. *Form*. Identifies formal argument devices encouraged during CR.
6. *Repeat*. Represents an idea unit that adds no new information to what is already stated in the essay.

Fourth, units categorized as argument, counterargument, and rebuttal may be additionally classified as *textual information*. Textual information is a quotation from the story or a close paraphrase.

Finally, units designated as form include the following subcategories:

1. *Explicit Reference.* Labeling information as coming directly from the story. For example, "It said in the story [EVIDENCE]" or "At the end it said [EVIDENCE]."
2. *Perspective.* Recognition of the alternative viewpoints through the use of a formal argument device emphasized in CR. The idea units that approximate CR form "Other people might say [COUNTERARGUMENT]" are included in this category.

Idea units are classified as form if they express the conceptual notion of labeling information as coming from the story or acknowledging the existence of alternative perspectives. The specific wording can differ from that typical during CR discussions. For example, statements such as "Then people would argue and say, well, [COUNTERARGUMENT]" or "Probably the only reason why anyone else would want to disagree is [COUNTERARGUMENT]" are scored as form.

The coding system was applied to the data using NUD*IST[1] computer software. All essays were scored by one rater blind to whether the essay was written by a student from a CR classroom or a contrast classroom. Scoring was checked at least twice to ensure agreement with the coding system. Twenty-nine essays were randomly selected to check interrater reliability. These essays were scored by a second rater who had been trained in applying the coding system. The correlation coefficient for the coded category between the two raters was .96. The correlation coefficient for the irrelevant category was .99.

## Hypothesis

The primary hypothesis (Test 1) is that, on the average, CR students will outperform contrast students in the total number of arguments, counterarguments, rebuttals, uses of textual information, and formal argument devices.

Three alternative definitions of the primary hypothesis are also tested. First, it might be argued that adding textual information units to the total measure overweights students' claims that refer to story information. To address this point, the second analysis (Test 2) omitted textual information units from the total measure. The resulting measure consisted of only arguments, counterarguments, rebuttals, and forms.

Second, to analyze the extent to which the primary measure is affected by students' disposition to use formal argument devices, units coded as form are dropped from the analysis in Test 3. The dependent measure in Test 3 consists of arguments, counterarguments, rebuttals, and textual information.

Finally, it may be argued that units classified as irrelevant constitute valid parts of arguments and should not be excluded. That is, the rater may have missed the connection of certain students' claims to the main topic of the essay. In this analy-

---

[1]NUD*IST stands for Non-Numerical Unstructured Data * Indexing Searching and Theorizing.

sis (Test 4), student essays were compared on a measure that includes the units classified as irrelevant.

## RESULTS

The data were first analyzed using an analysis of variance (ANOVA) with two fixed factors. The first factor was whether students engaged in CR discussions, which was given the short label discussion (Factor A). The second factor was school type (Factor B). Schools C and D were combined into one level of the latter factor, as the contrast classroom in School D was chosen to match the student population and the school culture of the CR classroom in School C. Hence, it was assumed that six classrooms came from three school types, two classrooms from each type. The treatment in this study was group oriented, and could result in nonindependence among students. However, we used an individual student as a unit of analysis in this study. The probability of Type I error was set to .05.

The dependent variable, including its primary and alternative definitions, was transformed to achieve greater homogeneity of error variance and normality of residuals. The transformed score was set equal to the square root of the sum of the original score and 0.5. Transformed scores were regressed on the factors in the model and the residuals were assessed in terms of their conformity with ANOVA assumptions. The examination of histogram plots did not reveal substantial departures from normality. Also, according to Kolmogorov–Smirnov tests, the hypothesis that the sample comes from a normal distribution, was retained ($p < .617$ for primary measure, $p < .745$, $p < .424$, and $p < .929$ for the alternative measures).

The hypothesis regarding homogeneity of error variance was tested using the Cohran $F$ test. For the primary measure the observed value equaled 3.67. This is close to a critical value of 3.76 ($\alpha = .05$), but does not exceed it. The $F$ statistics for three alternative measures were 5.17, 6.61, and 6.00, and exceeded the critical value. Therefore, the $F$ test for the primary measure is more trustworthy than those for alternative definitions of the dependent variable. The number of observations is approximately equal within each treatment level, so violations of the homogeneity of variance assumption should have only a slight effect on Type I error rates. As we show shortly, the omnibus $F$ tests for the discussion factor far exceeded the critical value corresponding to $\alpha = .05$. Therefore, violating the homogeneity of variance assumption in the case of the alternative measures should not affect the conclusions.

### Primary Measure of Reasoned Argumentation

The dependent variable for the primary measure represented the total number of idea units coded as arguments, counterarguments, rebuttals, formal argument devices, and textual information. According to the two-factor ANOVA (Test 1), ef-

TABLE 1
Analysis of Variance for Primary Measure (Test 1)

| Source | df | Ms | F |
|---|---|---|---|
| Discussion [A] | 1 | 9.94 | 9.34* |
| School type [B] | 2 | 9.23 | 8.68* |
| Interaction [A] × [B] | 2 | 0.50 | 0.47 |
| Within cells | 109 | 1.06 | |
| Total | 114 | | |

*$p < .01$.

TABLE 2
Follow-Up Tests Comparing Collaborative Reasoning
(CR) and Contrast (C) Classrooms Within Schools

| Classrooms Within | M CR–C Difference | df | t |
|---|---|---|---|
| School A | 0.82 | 109 | 2.39** |
| School B | 0.36 | 109 | 1.12 |
| School C/D | 0.61 | 109 | 1.83* |

*$p < .05$. **$p < .01$.

fects of both the discussion and school type factors were statistically significant, although the interaction was not (see Table 1).

The omnibus $F$ test was followed up with three directional a priori orthogonal contrasts to determine whether the effects of CR discussion were consistent within different school types. The mean differences were significant in two schools. In School B, the mean difference was not significant, but it was in the expected direction; that is, the CR group had a higher mean than its contrast (see Table 2).

Finally, the effect size of the discussion factor was assessed using Cohen's (1992) guidelines. The effect size of discussion was .27, which Cohen categorized as a medium effect.

## Alternative Definitions of Reasoned Argumentation

For all three alternative measures, the results of the two-factor ANOVA and the follow-up tests were fully consistent with those presented for the primary measure. In Test 2, the dependent variable represented the total number of idea units coded as arguments, counterarguments, rebuttals, and formal argument devices. Textual information has been excluded. The discussion effect in Test 2 was statistically significant, $F(1, 109) = 9.96, p < .01$. In Test 3, the dependent variable included textual information, but excluded the units coded as form. The means for CR and contrast groups were significantly different, $F(1, 109) = 8.25, p < .01$. The dependent variable in Test 4 consisted of the total number of arguments, counter-arguments, rebuttals, formal argument devices, textual information, and irrelevant idea units. Again, CR students had a significantly higher mean on the dependent measure, $F(1, 109) = 9.91, p < .01$. The school type effect was significant for all three alternative measures. In order, $F$ statistics and probability levels for Test 2 through Test 4 were $F(2, 109) = 5.79, p < .01$; $F(2, 109) = 8.21, p < .01$; and $F(2, 109) = 11.61, p < .01$. The interaction between the school type and the discussion factors was not significant for the alternative measures, $F(2, 109) = 0.51, ns$; $F(2, 109) = 0.49, ns$; and $F(2, 109) = 1.98, ns$, respectively.

Consistent with the primary measure, the follow-up tests for the alternative measures reveal that the differences between the means were significant for Schools A and C–D, but not for School B. The mean differences and corresponding $t$ values are presented in Table 3.

## Vocabulary Knowledge

To determine whether classrooms differed in terms of their average vocabulary knowledge, a two-factor ANOVA was performed, using vocabulary scores as the dependent variable. There was no significant difference in mean vocabulary scores of CR and contrast classrooms, $F(1, 111) = 0.51, ns$. Means for CR and contrast classrooms were 0.38 ($SD = 0.22$) and 0.40 ($SD = 0.25$), respectively. The fact that groups were comparable increases confidence that the differences between the groups on measures of reasoned argumentation were due to the CR discussions.

## Adjustment for Variation in Vocabulary Knowledge

Although Pedhazur (1997) advised against applying analysis of covariance (ANCOVA) to intact groups, another analysis of the data was performed using the

TABLE 3
Follow-Up Tests for Alternative Measures Comparing Collaborative Reasoning (CR) and Contrast (C) Classrooms Within Schools

| Test | Classrooms Within | M CR–C Difference | t (df = 109) |
|---|---|---|---|
| Test 2 | School A | 0.78 | 2.53** |
| | School B | 0.35 | 1.21 |
| | School C/D | 0.53 | 1.76* |
| Test 3 | School A | 0.76 | 2.26* |
| | School B | 0.31 | 0.96 |
| | School C/D | 0.59 | 1.79* |
| Test 4 | School A | 1.09 | 2.97** |
| | School B | 0.12 | 0.34 |
| | School C/D | 0.79 | 2.22* |

*$p < .05$. **$p < .01$.

vocabulary score as a covariate. The primary goal of the analysis was to remove the error variance associated with vocabulary knowledge, rather than to equate groups on vocabulary knowledge.

The test of homogeneity of regression coefficients for the covariate was very close to exceeding the allowed critical value. Therefore, the analysis should be interpreted with caution. The results of the ANCOVA were again fully consistent with the ANOVA analysis for the primary and alternative measures. The discussion effect was significant, $F(1, 103) = 12.60, p < .01$. The school type effect was also significant, $F(2, 103) = 5.95, p < .01$, but the two-way and three-way interactions were not, $F(2, 103) = 0.43$, $ns$; and $F(5, 103) = 2.14$, $ns$, respectively. The mean differences were significant for School A, $t(103) = 2.56, p < .01$, and School C–D, $t(103) = 2.09, p < .05$, but not for School B, $t(103) = 1.40$, $ns$. The effect size for the CR discussion variable was equal to 0.32, which is still a medium effect size.

## Subcategories of Reasoned Argumentation

Means and standard deviations for the variables that comprise the dependent measures are presented in Table 4. It is apparent that CR groups had higher means in all argument subcategories. The essays of CR students also contained a higher total number of words ($M = 152$) than the essays of contrast students ($M = 97$). Total number of words was most highly correlated with the alternative measure that included irrelevant units ($r = .81$). The correlation between number of words and the primary measure was .63. These results are consistent with the intended function of the coding system, which was designed to count only propositions that relate to argumentation.

Although there were more words written by students in CR groups, we do not suppose that CR students were merely more verbose, and were stumbling on ideas relevant to argumentation unwittingly. Our interpretation is that, through participation in CR discussions, students were able to internalize an argument schema,

TABLE 4
Means and Standard Deviations of Argumentation Subcategories

| Measure | CR | | Contrast | |
|---|---|---|---|---|
| | M | SD | M | SD |
| Arguments | 8.70 | 6.74 | 6.95 | 4.41 |
| Counterarguments | 2.02 | 2.63 | 0.94 | 1.62 |
| Rebuttals | 0.88 | 1.68 | 0.50 | 0.97 |
| Form | 0.62 | 1.38 | 0.16 | 0.45 |
| Textual information | 3.62 | 3.15 | 2.68 | 2.34 |
| Irrelevant | 3.36 | 9.88 | 1.63 | 3.87 |

*Note.* CR = collaborative reasoning.

which in turn allowed them to construct a more complete argument. In other words, having an argument schema enabled students to consider and present more arguments, counterarguments, rebuttals, and formal argument devices.

## DETAILED ANALYSIS OF SELECTED ESSAYS

A detailed examination of selected essays was performed to illustrate the nature of differences between essays written by CR students and contrast students. Two essays were selected from each school, one from the CR class and one from the contrast class. We judged that these essays exemplified the set of essays in each classroom and had a total number of coded units that approximated the means for their respective groups. The spelling in essays has been corrected, but the content and the grammar have been left unchanged.

School A

*Essay 1 (CR, mean for the classroom = 22, units for selected essay = 28).*

> I think Jack should not tell on Thomas. It said in the story that he had never won anything. It looked like Thomas was getting some friends and if Jack tattled Thomas would lose them. There would be other chances for Jack to win something. Some people might say that Thomas doesn't deserve the prize. But Thomas was poor because it said he smelled strange. Thomas was mean because he didn't have any friends. I think Jack should let Thomas win the prize. But someone might say that Thomas has been mean and Jack should tell. The reason Thomas is mean is because no one is nice to him. But some people might say that it meant a lot to Jack and that Thomas did not put much effort. (Which is true). This might change my mind.

In this essay, the student shows a firm grasp of an argument schema. He is able to clearly state his position, provide supporting arguments, and consider and rebut counterarguments. The student's claims are unambiguous, complete, and relevant to the main issue. They are supported with story evidence that is accurate, differentiated from claims, and related to propositions. In addition to employing textual evidence, the student appeals to hypothetical situations and general principles (i.e., "It looked like Thomas was getting some friends and if Jack tattled Thomas would lose them. There would be other chances for Jack to win something.").

The essay contains a systematic anticipation and recognition of opposing arguments. In a way, it represents a dialogue between "some people" and the student. Counterarguments are not simply dismissed, they are seriously considered and responded to. The student is open to alternative perspectives, which, through the use of rebuttals, are being integrated with the chosen position. Interestingly, the student's opinion on the issue is tentative, as indicated by the last sentence. He is willing to reevaluate his position when presented with compelling arguments.

The essay also exhibits two other characteristics desirable in argumentative discourse. First, textual information is specifically marked as coming from the story through the use of such phrases as "it said in the story" and "it said [EVIDENCE]." Second, the student frequently utilizes the CR form "some people might say [COUNTERARGUMENT]." Perhaps it is this form that provides the student with a tool, prompting him to have a dialogic argument that enhances and corrects otherwise egocentric thinking.

*Essay 2 (Contrast, mean for the classroom = 12, units for selected essay = 12).*

> Jack should of told on Thomas because Thomas cheated and also it would of helped his self-esteem because if he doesn't he won't be able to forgive himself knowing he could be the one with that trophy or maybe somebody who deserved it not Thomas and also the only friends he's gonna loose are the ones who would probably cheat themselves so he's better off. If they say they're mad I'd just ask them if they wanted to live a lie.

This essay represents a good attempt at persuasive writing. The position is clearly stated and several supporting arguments are presented. The student, however, does not directly appeal to the primary source, the story, for supporting evidence. Similar to the first essay, the arguments in this essay include hypothetical situations and general principles. Yet, compared to the first essay, the hypothetical situations are not as easily inferred from the story information. They represent bigger leaps and are less convincing (i.e., "also the only friends he's gonna loose are the ones who would probably cheat themselves so he's better off").

In the last sentence, the student makes an attempt at a counterargument (i.e., "If they say they're mad"), but it is neither specific nor articulate. The student tries to respond to the opposing position (i.e., "I'd just ask them if they wanted to live a lie"), but the response is vague and merely represents a denial of the opposing claim. The student's writing is egocentric. There is no reflection or critical evaluation of the chosen position. Alternative perspectives are not given much consideration.

School B

*Essay 1 (CR, mean for the classroom = 15, units for selected essay = 17).*

> I think that Jack should tell on Thomas because he cheated. The reason is that the teacher said to build it by yourself. Thomas did not build the car by himself and that

was very wrong because his brother helped him and the teacher said not to get help to do it on your own. Thomas's brother should not have helped him build that car. Everyone else had made their cars on their own and Thomas should have made the car by him self too. I think Jack should tell because it was wrong to cheat like that and because he was in the race to and he got cheated. That is what I thank about the story.

*Essay 2 (Contrast, mean for the classroom = 10, units for selected essay = 11).*

Yes I think Jack should tell on Thomas because Thomas cheated his brother helped him and he was supposed to do it by himself and he pick on kids a lot. I would have told on him as soon as he told me and got him in trouble and then laugh at him and someone else would have got the prize however it was how won the prize so I would have told on him.

The preceding two essays differ mainly in the number and type of reasons advanced by students in support of their positions. In the first essay, the student presents more relevant and compelling reasons. For example, the conclusion that "Thomas cheated" is supported by the explicit mentioning of the rules of the game (i.e., "the teacher said to build it by yourself"), as well as by identifying Thomas's actions, which go against the rules (i.e., "Thomas did not build the car by himself"). Although not directly citing the source, the student from the CR group frequently appeals to the story information for evidence, compared to appeals to personal intuition by the student in the contrast group (i.e., "I would have told on him as soon as he told me and got him in trouble and then laugh at him"). On the formal level, the first essay utilizes reasoned discourse more effectively, which is exemplified by such statements as "The reason is that [REASON]," and the frequent use of the CR form "[CONCLUSION], because [REASON]." Neither essay, however, gives consideration to an alternative position.

## Schools C and D

*Essay 1 (CR, mean for the classroom = 12, units for selected essay = 11).*

I don't think Jack should tell on Thomas because if Thomas had never won a thing like a trophy or a race, I think he should just let Thomas be happy and have the trophy even though Thomas did not make the model car and Thomas's older brother did I think he should just let it slip by.

I think other thought are that Jack should tell and that he should not get the trophy because he did not make the car.

*Essay 2 (Contrast, mean for the classroom = 9, units for selected essay = 11).*

> I think Jack should tell on Thomas because he didn't build the car his brother did half of it and Thomas won all of the races and jack was working very hard. Thomas did half of his car like painting and the stickers and stuff. Mr. Howard passed out instructions to the whole class. Thomas won his first prize.

These two essays are similar in terms of the number and type of arguments used to support a chosen position. Both essays present relevant reasons and both effectively utilize story information to justify conclusions. However, the CR student reflects on alternative perspectives (i.e., "even though Thomas did not make the model car and Thomas's older brother did" and "I think other thought are that Jack should tell and that he should not get the trophy because he did not make the car."). The CR student, however, is not successful at either responding to the opposing claims or reconciling the chosen position and counterarguments. As for the contrast essay, it lacks a coherent consideration of the opposing position. The last sentence (i.e., "Thomas won his first prize.") may be an attempt at counterargument, but it is vague.

In summary, a detailed analysis of several student essays further illustrates the differences between the groups. CR students are generally more successful at generating and articulating an argument, considering alternative perspectives, marshaling text information, and effectively utilizing certain formal argument devices.

## DISCUSSION

In this study, students who participated in CR discussions wrote essays that contained a significantly greater number of arguments, counterarguments, rebuttals, uses of formal argument devices, and references to text information than the essays of similar students who did not experience CR. Evidently, reasoning skills acquired in discussion transferred to a different context, from collaborative oral discussions to the individual task of persuasive writing. This finding is consistent with the more general thesis that participation in oral argumentation promotes individual reasoning.

To explain these findings, we invoke the concept of an argument schema. An argument schema incorporates knowledge of the rhetorical structure of an argument, the inferential rules of reasoning, and other cognitive and social practices useful in argumentation (e.g., Anderson et al., 2001; Chambliss, 1995; Cheng & Holyoak, 1985, 1989; Crowhurst, 1988; Hidi & Hildyard, 1983; Politzer & Nguyen-Xuan, 1992; Scardamalia & Bereiter, 1986). Because an argument schema is abstract, it enables transfer between different contexts and communicative modes.

Argument schemas are comprised of the structural and functional communalities people have abstracted from their experience with argumentation. The richer and more extensive the experience the more refined and complete the schema. With suitable experience, even children as young as the participants in this study can make considerable progress in the elaboration of a useful schema. Our theory is that children generalize elements common in CR discussions. These common elements include formulating an opinion, supporting it with reasons, presenting and responding to counterarguments, and using certain rhetorical forms.

Within the limits that this was a quasi-experiment, without random assignment of participants to conditions, the study provides fairly strong evidence that students acquired some generalized knowledge of argumentation. The CR and contrast classrooms were matched on ethnicity and socioeconomic status and were nearly identical in average vocabulary knowledge. Effects were obtained not only on the primary measure of reasoned argumentation, but also on each of three alternate measures that excluded different subcategories of essay propositions that, according to some ways of thinking, might have biased the study. For instance, the fact that there was a strong effect favoring CR on the alternate measure that excluded formal argument devices rules out the interpretation that CR students were simply learning catch phrases such as "In the story it said [EVIDENCE]."

The persuasive writing task probably did not tap everything children know about reasoned argumentation. The communication channel can influence the quality of arguments people are able to produce (Pellegrini, Galda, & Rubin, 1984). This may be especially true for younger children, as "the written channel may interfere with children's cognitive role-taking and communicative performance" (Kroll, as cited in Pellegrini et al., 1984, p. 287). Interestingly, there was not a significant difference between CR and contrast groups in School B, which may be due to the fact that these students were the only fourth graders in the study. In any case, it is not clear whether the reasoning abilities and dispositions acquired by CR students were fully displayed in their writings. Having an individual oral argumentation task in addition to a writing task would help to determine the effect of the communication channel on students' performance. Future research needs to examine whether the results of this study can be replicated over a longer retention interval, as well as using a different kind of text, different kinds of writing prompts, and assessment tasks that involve a different communication channel.

The coding system used in this study did not take into consideration the relations between the propositions comprising an argument. In other words, only the number of relevant propositions was assessed, and not the manner in which they were linked. Analyzing argument depth, or the extent to which individual arguments are elaborated, is an interesting direction to take in future studies. Chinn and Anderson (1998) proposed an argument network method that enables assessment of the depth of an argument.

We have stressed the role of oral argumentation in producing the results observed in this study. It is true that students engaged in written discussions via Web forums, as well as oral face-to-face discussions, but we are inclined to discount the influence of the Web discussions. Argument development was meager in most of the Web discussions because of students' generally poor keyboarding skills and, perhaps, the unfamiliarity of the communication channel. Web discussions were supposed to resemble the oral discussions and, in fact, student contributions were written in a conversational style rather than the essay style required by the persuasive writing task.

In conclusion, the findings of this study should be interpreted with the caution due in any quasi-experimental research. However, these findings add to an emerging picture of social and cognitive processes that underlie the development of reasoning. Collaborative discussion appears to be an effective training ground for the development and internalization of generalized knowledge of argumentation.

## REFERENCES

Anderson, R. C., Chinn, C., Chang, J., Waggoner, M., & Yi, H. (1997). On the logical integrity of children's arguments. *Cognition and Instruction, 15,* 135–167.

Anderson, R. C., Chinn, C., Waggoner, M., & Nguyen, K. (1998). Intellectually stimulating story discussions. In J. Osborn & F. Lehr (Eds.), *Literacy for all: Issues in teaching and learning* (pp. 170–186). New York: Guilford.

Anderson, R. C., & Freebody, P. (1983). Reading comprehension and the assessment and acquisition of word knowledge. In B. Hutson (Ed.), *Advances in reading/language research* (Vol. 2, pp. 213–256). Greenwich, CT: JAI.

Anderson, R. C., Nguyen-Jahiel, K., McNurlen, B., Archodidou, A., Kim, S., Reznitskaya, A., Tillmanns, M., & Gilbert, L. (2001). The snowball phenomenon: Spread of ways of talking and ways of thinking across groups of children. *Cognition and Instruction, 19,* 1–46.

Anderson, R. C., & Pearson, D. (1984). A schema-theoretic view of basic processes in reading comprehension. In P. D. Pearson, R. Barr, M. L. Kamil, & P. Mosenthal (Eds.), *Handbook of reading research* (pp. 255–292). New York: Longman.

Applebee, A. N., Langer, J. A., Mullis, I. V., Latham, A. S., & Gentile, C. A. (1994). *The national assessment of educational progress 1992 report card.* Princeton, NJ: Educational Testing Service.

Au, K. H., & Mason, J. M. (1981). Social organizational factors in learning to read: The balance of rights hypothesis. *Reading Research Quarterly, 17,* 115–152.

Bakhtin, M. M. (1981). *The dialogic imagination: Four essays by M. M. Bakhtin* (M. Holquist, Ed. & Trans., C. Emerson, Trans.). Austin: University of Texas Press.

Bakhtin, M. M. (1986). *Speech genres and other late essays by M. M. Bakhtin* (M. Holquist & C. Emerson, Eds., V. McGee, Trans.). Austin: University of Texas Press.

Burnes, B. (1981). Harry Stottlemeier's discovery—The Minnesota experience. *Thinking, The Journal of Philosophy for Children, 3*(1), 8–11.

Cazden, C. B. (1988). *Classroom discourse: The language of teaching and learning.* Portsmouth, NH: Heinemann.

Cheng, P., & Holyoak, K. J. (1985). Pragmatic reasoning schemas. *Cognitive Psychology, 17,* 391–416.

Cheng, P., & Holyoak, K. J. (1989). On the natural selection of reasoning theories. *Cognition, 33,* 285–313.

Chi, M. T. H., de Leeuw, N., Chiu, M., & LaVancher, C. (1994). Eliciting self-explanations improves understanding. *Cognitive Science, 18,* 439–477.

Chinn, C. A., & Anderson, R. C. (1998). The structure of discussions that promote reasoning. *Teachers College Record, 100,* 315–368.

Chinn, C. A., Anderson, R. C., & Waggoner, M. A. (2001). Pattern of discourse in two kinds of literature discussion. *Reading Research Quarterly, 36,* 378–411.

Chinn, C. A., O'Donnell, A. M., & Jinks, T. S. (in press). The structure of discourse in collaborative learning. *Journal of Experimental Education.*

Cohen, J. (1992). A power primer. *Psychological Bulletin, 112,* 155–159.

Commeyras, M. (1994). Promoting critical thinking through dialogical reading thinking lessons. *Reading Teacher, 46,* 486–494.

Crowhurst, M. (1988). *Research review: Patterns of development in writing persuasive/argumentative discourse* (Rep. No. 506374). (ERIC Document Reproduction Service No. ED 299 596) Vancouver, Canada: The University of British Columbia.

Crowhurst, M. (1990). Teaching and learning the writing of persuasive/argumentative discourse. *Canadian Journal of Education, 15,* 348–359.

Goldman, S. R., & Rakestraw, J. A. (2000). Structural aspects of constructing meaning from text. In M. L. Kamil, P. B. Mosenthal, P. D. Pearson, & R. Barr (Eds.), *Handbook of reading research* (Vol. 3, pp. 311–335). Mahwah, NJ: Lawrence Erlbaum Associates, Inc.

Govier, T. (1987). *Problems in argument analysis and evaluation.* Providence, RI: Foris.

Hidi, S., & Hildyard, A. (1983). The comparison of oral and written productions in two discourse types. *Discourse Processes, 6,* 91–105.

Higa, W. (1980). Philosophy for children in Hawaii: A quantitative evaluation. *Thinking, The Journal of Philosophy for Children, 2*(1), 21–31.

Karp, W. (1985). Why Johnny can't think? *Harper's Magazine, 270*(1621), 69–73.

King, A., Staffieri, A., & Adelgais, A. (1998). Mutual peer tutoring: Effects of structuring tutorial interaction to scaffold peer learning. *Journal of Educational Psychology, 90,* 134–152.

Kirch, I., Jungleblut, A., Jenkins, L., & Kolstad, A. (1993). *Adult literacy in America.* Princeton, NJ: Educational Testing Service.

Knudson, R. E. (1992, December). *An analysis of persuasive discourse: Learning how to take a stand.* Paper presented at the National Reading Conference, San Antonio, TX. (ERIC Document Reproduction Service No. ED 353 381)

Kuhn, D. (1991). *The skills of argument.* Cambridge, England: Cambridge University Press.

Kuhn, D. (1992). Thinking as argument. *Harvard Educational Review, 62,* 155–177.

Kuhn, D., Shaw, V., & Felton, M. (1997). Effects of dyadic interaction on argumentative reasoning. *Cognition and Instruction, 15,* 287–315.

Langer, J. A., Campbell, J. R., Neuman, S. B., Mullis, I. V. S., Persky, H. R., & Donahue, P. L. (1995). *Reading assessment redesigned.* Princeton, NJ: Educational Testing Service.

Lipman, M. (1997). Education for democracy and freedom. *Wesleyan Graduate Review, 1*(1), 32–38.

McCann, T. M. (1989). Student argumentative writing knowledge and ability at three grade levels. *Research in the Teaching of English, 23,* 63–77.

Means, M. L., & Voss, J. F. (1996). Who reasons well? Two studies of informal reasoning among children of different grade, ability, and knowledge levels. *Cognition and Instruction, 14,* 139–178.

Nickerson, R. S., Perkins, D. N., & Smith, E. E. (Eds.). (1985). *The teaching of thinking.* Hillsdale, NJ: Lawrence Erlbaum Associates, Inc.

O'Donnell, A. (1999). Structuring dyadic interaction through scripted cooperation. In A. M. O'Donnell & A. King (Eds.), *Cognitive perspectives on peer learning* (pp. 179–196). Mahwah, NJ: Lawrence Erlbaum Associates, Inc.

Okada, T., & Simon, H. A. (1997). Collaborative discovery in a scientific domain. *Cognitive Science, 21,* 109–146.

Onosko, J. J. (1990). Comparing teacher's instruction to promote students' thinking. *Journal of Curriculum Studies, 22,* 443–461.

Paul, R. W. (1986). Dialogical thinking: Critical thought essential to the acquisition of rational knowledge and passions. In J. B. Baron & R. J. Sternberg (Eds.), *Teaching thinking skills: Theory and practice* (pp. 127–148). New York: Freeman.

Pedhazur, E. J. (1997). *Multiple regression in behavioral research.* New York: Harcourt Brace.

Pellegrini, A. D., Galda, L., & Rubin, D. (1984). Persuasion as a social-cognitive activity: The effects of age and channel of communication on children's production of persuasive messages. *Language and Communication, 4,* 285–293.

Politzer, G., & Nguyen-Xuan, A. (1992). Reasoning about conditional promises and warnings: Darwinian algorithms, mental models, relevance judgments or pragmatic schemas. *Quarterly Journal of Experimental Psychology, 44A,* 401–412.

Scardamalia, M., & Bereiter, C. (1986). Research on written composition. In M. Wittrock (Ed.), *Handbook of research on teaching* (3rd ed., pp. 778–803). London: Macmillan.

Simon, C. (1975). Philosophy for students with learning disabilities. *Thinking, The Journal of Philosophy for Children, 1*(1), 21–27.

Teasley, S. D. (1995). The role of talk in children's peer collaborations. *Developmental Psychology, 31,* 207–220.

Vygotsky, L. (1981). The genesis of higher order mental functions. In J. W. Wertsch (Ed.), *The concept of activity in Soviet psychology* (pp. 144–184). Armonk, NY: Sharpe.

Waggoner, M., Chinn, C., Yi, H., & Anderson, R. C. (1995). Collaborative reasoning about stories. *Language Arts, 72,* 582–588.

# Changing Stances on Abortion During Case-Based Reasoning Tasks: Who Changes and Under What Conditions

Ronan S. Bernas
*Department of Psychology*
*Eastern Illinois University*

Nancy L. Stein
*Department of Psychology*
*The University of Chicago*

College students who supported opposing positions on abortion were asked to state their reasons for and against their own position as well as their reason for and against the opposition. Students then served as judges on 4 cases in which women were seeking an abortion. The circumstances motivating a woman varied across the 4 cases. Case information either challenged or supported prototypic assumptions and beliefs that underlie a prolife or prochoice stance. Students who received information directly challenging their position on abortion changed stances more frequently than those who did not. Three additional factors also predicted changes in stances: (a) taking a prochoice rather than a prolife position, (b) being able to cite more problems with one's own position, and (c) receiving challenging cases that present novel rather than anticipated conditions motivating a woman's desire for abortion. The results are discussed in terms of a process model of conceptual change and learning, where changes in stances come about because of awareness of new information about the harms and benefits of each position, which in turn causes a shift in the relative ranking of important moral tenets that an arguer uses to support a position.

The goal of this article is to examine the nature of taking a stance on a controversial issue such as abortion. College students who held conditional or nonconditional stances on abortion, either pro or con, were asked to explain why they

---

Correspondence and requests for reprints should be sent to Ronan S. Bernas, Department of Psychology, Eastern Illinois University, 600 Lincoln Ave., Charleston, IL 61920. E-mail: cfrsb@eiu.edu

supported a position and why they found problems with the opposing position. They were also asked to generate reasons for supporting the opposing view and problems that they found with their own position. Students were then asked to be a judge in four cases in which women wanted to undergo an abortion. The cases were designed to either challenge or support prolife and prochoice stances. Our goal was to determine those dimensions of thinking and reasoning that predicted whether students would change or adhere to their general stance on abortion.

## THE NATURE OF CONSISTENCY IN TAKING ARGUMENTATIVE STANCES

The ease and process by which people change their stances on controversial issues has been a subject of debate for many years. Ross and Lepper (1980; Vallone, Ross, & Lepper, 1985) noted that asking people to reconsider or alter their positions on controversial issues often results in the person taking a more entrenched, committed stance. Under these conditions, differences of opinion become more extreme, and opponents end up disagreeing more than they did before the reappraisal was considered. As Sherif and Sherif (1953) observed, discussing and explaining one's position does not necessarily lead to greater understanding of and sensitivity to the opposite position. In the face of new evidence introduced by an opponent, an arguer often focuses on constructing counterarguments to the new evidence, devaluing legitimate new information as inappropriate, and stating that even greater negative consequences will occur if an opposing stance is supported.

On the other hand, many investigators have argued that conflict and argument situations are ideal for inducing a change of opinion on a specific issue. Dunn (1989, 1992), Murray (1972), Piaget (1932), and Valsiner and Cairns (1992) all argued that conflict situations provide a forum for considering new information about an issue and an opportunity to compare the positive and negative consequences of both positions. Investigators such as Stein and Miller (1990, 1993a, 1993b) provided empirical demonstrations of arguers switching their opinions in many different types of situations. The ability to switch positions occurs in both adults (Fisher & Brown, 1988; Stein, Bernas, & Calicchia, 1997) and children (Stein & Miller, 1993a, 1993b).

Our examination of past studies suggests that both entrenchment and change may occur, but under different sets of conditions. The nature of the circumstances motivating support for a position, the stakes involved, and the negative consequences of supporting a particular stance should be critical in predicting whether entrenchment or conceptual change occurs. We use a theory of argumentative thinking and reasoning (Stein & Bernas, 1999; Stein et al., 1997; Stein, Bernas, Calicchia, & Wright, 1995; Stein & Miller, 1990, 1993a, 1993b) to predict whether changes in positions will occur in making decisions to support a woman's right to seek an abortion.

## THE NATURE OF ARGUMENTATIVE REASONING AND TAKING A STANCE

Arguments arise when two people recognize that their goals and positions are mutually exclusive of one another (Stein & Miller, 1990, 1993a, 1993b), such that support for both positions cannot coexist at the same time. In the initial phases of an argument, both participants are motivated to defend their point of view by convincing their opponent of the superiority of their favored position (Fisher & Brown, 1988; Gottman, 1979; Stein & Miller, 1990). Both participants justify their positions by offering reasons that support their claims and by raising criticisms of the opposing side. The supporting evidence that arguers offer for their position is often linked directly to personal values, desired states of being, sociomoral principles, and knowledge about the costs and benefits of upholding their position oven their opponents (Shantz, 1987; Sillars & Garner, 1982; Stein & Miller, 1990, 1993a, 1993b; Voss, Fincher-Kiefer, Wiley, & Silfies, 1993; Voss, Wolfe, Militello, Fincher-Kiefer, & Ney, 1991).

In defending their position, arguers believe that the values and sociomoral principles supporting their own position are more important than those supporting the opposite stance (Stein & Miller, 1990, 1993a, 1993b). For example, on issues of abortion, arguers on opposing sides assign different degrees of value and importance to a woman's right to make the best choice for her physical and psychological well-being. A prochoice supporter assigns the highest value to this belief, whereas a prolife supporter assigns less value to this belief.

Arguers opposing each other also believe that more positive consequences will result from upholding their stance than from upholding the opposite stance (Stein & Miller, 1990, 1993a, 1993b). In many situations, both opponents contend that major disasters will occur (Stein et al., 1997; Stein & Miller, 1993b) if the opposing stance is allowed to prevail. As an example, prolife advocates often argue that abortion would result in the wanton killing of unborn children.

Although arguers tend to be committed to a particular position, they do differ on the unconditional nature of their stance. Some express an unconditional commitment to a prolife or prochoice stance, whereas others express conditional support, depending on the conditions and circumstances in a given situation (Stein & Miller, 1990, 1993a, 1993b). The conditional nature of support for abortion is even acknowledged by certain institutions, religions, and countries that support a consistent prolife stance. Although prolife supporters have strong beliefs about preserving the unborn child's life, situations do exist when prolife advocates must reevaluate the tenets of their support.

When a woman's life is threatened during pregnancy, for example, a dilemma exists as to whose life should be preserved—the woman's or the unborn child's. Many supporters of a prolife position favor an abortion when the mother's life is in danger because they believe that the negative consequences to the infant, should the mother not survive, could result in continual suffering and a poor quality of life for the child. They also believe that the mother's life is as important as the unborn child's life. Thus, the circumstances surrounding a case often necessitate a reevaluation of situations and moral principles not previously considered. A shift in terms of which moral principle is most important causes a shift in the position supported.

On the other hand, support for a position can be unconditional. These types of stances, however, are often based on inadequate knowledge of and familiarity with the opposing position (Stein & Miller, 1993a, 1993b). Arguers who are unconditionally committed to a position often lack knowledge and understanding about the reasons their opponents support the opposing position. They also lack knowledge about the limitations of and problems with their own position. Stein and her colleagues (Stein & Albro, 1997; Stein & Miller, 1990, 1993a, 1993b; Stein & Ross, 1996; Stein et al., 1997; Stein et al., 1995) showed that arguers of all ages offer more reasons to support their favored position than they do for their opponent's position. They also generate more counterarguments against the opposition than against their own position. Stratman (1990) also showed this bias to exist in lawyers who prepare and write briefs in courts of law. Judges who depend on unbiased summaries of a case are often disappointed when lawyers fail to introduce negative evidence against their own case. Even expert lawyers who should have more knowledge of an issue rarely raise any counterarguments against their own position (Kuhn, 1991).

The presence or absence of biased knowledge for and against each side of an issue has important theoretical and empirical implications for the outcomes of argumentation. Stein et al. (1997) demonstrated that understanding supporting reasons for the opposing side, in combination with criticisms of one's own stance, enables an arguer to compromise with an opponent more frequently. When arguers have a limited understanding of the issues, they are more likely to end their arguments in a win–loss situation or in a standoff.

## THE PROCESS OF CONCEPTUAL CHANGE IN ARGUMENTATION

Our model of arguing proposes that decision making and argumentative reasoning are dynamic processes in which beliefs, although retaining some stability, constantly undergo updating, revision, and change, as new information is considered (Stein & Miller, 1990, 1993a, 1993b; Stein et al., 1997; Stein et al., 1995). Several studies on conceptual change (e.g., Chinn & Brewer, 1993; Duit, 1991; Vosniadou & Brewer, 1992) have shown that the greatest amount of change or revision in beliefs occurs when people encounter information that is anomalous or inconsistent with their current beliefs. Conceptual change occurs when people update their current beliefs in response to new challenging information.

When people are confronted with information that challenges their beliefs, they experience difficulty in applying their prior knowledge to the new information. A prochoice supporter, for example, may initially advocate abortion in all cases, believing that a woman always has the right to decide. When presented with a case in which a woman has been using abortion as a means of birth control and has a wanton disregard for life, a prochoice adherent may decide that the negative social consequences and lack of moral responsibility are more important than ensuring absolute choice. Using new principles in one case may facilitate further change in the stance when other cases are considered.

In this study, we examined the conditions under which people switched or maintained their stances on abortion. College students were first asked to report and justify their positions on abortion. We identified the particular stances that students took, the degree of support they offered for their stances, their knowledge of the pros and cons of both sides of the abortion issue, and their knowledge of specific cases or concrete examples of women seeking abortion that might challenge or make their stance conditional.

Students were then presented with cases that differed in terms of the circumstances and conditions that motivated a woman to seek an abortion. The cases were designed to either confirm or challenge prototypic expectations underlying prolife or prochoice stances, thereby forcing students to consider situations, consequences, and moral principles normally not considered. Students were asked to act as judges on each case, deciding and justifying whether a woman could seek an abortion.

## METHOD

### Participants

The participants were 186 undergraduate (77%) and graduate students (23%) from the University of Chicago. Approximately half were men ($n = 92$) and half were women ($n = 94$), with an average age of 22. The participants were recruited through campus ads and were paid $10 for their involvement.

### Procedure

The participants were asked to choose which stance best characterized their position on abortion. The choices were: (a) would support abortion in all cases (subsequently labeled a nonconditional prochoice stance; (b) would support abortion in most cases, except for a few ones (conditional prochoice); (c) would oppose abortion in most cases, except for a few ones (conditional prolife); and (d) would oppose abortion in all cases (nonconditional prolife). Participants were then asked to state reasons that would support their chosen position, go against their position, support the opposed position, and go against the opposed position. Because the generation of reasons for each stance could have affected the decisions that participants made during consideration of each case, only half of the participants were asked to generate reasons for and against each position before the case-based decision-making tasks. The remaining half completed the case-based decision-making tasks as soon as they declared which of the four positions most accurately represented their point of view.

All participants were asked to read four different cases. Each case depicted a woman who wanted to have an abortion. Four of the cases were designed to challenge the prototypic expectations and principles of a prolife position and four were designed to challenge the prototypic expectations and principles of a prochoice position. The cases challenging a prolife position were about a woman whose physical health and life were in danger if the pregnancy continued, a woman whose mental state was unstable and who was suicidal during pregnancy, rape, and incest. The cases that challenged a prochoice position were about a woman who had multiple abortions in the past and was using abortion as birth control, a woman whose life was in jeopardy if she underwent an abortion, a woman who wanted to abort because the unborn was of an undesired gender, and a woman who wanted to abort because her husband threatened to leave her if she carried the pregnancy to term.

One third of the participants supporting each position received a set of four cases that supported their initial positions. Another third received four cases that challenged their position. The remaining third received cases that were mixed, two supportive and two challenging of their position. After reading each case, participants were asked to make decisions in favor of or against the woman having an abortion. They were also required to justify their decisions orally. After participants were presented with all four cases, they were again asked to specify their general stance on abortion, choosing one of the four options they were given in the beginning of the study. They were asked to explain why they took the stance they did, providing reasons for and against their stance and reasons for and against the opposition. Verbal responses to all the tasks were audiotaped and transcribed.

## Data Coding

Participants' decisions for each case were coded in terms of whether they maintained their initial stance or whether they changed their stance. A change or shift from a position occurred when participants chose to support a position opposite to the one they initially supported. Coding the decisions of the nonconditional supporters of each position was nonproblematic. A shift occurred when participants supported the position opposite to the one they initially supported (before the four cases were presented). Agreement occurred when participants maintained the same position that they took before the cases were presented.

For individuals who acknowledged that under certain conditions they would not support their favored position, changes and shifts were scored according to the following criteria: For participants who explicated, before the decision-making tasks, the conditions under which they would switch positions, only those changes they did not mention were scored as shifts in position.

Participants' knowledge of the pros and cons of both sides of the abortion issue was also scored. Criteria of causal consistency, coherence, and understandability (Stein et al., 1995; Trabasso, Van den Broek, & Suh, 1989) were used to determine the validity of each reason for and against each position. Two coders worked independently in classifying reasons into the following four categories: supporting reasons for the favored side, supporting reasons for the opposed side, opposing reasons for the favored side, and opposing reasons for the opposed side. Supporting reasons provided evidence for a position by pointing out the values, principles, and beliefs that underlie the position. Supporting reasons also referred to the benefits or positive outcomes of holding a position. If, for example, the participant was a prolife advocate and he or she asserted that the "fetus is alive" and that sanctity of life is the most important principle, this reason was classified as a supporting reason for the favored position. If the same participant also acknowledged that "the woman had a right to choose," then the reason was coded as a supporting reason for the opposed side.

Opposing reasons (counterarguments and conditionals) limit, undermine, or negate a specific stance. These reasons include principles and beliefs that counter a position, or they point out the harms and negative outcomes that would occur if a position were upheld. Prolife adherents, for example, criticized their stance when they acknowledged that banning abortion could lead to back-alley abortions (coded as an opposing reason for the favored side). The interrater reliability was 87% for all coded reasons.

## RESULTS

### Gender Differences in Positions on Abortion

In the design of our study, we included an equal number of participants who supported each position on abortion. Of the 186 participants, 47 supported a nonconditional prochoice position, 48 supported a conditional prochoice position, 45 supported a conditional prolife position, and 46 supported a nonconditional prolife position.

Approximately half of the volunteers were men ($n = 92$) and half were women ($n = 94$). No gender differences were found in the proportion of men and women supporting prochoice or prolife stances, nor were there any differences in the proportion of men and women supporting conditional and nonconditional prochoice stances. Among those who supported prolife stances, however, more men supported nonconditional stances (65% vs. 40%), whereas more women supported conditional stances (60% vs. 35%), $\chi^2(1, N = 91) = 4.84, p < .05$.

### Who Changed the Most and in What Types of Cases

The first analysis in this set was carried out on the 91 participants who generated reasons for supporting a particular stance before and after the decision-making task. Although we included only half of our sample in this analysis, the results provided a more sensitive index of the amount of change conditional supporters underwent. A three-way analysis of variance (ANOVA) was carried out on the number of times the participants switched stances over all of the cases presented. The initial position taken (prochoice vs. prolife), the degree of support for the position (nonconditional vs. conditional), and the types of cases considered (supportive vs. mixed vs. challenging) were the between-subject variables.

A main effect of position was found, $F(1, 79) = 9.82, p < .01$. Prochoice supporters changed their stances more frequently ($M = 1.24$) than did prolife supporters ($M = 0.69$). A main effect of type of case was also found, $F(2, 79) = 28.40, p < .001$. Participants changed very little when responding to cases that supported their position ($M = 0.12$). They changed their stances on at least one case, however, when reading a set of mixed cases ($M = 1.04$). When they read a set of challenging cases, they changed stance more frequently ($M = 1.74$).

Were the rates of changes on challenging cases different in mixed and challenging conditions? For participants who received a set of mixed cases, the rate of change on challenging cases was 55%. Thus, of the two challenging cases they read from the set of four, they switched positions, on average, on one of the cases. Participants who received a complete set of four challenging cases also switched stances on about half of the cases (51%). Thus, the degrees of change in the two conditions that included challenging cases were not different. The number of challenging cases presented did not influence the proportion of decisions that indicated a change in stance. A series of subsequent analyses on gender also showed no effect of gender on the rate of change in any condition.

### Frequency of Generating Arguments for and Against a Position

The frequency of generating each of four types of reasons (for and against each position on abortion) is displayed in Table 1. We examined whether the four groups of participants differed in how much of each type of reason they produced. For each type of reason, a two-way ANOVA was conducted with the initial position taken (prochoice vs. prolife) and the degree of support (nonconditional vs. conditional) as the between-subject variables. No significant differences were found across the four different types of stances in generating supporting and opposing reasons for either side of the abortion issue.

Across the four different stances on abortion, participants generated significantly more supports for their favored side ($M = 2.29$) than for the opposed side

TABLE 1
Distribution of Arguments for and Against Both Sides of the
Abortion Issue by Position Taken on Abortion

| Position Taken on Abortion | Supporting Reason | | Opposing Reason | |
|---|---|---|---|---|
| | Favored Side | Opposed Side | Favored Side | Opposed Side |
| Nonconditional prochoice | 2.64 | 1.68 | 3.32 | 3.73 |
| Conditional prochoice | 2.46 | 1.75 | 4.38 | 3.88 |
| Conditional prolife | 1.78 | 1.87 | 4.70 | 4.35 |
| Nonconditional prolife | 2.27 | 1.55 | 3.96 | 4.59 |
| All participants | 2.29 | 1.71 | 4.10 | 4.13 |

($M = 1.71$), $t(90) = 2.18, p < .05$. No significant differences were found in the number of problems or criticisms raised against the favored ($M = 4.10$) versus the opposed ($M = 4.13$) position. Over all positions, more criticisms were generated ($M = 8.23$) than supports ($M = 4.00$), $t(90) = -9.66, p < .001$. All participants, despite the conditional or nonconditional nature of their stances, were very adept at pointing out the faults of both positions on abortion. Participants consistently framed the abortion issue in negative terms, opting to find faults with both sides and infrequently referring to reasons for supporting each position.

### Correlations Between Amount of Position Knowledge and Changes in Stances

Although all participants exhibited similar patterns of generating supports and problems for each position, individual differences did exist in terms of the number of supports and problems generated for each position. A correlation was carried out to determine whether the frequency of generating one of four different types of reasons was related to the number of changes made in a stance during decision making. This analysis was carried out only on those data from participants who received challenging information during decision making ($n = 31$). The results are summarized in Table 2.

Among the prochoice advocates, the only significant correlation found was between the number of criticisms initially raised about one's own position and the number of times a participant switched positions ($r = .64, p < .01$). The more the prochoice supporters found fault in their own position, the more willing they were to shift positions when presented with challenging information. This correlation, however, was not present among the prolife participants. Thus, patterns of generating supports and problems for each position were not predictive of changes in stance among the prolife participants during case-based decision making.

TABLE 2
Types of Reason and Frequency of Changes During Case Deliberation

| Type of Reason | Correlations With the Number of Changes Made During Case Deliberation (Pearson's r) | |
|---|---|---|
| | Prochoice | Prolife |
| Supporting reason for the favored side | .12 | −.11 |
| Supporting reason for the opposed side | −.22 | −.07 |
| Opposing reason for the favored side | .64* | .14 |
| Opposing reason for the opposed side | .48 | −.24 |

*$p < .01$.

## Prior Knowledge of the Study's Challenging Cases and Changes in Stances

We examined if, before deliberating on the cases, the participants spontaneously talked about and anticipated any of the cases that we designed to challenge their views. For the prolife participants, the number of challenging cases (those we constructed to challenge the prolife view) that they anticipated was counted. Likewise, for the prochoice participants, we obtained the number of challenging cases (those designed to challenge the prochoice view) they foresaw. To test if the four groups of participants differed in their ability to anticipate the challenging cases, a two-way ANOVA was conducted with the initial position taken (prochoice vs. prolife) and the degree of support (nonconditional vs. conditional) as between-subject variables. This analysis was conducted on the 61 participants who received a set of mixed or challenging cases. A main effect of position was found to be significant, $F(1, 57) = 9.44$, $p < .01$. Prolife advocates anticipated at least one of the cases designed to challenge the prolife position ($M = 1.03$), whereas the prochoice adherents hardly anticipated any of the cases designed to challenge the prochoice view ($M = 0.37$).

We then examined whether prior knowledge of the challenging cases in the study predicted the likelihood of changing stances during case decision making. A Pearson's $r$ was used to test the relation between number of foreseen challenging cases and the number of changes, but was not found to be significant. Individual differences in ability to anticipate the study's challenging cases were not predictive of willingness to modify stances. However, when the previous results on position differences in shifts are taken into account, we find an inverse relation. Prolife supporters, who were more likely than the prochoice advocates to anticipate the study's challenging cases, were the ones who changed less frequently (see Table 3).

TABLE 3
How Many of the Challenging Cases in the Study Were
Foreseen and the Frequency of Changes

| Position on Abortion | Average Number of Challenging Cases in the Study Foreseen | Average Number of Changes During Case Deliberation |
|---|---|---|
| Prochoice | 0.37 | 1.24 |
| Prolife | 1.03 | 0.69 |

## Summary

The participants' willingness to modify their stances on abortion depended on a number of factors. Students who received information directly challenging their position on abortion changed stances more frequently. Three additional factors also predicted changes in stance: taking a prochoice rather than a prolife position, being able to find more problems with the favored position, and being unable to anticipate the challenging information received.

## DISCUSSION

In this study, we examined the conditions under which people shift or maintain their stances on the issue of abortion. Despite the fact that some of our participants held unconditional commitments to their chosen positions, they displayed a willingness to modify their stance when presented with information that challenged the prototypic assumptions and beliefs of the stance. More than half of the nonconditional prolife and nonconditional prochoice supporters acknowledged the validity of the opposite stance on at least one of the challenging cases they received. As expected, position changes were more frequent when presented with challenging rather than supportive information. The rate of change, however, differed by position. The prochoice adherents modified their stances more frequently than the prolife advocates did. What accounts for the differences between prochoice and prolife individuals?

Our prolife and prochoice participants differed on two accounts: how they anticipated the challenging cases they received, and whether their ability to cite problems with their own stance predicted how they switched positions. The prolife supporters were more likely than the prochoice supporters to foresee some of the challenging cases that we presented to them. Some of the study cases may not have offered them new information that could challenge the beliefs and assumptions of their prolife position. In fact, being able to anticipate these cases may have actually prepared them to defend themselves. Their prior knowledge of such circumstances gave them the opportunity to refute the limitations and weaknesses of their stance posed by these cases.

The prochoice participants were different from the prolife participants on a second point. Although they were highly capable of finding fault with the opposite stance, as were the prolife individuals, they seemed to exhibit a certain degree of openness. Their ability to cite problems with their own stance predicted how much they were willing to modify their views. The more they found fault in their own views, the more they changed. This was not true among the prolife participants, however. Although the prolife supporters also raised ample criticisms for the prolife stance, this did not necessarily weaken their position. Although they were able to find fault with their own views, they also had high knowledge of problems for the opposite stance and used this knowledge to further build the prolife case.

Such arguers may criticize their own stances for a strategic purpose. They criticize themselves to eventually demonstrate that more is wrong with the opposite stance than their own. Even though the arguers are able to generate criticisms for their favored stances, they may not believe them or they may not even use them during case-based decision making. A close look at the arguments revealed that some participants did not often identify themselves as the actual source of the criticisms raised. As an example, we present a nonconditional prolife individual's response to a request for criticisms to his stance:

> In terms of the arguments that people throw at me, I think one of the problems is something in that situation when it's either the mother's life or the fetuses'. You say ... why should the mother die when she can have a very simple operation and be safe?

Our prochoice and prolife participants argued about abortion in very negative terms. They emphasized the problems and costs of both sides of the issue rather than citing the benefits and advantages. Moreover, when asked to justify the opposing stance, they were unable to talk about how the opposite side views things and what is reasonable about the other side. Instead, the participants criticized their own stances. In fact, the production of supports for the opposite side was the lowest across all participants. This observation is particularly significant because knowledge of the supports for the opposite side forms the basis for understanding and appreciating the opposite view. Supporting reasons provide information about what really motivates the opposing side. They are the fundamental beliefs, principles, or assumptions that underlie a stance on an issue. True understanding occurs when one can arrive at a coherent understanding and a deep comprehension of the values and beliefs that motivate the opposing side. When this happens, arguers are more likely to embrace true change in stances.

Our goal in this study was to determine those dimensions of thinking that predict whether people would change or adhere to their general stance on abortion.

Our results show that prior knowledge of the pros and cons of an issue, as well as the novelty of the information used to confront a person's views, predict whether conceptual change and learning will occur.

## REFERENCES

Chinn, C. A., & Brewer, W. F. (1993). The role of anomalous data in knowledge acquisition: A theoretical framework and implications for science instruction. *Review of Education Research, 63*(1), 1–49.
Duit, R. (1991). Students' conceptual frameworks: Consequences for learning science. In S. Glynn, R. Yeany, & B. Britton (Eds.), *The psychology of learning science* (pp. 65–85). Hillsdale, NJ: Lawrence Erlbaum Associates, Inc.
Dunn, J. (1989). *The beginnings of social understanding.* Cambridge, MA: Harvard University Press.
Dunn, J. (1992). *Young children's close relationships: Beyond attachment.* London: Sage.
Fisher, R., & Brown, S. (1988). *Getting together: Building a relationship that gets to yes.* Boston: Houghton Mifflin.
Gottman, J. M. (1979). *Marital interaction: Experimental investigations.* New York: Academic.
Kuhn, D. (1991). *The skills of argument.* Cambridge, England: Cambridge University Press.
Murray, F. B. (1972). Acquisition of conservation through social interaction. *Developmental Psychology, 6,* 1–6.
Piaget, J. (1932). *The moral judgment of the child.* New York: Free Press.
Ross, L., & Lepper, M. (1980). The perseverance of beliefs: Empirical and normative considerations. *New Directions for Methodology of Social and Behavioral Science, 4,* 17–36.
Shantz, C. U. (1987). Conflicts between children. *Child Development, 58,* 283–306.
Sherif, M., & Sherif, C. W. (1953). *Groups in harmony and in tension.* New York: Harper & Row.
Sillars, M., & Garner, P. (1982). Values and beliefs: A systematic basis for argumentation. In J. R. Cox & C. A. Willard (Eds.), *Advances in argumentation theory and research* (pp. 184–201). Carbondale: Illinois University Press.
Stein, N. L., & Albro, E. R. (1997, April). *The structure and content of parent–child conflict negotiations.* Paper presented at the annual meeting of the Society of Research on Child Development, Washington, DC.
Stein, N. L., & Bernas, R. S. (1999). The early emergence of argumentative knowledge and skill. In J. Andriessen & P. Coirier (Eds.), *Foundations of argumentative text processing* (pp. 97–116). Amsterdam: Amsterdam University Press.
Stein, N. L., Bernas, R. S., & Calicchia, D. J. (1997). Conflict talk: Understanding and resolving arguments. In T. Givon (Ed.), *Conversation: Cognitive, communicative and social perspectives* (pp. 233–267). Amsterdam: John Benjamins.
Stein, N. L., Bernas, R. S., Calicchia, D. J., & Wright, A. (1995). Understanding and resolving arguments: The dynamics of negotiation. In B. Britton & A. G. Graesser (Eds.), *Models of understanding* (pp. 257–287). Hillsdale, NJ: Lawrence Erlbaum Associates, Inc.
Stein, N. L., & Miller, C. A. (1990). I win—You lose: The development of argumentative thinking. In J. Voss, D. Perkins, & J. Segal (Eds.), *Informal reasoning and instruction* (pp. 265–290). Hillsdale, NJ: Lawrence Erlbaum Associates, Inc.
Stein, N. L., & Miller, C. A. (1993a). The development of memory and reasoning skill in argumentative contexts: Evaluating, explaining, and generating evidence. In R. Glaser (Ed.), *Advances in instructional psychology* (Vol. 4, pp. 285–335). Hillsdale, NJ: Lawrence Erlbaum Associates, Inc.
Stein, N. L., & Miller, C. A. (1993b). A theory of argumentative understanding: Relationships among position preference, judgments of goodness, memory, and reasoning. *Argumentation, 7,* 183–204.

Stein, N. L., & Ross, M. (1996, November). *Discussion conflicts: Similarities and differences in husband's and wife's description of the same conflicts*. Paper presented at the annual meeting of the Psychonomic Society, Chicago.

Stratman, J. (1990). The emergence of legal composition as a field of inquiry: Evaluating the prospects. *Review of Educational Research, 60*, 153–235.

Trabasso, T., Van den Broek, P., & Suh, S. Y. (1989). Logical necessity and transitivity of causal relations in stories. *Discourse Processes, 12*, 1–25.

Vallone, R. P., Ross, L., & Lepper, M. R. (1985). The hostile media phenomenon: Biased perception and perceptions of media bias in coverage of the Beirut massacre. *Journal of Personality and Social Psychology, 49*, 577–585.

Valsiner, J., & Cairns, R. (1992). Theoretical perspectives on conflict and development. In C. U. Shantz & W. W. Hartup (Eds.), *Conflict in child and adolescent development* (pp. 15–35). New York: Cambridge University Press.

Vosniadou, S., & Brewer, W. F. (1992). Mental models of the earth: A study of conceptual change in childhood. *Cognitive Psychology, 24*, 535–538.

Voss, J. F., Fincher-Kiefer, R., Wiley, J., & Silfies, L. N. (1993). On the processing of arguments. *Argumentation, 7*, 165–181.

Voss, J. F., Wolfe, C. R., Militello, L. G., Fincher-Kiefer, R., & Ney, L. G. (1991). *What is a good argument? On the structure and content of arguments involving social issues*. Unpublished manuscript.

# Science on the Web: Student Evaluations of Scientific Arguments

Sarah K. Brem
*Division of Psychology in Education*
*Arizona State University*

Janet Russell
*School of Educational Policy and Leadership*
*Ohio State University*

Lisa Weems
*Educational Leadership*
*Miami University*

The World Wide Web is rapidly growing as a source of scientific information for the layperson. We analyzed Web presentations of scientific arguments and how students evaluate those arguments. Our findings suggest that argumentation can be described as a situated activity. Web sites presented challenges relating to multiple layers of argument, missing evidence and evidence that cannot be corroborated, and insufficient detail. These characteristics of Web sites exacerbated weaknesses in students' skills of argument. Student weaknesses stemmed from their epistemological stance, their overreliance on surface features rather than systematic analysis, metacognitive failures, and a failure to understand the nature of science and publishing.

As a source of scientific information, the Web presents both challenges and opportunities. Almost anyone can publish on the Web; there is no peer review, no editors, and Web publishing is relatively inexpensive. However, as misinformation becomes more readily accessible, so do the tools for uncovering it. Search engines allow us to locate additional information and alternative viewpoints; examining uniform resource locators (URLs), hyperlinks, source code, and page

---

Correspondence and requests for reprints should be sent to Sarah K. Brem, Division of Psychology in Education, P.O. Box 870611, Arizona State University, Tempe, AZ 85287–0611. E-mail: Sarah.Brem@asu.edu

properties provides clues as to who created it, when, and why. Authors are accessible by e-mail, and discussion forums permit active examination of issues. These concerns and opportunities have led to a proliferation of critical thinking curricula and guidelines, and the skills of argument play a prominent role in these. Somewhat less attention has been paid to students' ability to use these tools. This is the focus of our article.

We examine student activities that center on a critical thinking module implementing commonly prescribed techniques for evaluating Web sites. Authored in Web-Based Integrated Science Environment (WISE; Linn, Bell, & Hsi, 1999), the module allowed students to visit third-party Web sites proffering scientific claims while remaining within a framework that provides explicit instruction in assessing arguments, note-taking capabilities, and graphical argumentation tools.[1] Through qualitative and quantitative analysis, we describe the interactions among Web-based accounts of science, students, tools, and classrooms. We evaluate the effectiveness of critical thinking techniques and suggest that scarce resources may exacerbate weaknesses in student argument skills. We document these dynamics to inform both cognitive models of argument and curriculum development.

## WHAT MAKES A GOOD ARGUMENT? EVALUATIVE CRITERIA AND THE CHALLENGES THEY PRESENT

The terms *argumentation* and *critical thinking* are sometimes used interchangeably, although argumentation is perhaps better regarded as employing critical thinking skills in service of assessing a set of claims. (Later, we discuss the specific skills our curriculum drew on.) Ennis (1992) characterized current approaches to critical thinking as falling into three categories, although they are perhaps better thought of as points along a continuum: general skills approaches, infusion approaches, and immersion approaches. General skills approaches advocate separate courses in abstract skills such as syllogism analysis and diagramming arguments (e.g., Halpern, 1996). Infusion approaches embed critical thinking activities in existing content and encourage cross-disciplinary transfer (e.g., Resnick, 1987). Immersion advocates argue for teaching critical thinking in the context and lexicon of each discipline separately, because the differences between them are so great (McPeck, 1981, 1990).

Understanding the interactions of thinkers, tools, and resources plays a central role in this debate. To the extent that critical thinking abilities vary by domain and environment, infusion and immersion approaches become more necessary. To the extent that cross-domain transfer and abstraction is feasible, general skills approaches become more viable. The evidence is mixed. A number of studies have reported domain-general critical thinking skills that remain relatively stable across

---

[1] A demo version of the module can be viewed at http://wise.berkeley.edu/WISE/demos/trash.

contexts (e.g., King & Kitchener, 1994; Kuhn, 1991). Popular assessment tools (e.g., Ennis, Millman, & Tomko, 1985; Watson & Glaser, 1980) employ items similar to algebra word problems; these provide little information about a domain and are most consistent with a general skills approach. However, the effectiveness of curricula and assessment tools varies considerably (Sternberg & Bhana, 1986; VanGelder, 2000), evaluations are often closely aligned with the curriculum, and they are often limited to materials created for an academic setting.

Furthermore, situated cognition (e.g., Hutchins, 1997; Lave, 1988) has not received much attention in the critical thinking literature. Situated approaches to reasoning stress the ways that environment, social interactions, and personal skills and knowledge come together to create a unique situation with limited possibilities for transfer. Situated cognition is thus most compatible with the immersion approach. Although there is little evidence, some studies suggest a relation between contexts and reasoning. For example, available information influences argument strategies and argument quality (Brem & Rips, 2000; Voss, Greene, Post, & Penner, 1983; Voss, Tyler, & Yengo, 1983). Likewise, King and Kitchener (1994) noted that "functional" ability runs considerably below "optimal" performance, although the influential factors remain unclear. Using a naturalistic methodology, we consider to what extent situated models of cognition apply to argumentation, examining how tools, students, and learning environments come together to produce argument evaluations.

Critical thinking prescriptions tend to be domain general, and thus fit the general skills model. The module reflects this tendency, as we chose criteria that typify online and offline works (e.g., Gilster, 1997; Halpern, 1996; Harris, 1997; Kirk, 1996). Labels for the four evaluation categories—credibility, accuracy, reasonableness, and support—are from Harris (1997), but the underlying categories do not reflect any one source.

### Credibility

Determining source credibility involves assessing expertise, detecting conflicts of interest or ulterior motives, and looking for signs of professional or unprofessional behavior. On the Web, such information may come from recognizing scientists, reporters, and their affiliations; page content's explicit statements regarding expertise; inferences based on URLs (e.g., .edu vs. .com); examining other pages at a Web site; and searches for additional information. Students must also understand the nature of science and Web publishing to identify conflicts and motives.

### Accuracy

Accuracy is one of the most difficult criteria. Ideally, assessing accuracy involves corroborating claims through independent sources. However, popular accounts are rarely independent, being variations on reports by a few services, such as the

Associated Press and Cable News Network; the only recourse may be consulting technical primary sources. Because this is beyond most laypeople, guidelines often include surface markers that substitute for systematic analysis. Criteria include the recency and currency of information, and whether accounts provide sufficient detail that one could verify them, if one had access to sufficient information (Gilster, 1997; Harris, 1997). Markers for these include dates of posting and modification, the inclusion of scientist and reporter e-mail addresses, links to technical archives and e-journals, and bibliographic references to print media. Students often treat markers as a guarantee of accuracy, a tendency we discuss.

## Reasonableness

Harris (1997) described reasonableness as "a test of the information against how the world really is." Similarly, Halpern (1996) warned against inappropriate assumptions and premises that seem clearly false. However, we frequently warn students against relying on common sense. How can we reconcile these messages?

Reasonableness measures how well information coheres with students' worldviews. Common sense is crafted from knowledge and experience, and thus can be highly coherent and a good guide. However, to the extent that this commonsense framework is flawed, inconsistent, or underdeveloped, reliance on it can be problematic. Students may not distinguish between a vague sense of plausibility and the use of either specific prior knowledge (Kuhn, 1991) or a rigorous measure of coherence (e.g., Thagard, 1989). In addition, people are quite good at inventing coherent explanations (e.g., C. A. Anderson, Lepper, & Ross, 1980; Ross, Lepper, Strack, & Steinmetz, 1977), and those with less information about a topic are more likely to accept such explanations (Brem & Rips, 2000); thus, students could be vulnerable.

A systematic approach to reasonableness involves evaluating the goodness of fit between bodies of information, but the Web also provides surface markers for reasonableness. For example, hyperlinks to other resources visually suggest that a page coheres with a larger framework of information; of course, these links may be tenuous or irrelevant to the user's purpose. To use either systematic approaches or surface markers, students must first recognize and evaluate what enhances or detracts from the reasonableness of a page.

## Support

We can conceptualize support, or evidence, using a simplified form of Toulmin's (1958) model of argument, consisting of claims supported by data and warrants, which permit inference from data to claims. The simplified model treats providing support for warrants as isomorphic to that of providing support for claims (R. C. Anderson, Chinn, Chang, Waggoner, & Yi, 1997).

For example, one site that students visited claimed that men are more effective than women in life-saving situations. In support of this, the author presented the datum:

> Every year, the Carnegie Hero Fund Commission reviews 800 to 1,000 incidents of selfless bravery in America and awards the 10 percent of the rescuers they deem truly heroic a medal and stipend. Since the awards were established in 1904, more than 90 percent of these citations have gone to men. (Real Men)

As is typical in everyday arguments (R. C. Anderson et al., 1997; Voss, Greene, et al., 1983), the warrant is not explicitly stated, but might be: "If men receive more awards, they must be behaving more heroically, and being heroic means being effective in life-or-death situations."

An attacker can strike data or warrants (Pollock, 1987). Attacks on data are *rebutting defeaters*. Questioning the accuracy of the Hero Fund statistic would be a rebutting defeater. Attacks on warrants are *undercutting defeaters*. Perhaps the committee is biased against women, so even if the statistic is accurate, it may not support the claim. In describing argument structure and defeasibility to students, we used plain English descriptions: "Is the evidence based on just a few cases, or many cases? Look for evidence that doesn't match with the claim."

Systematically analyzing support involves considering the quality of each element as well as the larger structure (e.g., Halpern, 1996; Ranney & Schank, 1995; Thagard, 1989). It often requires substantial background knowledge of the discipline to understand how an argument is constructed and to evaluate that argument. In addition, the medium influences argument structure. For example, Web arguments use links to evidence, which may or may not be annotated to layout warrants, and demand multimedia, multimodal coordination, such as matching written claims to supporting audio clips, or tracking online claims to offline media. In taking on these tasks, students may rely on surface markers. Scientific jargon may suggest that the work rests on sound evidence and good scientific practice; support is indicated by the mere presence of links or bibliographic references. Students may rely on such markers without assessing the materials in more detail.

## A Network of Layers and Criteria

A complete analysis requires a consideration of every layer of an argument. The most prominent layer is usually the scientific argument. We can assess the credibility of scientists, the accuracy of their descriptions and findings, the reasonableness of their claims, and the support backing those claims. However, scientists often transmit their arguments via news organizations and public relations personnel. Mishandling at the reporting level can make the science appear either stronger or weaker (Berry, 1967; Borman, 1978), and thus it is important to assess these conduits along with the scientific message. Reporter credibility and reporting accuracy should be examined. Commentary and analysis should be evaluated with respect to reasonableness and support for reporter claims.

The picture can be made far more complicated than this. Scientific arguments are stratified, with scientists building on previous research (Latour, 1987; Latour & Woolgar, 1979), and reposting causes reporting layers to multiply quickly on the Web. We examined only students' ability to make the first cut between reporting and science, and even this overwhelmed many.

In addition, the four criteria contribute to the overall reliability of an argument separately and in concert. We can parcel out their contributions: An unknown source may present a well-supported argument, an unreasonable argument can be accurately reported, and so on. Nevertheless, we can tie their contributions together: Sources earn credibility through their accuracy and the quality of their support; a well-supported argument may become more reasonable as our worldview changes to accommodate it. Although it is beyond the scope of this study, eventually a model of argument should represent these dynamics.

## CRITICALLY EVALUATING WEB SITES: A DESCRIPTION OF STUDENTS AND THEIR ENVIRONMENT

### The Students and Their Classroom

Eighty-one girls at a private, Midwestern, single-sex school participated. The school is ethnically diverse, but predominately White. Families are generally middle-class or upper middle-class. Grades 9 ($n = 43$), 11 ($n = 19$), and 12 ($n = 19$) were represented. We found little indication of developmental trends, consistent with the finding that critical thinking skills remain stable after the middle school years without educational intervention (Kuhn, 1991; Kuhn & Felton, 2000).

Students first completed a section introducing the four criteria already described, and then visited six Web sites. All information at the site on that topic was available to the students; in most cases, students visited the original site. The sites highlight three typical Web environments: hoaxes, weaker sincere sites, and stronger sincere sites.

Students were free to choose any three to evaluate, selecting one each at what they perceived to be high, moderate, and low levels of reliability.[2] At the end of the module, we asked students to reflect on the criteria and describe for a novice

---

[2] Because students could choose any of the sites to evaluate, they could have chosen one type of site to the exclusion of another. This does not appear to be the case. Responses were divided roughly equally between hoax (37%), weaker (27%), and stronger (36%) sites; we found no significant differences in this distribution, $\chi^2(2, N = 56) = 2.98, p = .23$.

how to use the criteria, which of the criteria were hardest and easiest to apply, and which were more or less important. Classes spent one period on the introductory section and one or two periods on the evaluation section, at the teachers' discretion. They worked alone or in small groups. Two of the authors were present in the classroom throughout the project, along with a science teacher from the school. Student work was posted to a central server, generating nearly 700 electronic notepads.

The two teachers involved in the project differed considerably in their pedagogical philosophies. Both have many years of experience and a good rapport with students. One preferred a direct instruction model. Students were encouraged to take detailed notes on her lectures, and she preferred well-structured activities that she could score unambiguously. The other teacher was more constructivist in her approach, preferring students to set their own agenda and encouraging them to accept some ambiguity as part of the argument process. This may have affected the learning outcomes, and we discuss this possibility later.

## The Web Sites

Across the three categories of sites, there were some commonalities. Overall, there was a dearth of information presented. Background about scientists and reporters was frequently unavailable, and claims were asserted with little attention to the evidence backing them. Such omissions have been noted in earlier work dealing with print media (Berry, 1967; Evans, Krippendorf, & Yoon, 1990; Pulford, 1981; Tankard & Ryan, 1974). As illustrated later, sites differ more in appearance of reliability than in their quality of argument. In such cases, we can expect people to rely on markers of quality to supplement or replace systematic approaches (Chaiken, Liberman, & Eagly, 1989; Maheswaran & Chaiken, 1991). There are more informative sites on the Web, but even rich sites seem anemic if we lack the expertise to navigate language and modalities (Lemke, 2000). Furthermore, McPeck (1990) argued that the underdetermination of everyday arguments frequently hampers critical thinking. Thus, we believe these sites are not unusual in the challenges they present or in the skills they call on.

### Hoax Sites

Fraud on the Web is a common concern. These fabrications were created for entertainment purposes, but students did not necessarily recognize this. Hoax sites evoked a sense of the ridiculous, yet maintained a superficial appearance of scientific professionalism. Hoaxes were relatively easy to detect if students went with reasonableness, relying on a lack of coherence between their prior knowledge and the site information. Hoaxes did not stand up well to systematic evaluation. However, at an intermediate level, students could become confused, noting surface markers of reliability, but unable (or unwilling) to delve deeply enough to discard them.

*Cats.* This site (Mahoney, Lichtblau, Karpook, Chou, & Arena-DeRosa, n.d.) appears to be a peer-reviewed study claiming that cats have a violent reaction to bearded men. Clues indicate humorous intent, with procedural details such as having to anesthetize the unfortunate assistant whose fate it was to hold the cats. The site does not win points on reasonableness; it gives no explanation for the cats' reactions and details such as the anesthetized assistant do not cohere with most people's model of a scientific environment. Systematic analysis of the evidence shows inconclusive data, with cats responding inconsistently. However, Cats displays the basic structure of a scientific report. The authors display affiliations with prestigious American universities. Support appears plentiful, with tables of data and scientific-sounding method and results sections. The information is uncorroborated but detailed, and so has the appearance of being accurate and verifiable. Identifying the reporting layer—an online humor magazine—would immediately reveal the hoax, but this layer is virtually invisible. Users can find the publisher only by browsing other pages at the site.

*Human Horse.* This site (Guthrie, n.d.) claims that Manny, the human-headed horse, has been cloned. Again, the story fails to cohere with the specifics of cloning technology as well as students' common sense of what is scientifically possible, so reasonableness is low. Still, reliability markers are present. It has the appearance and tone of a serious news story. For support, there is a photo depicting the human-headed horse, as well as quotes from alleged geneticists and ethicists. Credibility is lower than that of Cats; the reporting source is easily identified as a known tabloid and the scientist has fewer credentials. There are also fewer markers of accuracy; corroboration would be difficult to attempt, as the site does not provide scientist affiliations or references to the technical literature.

### Weaker Sincere Accounts

Weaker sincere sites are more ambiguous than either hoaxes or stronger sites, as they are more balanced between reputability and disreputability than the other two types of sites are. The claims are posted by respected reporting agencies, they were made by people who are sincere in their scientific efforts, and they are backed by existing evidence rather than mere fabrications. The scientists and their arguments do not stand up well to systematic examination, but such analysis requires both background information and coordination with other sources.

*Scottish Chapel.* Published online by the British Broadcasting Corporation (BBC), this is a serious news story about an anthropologist who has written a book to argue that the head of Jesus Christ was carried to Scotland by the Knights

Templar and buried under a chapel there (BBC Online Network, 1998). The BBC scores high in credibility with students. Accuracy and support are also high at the reporting level, with corroborating audio clips from the anthropologist and his critics. The only problem is reasonableness; the story does not cohere with students' notions of serious journalism.

In contrast, the scientific layers are rather weak. The anthropologist has no apparent professional affiliation, and, by his own admission, there is little or no physical evidence to support his claim. Accuracy is difficult to ascertain, as the site provides no links to corroborating scientific evidence. Conflicts between competing historical accounts as well as a failure of this account to cohere with Biblical accounts lower reasonableness. However, a motivated layperson who searches the Web for the scientist's book will find that it does indeed exist, and there are other books published by the same small press that feature similar theories. This cohering framework may thus enhance accuracy and reasonableness, if students put more effort into the matter. In addition, although Biblical accounts are not traditionally thought of as scientific evidence, they present a more coherent story than the scientific one presented here. Perceptions of accuracy and reasonableness may rise and fall with these additional complications.

*Real Men.* This MSNBC site (Segell, 1998) claims that men are evolutionarily adapted to be less emotional than women are. Again, there is a mismatch of science and reporting. MSNBC is a respected news organization, but the reporter is creating his own argument from scientific research and has no apparent scientific training. Thus, credibility varies depending on whether one focuses on the author as a professional reporter or as an amateur scientist. Regarding accuracy, the account is detailed—thus appearing verifiable—but there are no pointers to corroborating sources; systematic analysis will require an independent search. Support is weak (as illustrated by the earlier example), but detailed and filled with jargon. Reasonableness depends on student perspective, and at an all-girls school, many students are not well disposed toward gender stereotypes. In summary, as with Scottish Chapel, argument elements do not clearly point in a single direction.

### Stronger Sincere Accounts

Stronger sites present professional markers; the scientists are more credible, and the sites have an air of precision and authority. Systematic analysis would uphold this initial assessment, but limitations on the part of students and on the part of the Web sites create obstacles.

*Monkeys.* Posted by *Science News Online,* this site (Bower, 1998) describes research at Yerkes Regional Primate Research Center, suggesting that offspring abuse by monkeys can be used to model human child abuse. Both *Science News Online* and Yerkes are credible with students. Reasonableness is high with our students because primate models of human behavior cohere well with their model of "real science." At both the reporting and scientific level, corroboration and systematic evaluation of the evidence are possible, with complete bibliographic references and contact information for both the reporter and scientists.

However, *Science News Online* briefly describes the scientific evidence, but warrants are tacit and must be reconstructed. All references take students offline to primary sources such as *Psychological Bulletin*. Students could try to independently locate additional online material, but this is not an easy task. For example, to find information at Yerkes, students must not confuse it with Yerkes Observatory, and they must know how to get from the front door to the appropriate research program, only to turn up no mention of the study. Further investigation would reveal that the primary investigator has moved to a new institution. Students' lack of knowledge and the lack of resources create a challenging environment.

*Sex Reversal.* Posted by Reuters, this page (Reaney, 1998) presents the claim that an error in gene expression causes a mismatch between sex phenotype and genotype (e.g., male chromosomes, but female sex organs and sexual characteristics). Reliability markers are plentiful. Reuters is credible, and the research took place at institutions that seem appropriate, although they are overseas and unfamiliar. The site makes heavy use of jargon and textbook genetics.

Many elements preclude systematic analysis. The jargon is often impenetrable. With the exception of a passing reference to experiments involving "transgenic mice," there are no descriptions of data or warrants, only statements of claims. There are no pointers to corroborating materials, online or offline.

In conclusion, at all sites, missing information, knowledge requirements, and a failure to assist laypersons in locating and coordinating resources thwarts systematic analysis. Trying to delve deeper can be counterproductive and inefficient. Students who do not follow their initial reactions may not have the ability to resolve their confusion. Sites presenting weaker sincere science are the most ambiguous. Similar to hoax sites, they fail to cohere with students' prior knowledge and beliefs, but, similar to stronger sites, they are clearly marked as sincere attempts at legitimate science reported by credible news sources. Because there are many routes of evaluation, each with advantages and disadvantages, it is important that students not only make evaluations, but metacognitively analyze those evaluations.

## STUDENT INTERACTIONS WITH THE SITES: SITUATED CRITICAL THINKING

The sites made argument evaluation challenging, but weaknesses in student argument skills exacerbated these difficulties. In describing these dynamics, we use qualitative analysis to illustrate and catalog response types; descriptive statistics to give a sense of the relative frequency of certain problems and strategies; and, where appropriate, significance testing to compare how differences between sites influence student reasoning.

## Challenges Presented by Multiple Layers of Argument

Students need to assess both the scientific argument and the reporting conduits, but in only a few cases did they do this. At the Human Horse site, one group noted that although the scientists might have an ulterior motive, this did not apply at reporting level:

> (G28, human horse) If the writer of this page were selling these critters for 40,000$ a pop, I can imagine him wanting to advertise them. But as it is, there seems to be absolutely no reason for this person to be telling us this. The author is (or claims to be) a reporter of weekly world news. If this article was found in a newspaper, the object of it would be obviously to sell papers. But on the Internet, there isn't really any obvious motive.[3]

At the Sex Reversal site, a group noted that although the Reuters correspondent did not display any scientific credentials, the scientists seemed credible:

> (G7, sex reversal) 1. Author 2. Cite professionals [Here's why it raises or lowers the Credibility . . .] 1. The author is not a doctor. 2. These professionals seem knowledgeable of the human body.

In contrast, focusing solely on either reporting or science at Sex Reversal leads to diverging assessments:

> (G18, sex reversal) Patricia Reaney [the author] is not an established scientist or doctor [. . .] This lowers the credibility because we don't know her qualifications.

> (G46, sex reversal) The researchers . . . had credible titles and were researchers in that particular field. The places where they worked were stated, and reasonable for that kind of research. [. . .] Raises credibility because the research and titles matched.

Examining whether students reference science, reporting, or both when commenting on a site (Table 1),[4] science eclipses reporting across all site types. Reporting was, effectively, an invisible conduit for science.

---

[3]Students entered their notes into the computer, and the number of typographical errors was considerable. We do not believe that these are informative, and they make for difficult reading. Therefore, we have corrected student typographical errors, preserving other idiosyncrasies. Standardized prompts were present in the electronic notepads; these are included in quoted responses when necessary for the sense of the response.

[4]To assess interrater reliability for all quantitative codings of the texts, a second rater, blind to hypotheses, coded one third of all electronic notepads, drawing from all sites randomly and equally. Interrater agreement was 90%.

TABLE 1
Level of Analysis, by Percentage of Responses

|  | % Responses at Hoax Sites | % Responses at Weaker Science Sites | % Responses at Stronger Science Sites |
| --- | --- | --- | --- |
| Both | 16 | 13 | 15 |
| Reporting only | 13 | 14 | 22 |
| Science only | 70 | 73 | 64 |

## Challenges Presented by Student Epistemology and Metacognition

Also limiting was a frequent "absolutist" orientation (King & Kitchener, 1994; Kuhn, 1991; Kuhn, Weinstock, & Flaton, 1994), a belief that, given enough time and information, one can arrive at a "right answer" with complete certainty. Students looked for "true" arguments and "real" scientists. Some went so far as to see the task as distinguishing "real" science from hoaxes (Table 2). At Human Horse and Cats, such concerns are quite appropriate. However, absolutist and hoax-seeking orientations persisted at the other sites:

> (G4, real men) They used some specific numbers in this article to prove their point about bravery in America. For example, "Every year, the Carnegie Hero Fund Commission reviews 800 to 1,000 incidents of selfless bravery in America and awards the 10% of the rescuers they deem truly heroic a medal and stipend." [. . .] it is a real quote and it can be proven. If it wasn't real, then why would it be a quote?

> (G38, monkeys) It never really occurred to me that monkeys were abusive but, hearing what they have to say makes it believable. [. . .] When I read the headline, it seemed that this wasn't going to be true but now I realize that it is true because they had actual facts.

> (G20, monkeys) The fact that people from well-known facilities were quoted, and gave their own support for this experiment. [. . .] This raises the support because prestigious people would not support false information.

Students' epistemology could stem from several factors. King and Kitchener (1994) and Kuhn (1991) reported stable, consistent absolutist epistemologies across domains. This is consistent with the overall high levels in this study—the lowest levels are seen at the stronger science sites, where combined absolutist and hoax-seeking still comprise 44% of responses.

However, the percentage of absolutist and hoax responses at each type of site suggests that students' epistemology may also be partially situated. Groups were significantly more likely to take a hoax-seeking stance at hoax sites (hoax sites vs.

TABLE 2
Groups Exhibiting an Absolutist Orientation at Hoax and Nonhoax Sites

| Epistemological Stance | % Responses at Hoax Sites | % Responses at Weaker Science Sites | % Responses at Stronger Science Sites |
|---|---|---|---|
| Absolutist | 6 | 28 | 10 |
| Searching for a hoax | 76 | 31 | 34 |

weaker sites, $z = 3.14$, $p < .01$; hoax sites vs. stronger sites, $z = 3.19$, $p < .01$). Moreover, students were most likely to exhibit absolutist reasoning at weaker sites (weaker sites vs. hoax sites, $z = 2.27$, $p < .05$; weaker sites vs. stronger sites, $z = 2.06$, $p < .05$). Thus, the tone of the site influences the tone of inquiry. Students discuss hoaxes where hoaxes are likely; weaker sites, which may turn out to be false, lead to discussions of "right" and "wrong" answers. Stronger sites, "real science," is less likely to be simply right or wrong, and so absolutist criteria are less appropriate. These results are analogous to those of Lave (1988) and Scribner (1984) in their work on situated mathematics, with the environment influencing the choice of solution strategy.

A final epistemological influence may be the classroom environment. As we noted earlier, teachers voiced different philosophies. Some were pleased that students simply considered the possibility that not everything they see is true and worked for a clear-cut solution. This was reflected by classroom discussions of truth, proof, and real science. Classroom language may have set an absolutist agenda (see also Lemke, 1990; Zeidler & Lederman, 1989).

## Challenges Presented by the Evaluation Criteria

### Credibility

Students frequently relied on credentials as a marker of credibility:

(G13, sex reversal) MRC institute, Robert Lovell Badge, "nature" [...] MRC sounds like a respectable research center of science, Robert isn't explained so we don't know his educational background and he could really be anyone. "Nature" is a well established and known journal

This quote illustrates a problem that many students faced. The Web site does not describe the institute in any detail, and does not discuss Lovell Badge's role in the project, nor his area of expertise. Students can only ask whether a person or organization carries the markers of respectability. The problem of relying on affiliations and titles can be seen at the Cats site. Students assumed author expertise because of their university affiliation, although there was no information regarding their positions:

(G20, cats) There are many credible sources: doctors and scientists. [. . .] This raises the credibility because they know what they're talking about and they have been educated in this subject.

(G27, cats) The authors seem more reliable because there are more of them, and they are all at universities, or schools.

Reliance on markers also fell short when students did not understand how scientists produce arguments. For example, Cats is a multiauthored site; the preceding quotes show that some students treated having many authors as independent corroboration. Students also relied on incomplete conceptions of scientists and science in believing that "real" scientists have only humanitarian motives (Brem, 2000):

(G42, human horse) In the article, the author seemed to explain that the only thing gained by this project is money. They'll be sold as pets for $40,000. Yet it never really stated if this new "animal" could help the scientists learn more about cloning organs, etc. that would be put in good use to humans.

(G22, monkeys) I think that the only thing, which may be great to them, they have to gain is finding out information regarding child abuse. They seem as if they are trying to find out why child abuse starts (human and monkey) and how they can help. I feel that overall the article is credible.

Few recognized the motives of career goals and prestige:

(G25, member) Probably credibility [is most difficult], simply because most scientists want their theories to be published in a journal, and will staunchly fight against any research that goes against their original theory. So, why wouldn't they do everything possible to make their research seem ABSOLUTELY TRUE?

A lack of information may necessitate reliance on surface markers, but it is important that students be aware of the limitations this places on their analysis. In this regard, most students gave no indication that they reflected on the strategies they employed. Across all sites, metacognitive statements were present in only seven student evaluations of credibility (e.g., "We are not sure whether to believe this story or not, because we have never heard of something like this before, but it could be possible!").

### Accuracy

Given the obstacles to corroboration, a common prescription is to protect against information that is likely to be inaccurate or cannot be corroborated. Out-of-date pages, anonymous sources, and evidence like "hundreds of happy customers," should create suspicion. However, the presence of details is no guarantee of

TABLE 3
Student Responses Regarding Difficulty of Application

|  | Hardest to Apply | Easiest to Apply |
|---|---|---|
| Accuracy | 56.7% | 6.3% |
| Reasonableness | 18.3% | 39.7% |
| Credibility | 18.3% | 12.7% |
| Support | 6.7% | 41.3% |

their accuracy, and their absence means only that accuracy cannot be assessed. Thus, using details to mark accuracy is a fairly weak strategy.

Although they had access to the Web, only two groups ventured beyond the selected sites for corroborating information. Instead, students consistently acted as if details guaranteed accuracy:

(G25, monkeys) They discuss percentages of abuse and neglect in monkey "families," and how these relate to percentages of abuse and neglect in human families. [. . .] The fact that they used percentages (or any specific fact) makes their statements seem more accurate.

(G11, sex reversal) Here they used numbers to show how often it happens, and they used specific terms and explanations. [. . .] This raises the accuracy because they were precise and explained everything in detail.

Given students' willingness to rely on this marker, it was surprising that when we asked them at the end of the module which of the criteria was hardest to apply, 56.7% said accuracy (Table 3).[5] Their explanations consistently showed awareness of the limitations in their knowledge:

(G8, member) The hardest CARS [acronym for the four criteria] to apply is the accuracy. A lot of the articles have to do with high tech science information. Some of the terms you don't know or you have no idea about anything in the field that is being written about. So they could be telling you lies and you would not know if it was true or not, just because you don't know much in that field.

(G45, member) I think the hardest of the CARS to apply would be the A or Accuracy, because unless you are old and know everything there is to know you can't really tell if the info is accurate. And it might be hard to learn if it is accurate.

Students made these remarks within the same class period as their evaluations; we did not prompt them to focus on accuracy. Yet, if students were thinking about

---

[5]Cross-tabulation of Tables 3 and 4 did not reveal any significant relations between perceived difficulty and perceived importance of the criteria.

these issues, they gave virtually no evidence of this. Across all sites, students engaged in metacognitive reflection in only five evaluations of accuracy (e.g., "I feel I have not been supplied with the right amount of information needed to understand what's going on."). Metacognitive awareness would encourage discussion of strategies and their relative merits. Instead, we see reliance on questionable criteria.

### Reasonableness

Metacognition was also an issue in assessing reasonableness. Students should apply specific relevant knowledge and reflect on how the Web site does or does not cohere with their knowledge. They should recognize that plausibility is not the same as evidence. Some students showed such awareness, but others emerged with precisely the opposite position.

Although only 23.8% of students did so, reasonableness was the criterion most likely to be demoted. Those who demoted it pointed to the gulf between seeming reliable and being reliable:

(G1, member) They are all very important, but reasonableness is probably least [important] because I might think that something is unreasonable but I just don't know a lot about the topic and some things that are true can be off the wall.

(G32, member) The reasonability maybe [is less important] cause not everything sounds like it could have happened but the world is changing and hey you never know what people are doing these days.

At specific Web sites, students who displayed more desirable uses of reasonableness took it as an opportunity to import specific knowledge that cohered or did not cohere with the claims made at the site:

(G27, real men) The reference to ONLY male gorillas separating from troops is just plain false. I did a small study on gorillas in third grade and if my memory serves me correctly, both males and females switch tribes.

(G40, human horse) It does not fit because this information is unknown to us. So far the only animal we know has been cloned was "Dolly" the sheep and that was only a few years ago. As far as we know, scientists do not have the knowledge to clone two species into one.

However, as Table 3 shows, more students thought it easy to apply than hard. They found "gut instincts" trustworthy, and we gave them license to invoke these instincts:

(G8, member) I think reasonableness is the easiest because you get to use common sense to see if the article is even possible and you don't even need to have much background in the topic to be able to know how reasonable it is.

(G50, member) I found that reasonableness was easiest to apply because anyone can decide if an article sounds reasonable or not. If something is really weird, it's easy to tell that.

From this perspective, a plausible explanation receives approval without evidence:

(G52, real men) When he described how tears first came about, it just made sense. Also, it is true that if a man goes into battle and is crying, he will seem more vulnerable than someone who is not showing fear.

Unlike accuracy and credibility, for which virtually every response relied on surface markers, students' employment of reasonableness appears to have been influenced by site characteristics. We coded students' evaluations of reasonableness as to whether they relied on diffuse common sense or reference to specific knowledge (Table 4). The pattern is similar to that for epistemological stance. Reliance on specific knowledge is lowest at hoax sites and highest at weaker sincere sites (but this trend is not statistically significant). Nonsense was dismissed on common sense, whereas the ambiguous weaker sincere sites promoted a higher standard. Thus, the role of common sense may vary with context.

## Support

Assessing of claim–evidence structures is at the core of many models of argument (e.g., Kuhn, 1991; Siegel, 1988; Thagard, 1989; Toulmin, 1958). Likewise, students stress support. It was the criterion most often promoted (Table 5):

(G7, member) Support is the most important. If any idea is supported enough the idea can be taken seriously.

(G16, member) I think support is the most important, because no matter how credible the author and convincing their argument, if they can't back it up with examples and support from other people, it can't be trusted.

TABLE 4
Strategies for Assessing Reasonableness, by Group and Site Type

|  | % Responses at Hoax Sites | % Responses at Weaker Science Sites | % Responses at Stronger Science Sites |
|---|---|---|---|
| Reference to specific knowledge | 49 | 65 | 56 |

TABLE 5
Student Responses Regarding Criteria Importance

|  | Is There One Criterion That Is More Important Than the Others? | Is There One Criterion That Is Less Important Than the Others? |
|---|---|---|
| Accuracy | 10.0% | 1.6% |
| Reasonableness | 11.7% | 23.8% |
| Credibility | 16.7% | 14.3% |
| Support | 28.3% | 0% |
| None more or less important | 33.3% | 60.3% |

Students cited support as the easiest criterion to apply (Table 3). This is initially perplexing because systematic analysis of argument structures is not easy; critical thinking curricula work hard to convince students that it is worth the time (e.g., Halpern, 1996). Students, however, relied on surface markers, making use of what was available and expending little effort:

(G1, member) Support, because you can always tell if there is a lot of percentages and things that support the subject.

(G16, member) Support is the easiest because it is simple to see whether or not there was any research done. It is easy to find support right in the bibliography.

Almost every group relied on such markers as the presence of a bibliography, statistics, or quotes (Table 6), and most carried out systematic analyses of data at one or more sites; far fewer analyzed warrants.

Evaluations of data included analyzing its quality and sufficiency, or noting its absence:

(G2, monkeys) They have done studies over 35 years and in both pigtail macaques and sooty mangabey [...] this raises the support because they have done studies on more than one monkey over more than one year.

(G1, monkeys) There is ample detail and percentages to support the main idea of the monkeys being like humans and observing the monkeys to see how to help humans from abuse in families.

(G13, sex reversal) The conclusion wasn't strong, sounded like guesses instead of accurate information, Robert was not a doctor. The evidence they talk about they give no research history about their findings, they just state they have proof but don't explain what.

Warrants most often came to the forefront through undercutting defeaters; when they became problematic, they became noteworthy:

(G28, real men) The only evidence he offers to support his case is the award that is given to "Heroes" each year. These, he argues, are mostly awarded to men. He did not, however, mention that most of the awards were given to unemotional men. [...] This lowers the support because although it sounds logical and factual, and probably is, it has nothing to do with his topic, which is emotional vs. unemotional men, not men vs. women.

(G52, cats) The article says that all of the cats in the study were female. If some of the cats were in heat, that could have led to their reaction, and it might have not had anything to do with the bearded men.

Similar to reasonableness, there was sufficient variation to examine whether the environment influenced student strategies (Table 6). All sites show a heavy use of superficial markers ($zs \leq 1$). Weaker science sites receive the most attention regarding data and warrants; the warrant trend was not significant ($zs < 1$), whereas that involving data was (weaker sites vs. hoax sites, $z = 3.16, p < .01$; weaker sites vs. stronger sites, $z = 3.23, p < .01$). Similar to reasonableness, hoax sites are more easily dismissed and stronger science sites are more easily accepted based on surface markers; ambiguous sites require more attention.

Again, however, there was widespread metacognitive failure. Across all sites and responses, just one group acknowledged their reliance on surface markers of evidence:

(G22, sex reversal) "The evidence we have strongly suggest that DAX1 is the gene for human sex reversal syndrome." That is a fact because it can be backed up with proof. So I will assume that tests have been run to prove this info. Therefore it has support.

## TEACHING CRITICAL THINKING ON THE WEB RECOMMENDATIONS AND FUTURE INQUIRIES

We conceived this study as a naturalistic examination of the interaction between the electronic environment, the classroom, critical thinking guidelines, and stu-

TABLE 6
Categorization of Strategies for Assessing Support, by Case and by Group

| Type of Support Assessment (May Use More Than One Within a Case or Group) | % Responses at Hoax Sites | % Responses at Sincere Weaker Sites | % Responses at Sincere Stronger Sites |
|---|---|---|---|
| Use of surface markers | 80 | 71 | 79 |
| Systematic assessment | | | |
|    Discussion of warrants | 12 | 24 | 12 |
|    Discussion of data | 62 | 89 | 54 |

dents. The large number of books, curricula, and Web documents addressing the skills of Web argumentation show that this is an issue of some importance, but less attention has been paid to how well these attempts are serving the public. Key questions involve the extent to which argumentation is best pursued as the application of general skills or as a situated activity, and the determination of which strategies are most effective and productive. Next, we recapitulate the main findings and consider their relation to these issues.

## Argument as a Situated Activity

Several aspects of this study suggest that argument skills are a function of dynamic interactions as well as stable critical thinking skills. Students' epistemological stance and their methods for assessing support and reasonableness varied with the type of site, but this trend was not significant for reasonableness. At hoax sites, the goal was telling real from fake with as little effort as possible. Stronger sincere sites were more complex and fit students' conceptions of "real science." These sites were least likely to be simply divided into true and false, but they produced relatively low levels of systematic analysis—"scientific talk" stood in for or precluded deeper investigation. Ambiguous weaker science sites received the most attention, but with the possibility of serious flaws, students made absolutist attempts to sort right from wrong.

To better conceptualize argument as both general and situated, we need to better understand the extent and nature of the dynamics involved. For instance, it will be important to pin down ways that sites may be weaker or stronger, and how these differences are or are not marked. The interplay of science and reporting is another example. Regardless of the site type, students focused on the scientific argument, paying far less attention to the reporting. With the opportunity for countless repostings, it is particularly important on the Web that students recognize that conduits of information shape the science and create arguments of their own.

## Critical Thinking as Reflection

A recurring theme is the lack of metacognitive reflection. There is virtually no metacognition when assessing credibility or accuracy, although students did have access to the difficulties involved in assessing accuracy when prompted to reflect. Many students trusted common sense when assessing reasonableness, even though the goal was to produce the opposite response. Regarding support, nearly every group used surface markers and many noted their ease of use, but only one group reflected on the underlying assumptions.

It appears that students reacted to sites without reflecting on why they responded in a particular way. This is consistent with other findings suggesting a lack of reflection in argument (Kuhn, 1991; Kuhn & Felton, 2000) and a disconnect between reflection and reasoning (Bell, 2000). Improving student skills will not only be a matter of practicing evaluative strategies, but also of reflecting on the value and implications of particular moves.

## Markers as Argument?

As discussed earlier, incomplete resources are a problem across many media for disseminating science. Chi and her colleagues argued that this is inevitable; a source requiring no inferencing beyond common sense would have to be ridiculously long and tedious to meet the needs of every user (Chi, deLeeuw, Chiu, & LaVancher, 1994). However, what skills are most useful for assessing arguments when information is scarce? Placing a high priority on systematic analysis and eschewing more superficial strategies may not be in the best interests of learners, and it may not provide us with a complete and accurate model of argument. We need to determine what strategies are best for dealing with any particular confluence of factors, and how reliable we can expect a strategy to be. We also need to determine what sorts of metacognitive activity can assist students in choosing and using those strategies. We often think of systematic analysis as the "smart" sort of analysis, but coping and efficiency are also important, and metacognitive assessment is anything but mindless.

## ACKNOWLEDGMENTS

This research is supported by National Science Foundation Grant DGE–0001502 to Sarah K. Brem; National Science Foundation Grant DGE–9714444 to Janet Russell; and the Battelle Endowment for Technology and Human Affairs, Office of Academic Affairs, Ohio State University. We thank the teachers, students, and administrators who allowed us into their classrooms. Thanks also to Susan Goldman, Jim Voss, and an anonymous reviewer for their valuable comments.

## REFERENCES

Anderson, C. A., Lepper, M. R., & Ross, L. (1980). Perseverance of social theories: The role of explanation in the persistence of discredited information. *Journal of Personality and Social Psychology, 39,* 1037–1049.

Anderson, R. C., Chinn, C., Chang, J., Waggoner, M., & Yi, H. (1997). On the logical integrity of children's arguments. *Cognition and Instruction, 15,* 135–167.

BBC Online Network. (1998). *Christ's head in Scottish chapel.* Retrieved September 14, 2001 from the World Wide Web: http://news.bbc.co.uk/hi/english/uk/newsid_149000/149229.stm

Bell, P. (2000, April). *Refinement of middle school students' understanding of science resulting from argumentation and debate instruction.* Paper presented at the annual meeting of the American Educational Research Association, New Orleans, LA.

Berry, F. C. (1967). A study of accuracy in local news stories of three dailies. *Journalism Quarterly, 44,* 482–490.

Borman, S. C. (1978). Communication accuracy in magazine science reporting. *Journalism Quarterly, 55,* 345.

Bower, B. (May). *Monkeys provide model of child abuse.* Retrieved September 14, 2001 from the World Wide Web: http://www.sciencenews.org/sn_arc98/5_23_98/fob1.htm

Brem, S. K. (2000, April). *Using models of science to critically evaluate scientific arguments: A look at students, science education, and the popular media.* Paper presented at the annual meeting of the National Association of Research in Science Teaching, New Orleans, LA.

Brem, S. K., & Rips, L. J. (2000). Explanation and evidence in informal argument. *Cognitive Science, 24,* 573–604.

Chaiken, S., Liberman, A., & Eagly, A. (1989). Heuristic and systematic information processing within and beyond the persuasion context. In J. Uleman & J. Bargh (Eds.), *Unintended thought* (pp. 212–252). New York: Guilford.

Chi, M. T. H., deLeeuw, N., Chiu, M., & LaVancher, C. (1994). Eliciting self-explanations improves understanding. *Cognitive Science, 18,* 439–477.

Ennis, R. H. (1992). The degree to which critical thinking is subject specific: Clarification and needed research. In S. P. Norris (Ed.), *The generalizability of critical thinking: Multiple perspectives on an educational ideal* (pp. 21–37). New York: Teachers College Press.

Ennis, R. H., Millman, J., & Tomko, T. N. (1985). *The Cornell CT Test (Levels X and Z).* Pacific Grove, CA: Midwest.

Evans, W. A., Krippendorf, M., & Yoon, J. H. (1990). Science in the prestige and national presses. *Social Science Quarterly, 71,* 105–113.

Gilster, P. (1997). *Digital literacy.* New York: Wiley.

Guthrie, C. (n.d.). *Famed horse with human head cloned by scientists!* Retrieved September 14, 2001 from the World Wide Web: http://wise.berkeley.edu/WISE/evidence/20.html

Halpern, D. (1996). *Thought and knowledge: An introduction to critical thinking* (3rd ed.). Mahwah, NJ: Lawrence Erlbaum Associates, Inc.

Harris, R. (1997). *Evaluating Internet research sources* [Online]. Retrieved September 14, 2001 from the World Wide Web: http://www.virtualsalt.com/evalu8it.htm

Hutchins, E. (1997). *Cognition in the wild.* Cambridge, MA: MIT Press.

King, P. M., & Kitchener, K. S. (1994). *Developing reflective judgment: Understanding and promoting intellectual growth and critical thinking in adolescents and adults.* San Francisco: Jossey-Bass.

Kirk, E. E. (1996). Evaluating information on the Internet [Online]. Retrieved September 14, 2001 from the World Wide Web: http://milton.mse.jhu.edu/research/education/net.html

Kuhn, D. (1991). *The skills of argument.* Cambridge, England: Cambridge University Press.

Kuhn, D., & Felton, M. (2000, January). *Developing appreciation of the relevance of evidence to argument.* Paper presented at the Winter Conference on Discourse, Text and Cognition, Jackson Hole, WY.

Kuhn, D., Weinstock, M., & Flaton, R. (1994). How well do jurors reason? Competence dimensions of individual variation in a juror reasoning task. *Psychological Science, 5,* 289–296.

Latour, B. (1987). *Science in action: How to follow scientists and engineers through society.* Cambridge, MA: Harvard University Press.

Latour, B., & Woolgar, S. (1979). *Laboratory life: The social construction of scientific facts.* Beverly Hills, CA: Sage.

Lave, J. (1988). *Cognition in practice.* Cambridge, England: Cambridge University Press.

Lemke, J. L. (1990). *Talking science.* Norwood, NJ: Ablex.

Lemke, J. L. (2000, February). *Multimedia genres for science education and scientific literacy.* Paper presented at the Acquisition of Advanced Literacy conference, Davis, CA.

Linn, M., Bell, P., & Hsi, S. (1999). Using the Internet to enhance student understanding of science: The knowledge integration environment. *Interactive Learning Environments, 1,* 4–38.

Maheswaran, D., & Chaiken, S. (1991). Promoting systematic processing in low motivation settings: Effect of incongruent information on processing and judgment. *Journal of Personality and Social Psychology, 61,* 13–25.

Mahoney, C., Lichtblau, S. J., Karpook, N., Chou, C., & Arena-DeRosa, A. (n.d.). *Feline reactions to bearded men.* Retrieved September 14, 2001 from the World Wide Web: http://www.improbable.com/airchives/classical/cat/cat.html

McPeck, J. E. (1981). *Critical thinking and education.* New York: St. Martin's.

McPeck, J. E. (1990). *Teaching critical thinking: Dialogue and dialectic.* New York: Routledge.

Pollock, J. L. (1987). Defeasible reasoning. *Cognitive Science, 11,* 481–518.

Pulford, D. L. (1981). Follow-up study of science news accuracy. *Journalism Quarterly, 53,* 119–121.

Ranney, M., & Schank, P. (1995). Protocol modeling, textual analysis, the bifurcation/bootstrapping method, and *Convince Me*: Computer-based techniques for studying beliefs and their revision. *Behavior Research Methods, Instruments, and Computers, 27,* 239–243.

Reaney, P. (1998). *Researchers identify gene for human sex reversal syndrome.* Retrieved September 14, 2001 from the World Wide Web: http://archive.nandotimes.com/newsroom/ntn/health/021898/health14_8902_noframes.html

Resnick, L. B. (1987). *Education and learning to think.* Washington, DC: National Academy Press.

Ross, L., Lepper, M. R., Strack, F., & Steinmetz, J. (1977). Social explanation and social expectation: Effects of real and hypothetical explanations on subjective likelihood. *Journal of Personality and Social Psychology, 35,* 817–829.

Scribner, S. (1984). Studying working intelligence. In B. Rogoff & J. Lave (Eds.), *Everyday cognition: Its development in social context* (pp. 9–40). Cambridge, England: Cambridge University Press.

Segell, M. (1998). *Do big boys cry?* Retrieved September 14, 2001 from the World Wide Web: http://wise.berkeley.edu/WISE/evidence/14.html

Siegel, H. (1988). *Educating reason.* New York: Routledge.

Sternberg, R., & Bhana, K. (1986). Synthesis of research on the effectiveness of the intellectual skills programs: Snake-oil remedies or miracle cures? *Educational Leadership, 22,* 60–67.

Tankard, J. W., & Ryan, M. (1974). News perceptions of accuracy of science coverage. *Journalism Quarterly, 51,* 219–225.

Thagard, P. (1989). Explanatory coherence. *Behavioral and Brain Sciences, 12,* 435–502.

Toulmin, S. E. (1958). *The uses of argument.* Cambridge, England: Cambridge University Press.

VanGelder, T. (2000). *The efficacy of undergraduate critical thinking courses* [Online]. Retrieved September 14, 2001 from the World Wide Web: http://www.philosophy.unimelb.edu.au/reason/papers/efficacy.html

Voss, J., Greene, T., Post, T., & Penner, B. (1983). Problem-solving skill in the social sciences. In G. Bower (Ed.), *The psychology of learning and motivation* (Vol. 17, pp. 165–213). New York: Academic.

Voss, J. F., Tyler, S. W., & Yengo, L. A. (1983). Individual differences in the solving of social science problems. In R. F. Dillon & R. R. Schmeck (Eds.), *Individual differences in cognition* (Vol. 1, pp. 205–232). New York: Academic.

Watson, G., & Glaser, E. M. (1980). *Watson–Glaser Critical Thinking Appraisal, Forms A and B.* New York: Psychological Corporation.

Zeidler, D. L., & Lederman, N. G. (1989). The effect of teachers' language on students' conceptions of the nature of science. *Journal of Research in Science Teaching, 26,* 771–783.

# Narrative Structure, Information Certainty, Emotional Content, and Gender as Factors in a Pseudo Jury Decision-Making Task

James F. Voss and Julie A. Van Dyke
*Learning Research and Development Center
University of Pittsburgh*

Argumentation was studied in a courtroom context in which the prosecuting attorney's summary is assumed to be an argument with "X is guilty" as the claim and the narrative, which contains the evidence of the case, providing support for the claim. In Experiment 1, quality of evidence, narrative coherence, and gender were studied. In Experiments 2A and 2B the role of uncertainty of narrative information, emotional expressions in the narrative, and gender were studied. Both crime-related and non-crime-related uncertain information produced lower guilt ratings and lower ratings of narrative goodness than the baseline, suggesting jury doubt occurs with any narrative uncertainty. Victim-related emotional expressions produced lower guilt ratings than the baseline, although these were mediated by the particular story read. Effects of defendant-related emotional expressions depended on gender and narrative contents. The gender results suggest men respond more heuristically, focusing primarily on evidence, whereas women process the narrative more comprehensively.

Since at least the early Greek period, the courtroom has been an important venue for argumentation. Following a modified version of the dialectic procedure found in Plato's dialogues (van Eemeren, Grootendorst, & Snoeck Henkemans, 1996), it is assumed that questioning individuals who have sworn to tell the truth will lead to the correct knowledge of the events in a particular dispute, as well as to how, why, and by what agency the events occurred. Moreover, in today's courtroom, a defense or prosecuting attorney may deliver an opening or closing statement, with such statements frequently taking the form of narrative accounts of the available evidence. Such statements are structured as arguments with a prosecuting attor-

---

Correspondence and requests for reprints should be sent to James F. Voss, Learning Research and Development Center, 3939 O'Hara Street, Room 634, Pittsburgh, PA 15260. E-mail: voss@pitt.edu

ney's claim being "X is guilty," and the narrative, which includes a statement of the available evidence, being the support of the claim. This article, which follows from the work of Voss, Wiley, and Sandak (1999), is concerned with factors that influence the processing of a prosecuting attorney's hypothetical narrative in a pseudo jury decision-making task.

How narratives are processed has been the subject of considerable research, including studies of narrative structure (e.g., Mandler & Johnson, 1977), narrative use (e.g., Foucault, 1969/1972), and narrative comprehension (e.g., Trabasso, van den Broek, & Suh, 1989). That the narrative is important to jury decision making was established by Pennington and Hastie (1993), who showed that jurors use trial evidence to construct a narrative encompassing most of the case's important events. The narrative then is related to one of the possible verdicts the judge has explained. Our focus here, however, is not on the narratives constructed during jury deliberation, but on the narrative as provided by a prosecuting attorney's summary statement.

In these studies, after reading a hypothetical prosecuting attorney's statement, participants made judgments of the guilt of the defendant and of qualitative aspects of the prosecutor's narrative. These judgments were of the narrative's convincingness, evidence strength, and overall quality. We refer to these measures collectively as narrative goodness ratings.

In Experiment 1 we were concerned with how the coherence of the prosecutor's statement and the strength of evidence affected guilt and goodness ratings. The study also examined the possible performance differences of participant gender. In Experiments 2A and 2B, we studied the certainty of information and the emotional contents in the prosecutor's statement, as well as the gender of the participants.

## NARRATIVE COHERENCE AND EVIDENCE STRENGTH

Experiment 1 is an extension of a previous study (Voss et al., 1999) concerned with whether the quality of a prosecuting attorney's narrative could influence a juror's guilt judgments when narrative quality was varied and the evidence, stated within the narrative, was held constant. In the Voss et al. (1999) experiment, coherence–chronology were studied by comparing guilt and goodness judgments made following a 20-sentence prosecutor's statement, with sentences arranged in a coherent and normal chronological order or in a rearranged order. The rearrangement disrupted the narrative's coherence–chronology but contained the same contents as the normally ordered sentences. The results supported the hypothesis that guilt and goodness judgments would be significantly lower for the poorly ordered narrative, even though the evidence was constant in both types of narrative. The poor narrative thus worked against the prosecuting attorney's goal of achieving a guilt judgment.

Experiment 1 was designed to determine whether this finding would be upheld when coherence–chronology and evidence were both manipulated. Evidence, either strong or weak, and coherence–chronology, either normal or disrupted, were manipulated in a 2 × 2 design to investigate the role of each variable and their interaction. Of particular interest was whether having a good narrative structure would compensate for poor evidence; that is, whether higher guilt and goodness ratings would be obtained in a poor evidence, highly coherent condition than in a poor evidence, low coherent condition.

Kuhn (2001) recently showed that individual differences occur in juror decision-making situations, which suggests that gender, although it has not received much attention in juror decision-making research, could be a source of individual differences. Specifically, gender of the participant was held orthogonal to the manipulations in Experiment 1 to test a hypothesis derived from Meyers-Levy (1989). In summarizing the literature on gender differences, she suggested that males tend to process information by selecting a single feature, or *cue*, from the situation. The cue is usually regarded to be the most important aspect of the task. This selectivity hypothesis maintains that decision making will be guided primarily by the cue selected. Women, on the other hand, are presumed to be more comprehensive information processors, allowing a number of interrelated factors to influence their decision making. In the application, here, because the task was to determine guilt of the defendant, we assumed that the most relevant feature of the prosecutor's closing statement is the evidence. Thus, the Meyers-Levy hypothesis would predict men would likely use evidence as their cue, and therefore be more sensitive to its manipulation than women, who would be influenced by the broader text features embodied in part by the goodness ratings. Experiment 1 thus was designed to study three issues: the relative importance of evidence and narrative quality, whether a good narrative may compensate for poor evidence, and whether men are more influenced by evidence than women.

## INFORMATION UNCERTAINTY

Experiments 2A and 2B also constitute an extension of the Voss et al. (1999) study. Causal relations within a narrative had been determined as one of the characteristics of a good narrative (Leinhardt, Stainton, Virji, & Odoroff, 1994; Pennington & Hastie, 1993). In Voss et al., causal statements were manipulated to test the hypothesis that a prosecuting attorney's narrative with more explicit causal statements would produce higher guilt ratings and goodness judgments than a narrative having less explicit causal statements. An example of this difference is "Matthew's were the only fingerprints on the bat," as opposed to "Matthew's were the only fingerprints on the bat, indicating that he had touched it and, that no one else could have touched it, unless they were wearing gloves."

The results in the original study supported the hypothesis, but some of the changes made in the manipulation were not clearly related to causal factors involving the crime. For this reason, Experiments 2A and 2B were conducted with a refinement in the manipulation. In Experiment 2A, the variable that we hereafter refer to as information certainty or uncertainty involved two different narratives by the prosecutor. One stated definite information, whereas the other stated uncertain information in which only particular criminal- or crime-related statements were made uncertain. In Experiment 2B the same baseline narrative was employed, but uncertainty was created only in information that was irrelevant to the criminal or crime. Guilt and goodness judgments were obtained in both studies, so it was possible to determine whether, relative to a baseline containing definite statements, crime-related uncertainties produced lower than baseline guilt and goodness judgments and whether crime-irrelevant uncertainties produced similar effects. If the crime-related uncertain information produced lower guilt and goodness ratings than the baseline, but the irrelevant uncertainties did not, then the hypothesized effect of crime-related uncertainty influencing guilt and goodness judgments is supported. However, if the non-crime-related uncertain information also yielded lower guilt and goodness ratings, then the role of uncertain information may be regarded as general.

## NARRATIVE AFFECT OR EMOTION

Within the hypothesized courtroom context, a prosecutor's narrative may contain expressions that have affective or emotional contents. Moreover, there are at least two types of such statements, one set pertaining to the defendant and the other to the victim. For example, a prosecutor's argument may include, "He brutally smashed the victim on the back of his head." With respect to the victim, statements such as the "poor and unsuspecting victim" or "the blood-soaked shirt of the victim" may be included. In both cases, these statements are intended to convey a more vivid image of the crime and its severity, either of which may produce higher guilt and goodness ratings than the baseline. Moreover, previous research (Gernsbacher, Hallada, & Robertson, 1998) has shown that readers incorporate emotional information into their situational model of events described in the narrative. We assume therefore that this information becomes part of the representation that may be used by jurors in making their guilt and goodness decisions.

Experiment 2A involved a comparison of performance in two conditions: the baseline, in which the prosecutor's narrative contained no emotional statements, and a crime- or criminal-related condition that contained a number of crime-related (or criminal-related) emotional expressions. In Experiment 2B, there was the same nonemotional baseline condition as in Experiment 2A, but the narrative of the second condition contained emotional statements pertaining to the victim. The issue under study thus was whether emotional statements in the prosecutor's narrative, either crime-related, defendant-related, or victim-related, would act to produce higher guilt and goodness judgments than a baseline narrative void of emotional statements.

## PARTICIPANT GENDER

In Experiments 2A and 2B, gender of the participant was orthogonal to the other variables. Following the Meyers-Levy (1989) position, it was hypothesized that if, as previously suggested, men focus more on a specific cue such as evidence, then in Experiment 2A, when the information is crime-related and uncertain, men should provide lower guilt and goodness ratings relative to the baseline than women. However, in Experiment 2B, when the information uncertainty is not crime-related, men should not be influenced by the uncertainty (as compared to baseline performance). Women on the other hand should be influenced by the irrelevant uncertainty because they attend to a broader range of text factors in making their decision, and they would provide lower guilt and goodness ratings than focused in the baseline. Also, with respect to the emotion manipulation, men should not be influenced by either the Experiment 2A or Experiment 2B emotional statements because they are focusing on evidence. However, women in Experiment 2A should produce higher guilt and goodness judgments than men because their processing, assumed to be more comprehensive, would be influenced by the emotional content. In Experiment 2B the same result should occur; that is, there should be no influence of the narrative's emotional content for men, but higher guilt and goodness judgments for the victim-based emotion narrative than the baseline should be obtained for women.

## EXPERIMENT 1

Experiment 1 was designed to investigate the possible interaction of the level of coherence–chronology with evidence strength. In addition, gender was held orthogonal to both narrative structure and evidence quality to assess the likelihood that gender differences occur in interpreting the evidence.

### Method

*Participants.* Sixty-four undergraduates (32 men and 32 women) from the University of Pittsburgh psychology participant pool participated in the experiment. The participants received credit as part of their introductory psychology class.

*Design and materials.* The experiment had a 2 × 2 factorial design, with the variables evidence (strong, weak) and narrative structure (high coherent–chronology, low coherent–chronology). To allow each person to serve in each of the four conditions, four narratives were constructed, each with four versions. Each narrative version is appropriate to one of the four experimental conditions. Each of the four narratives described the events of a murder: One was about a man charged with murdering his ex-wife. Another is about a man who is killed because he accidentally hit the defendant's sister while driving home from work. A third story tells of a man who is killed on a hunting trip after the defendant discovers the victim had an affair with his wife. The last narrative is about a pharmacy owner who is killed while his store is being looted. See Appendices A, B, and C for the baseline conditions of the stories not discussed in the text. In all cases, the baseline story was written so that the evidence against the defendant is substantial but not conclusive. This judgment was confirmed by a pilot study. To construct the low-evidence condition, changes were introduced into each of the four baseline stories that admit an alternative explanation of the events and thus shed doubt on the defendant's guilt. For example, the baseline condition text for "The Earthquake" was as follows:

> We are all familiar with the earthquake that happened on Tuesday, December 15th. For hours it was pitch black throughout the city. In addition to the power outage, many shops in the downtown area had their windows broken and this led to widespread looting. Because they were concerned about losing their inventory, many shopkeepers stayed in their stores until the police came to secure the area. Vince Morelli was one of these shopkeepers, staying in his pharmacy in order to protect his goods.
>
> The defendant, Edward di Cicco, was looting Vince Morelli's pharmacy when he realized that the owner was present. He continued to loot the store anyway. Edward pointed his gun at Vince Morelli and demanded the keys to the drug cabinet. He was given the keys. Edward then went behind the counter where the drugs were kept, opened the cabinet, and began to put some drugs in a bag he had brought with him. Vince Morelli was not going to let this happen. When Edward was stuffing the drugs into his bag, Vince Morelli reached under the cash register where he kept his gun, but he was not quick enough. Edward di Cicco shot and killed him, and then attempted to flee. As he came out of the pharmacy, two police officers grabbed him. The officers found that the bag he was carrying contained morphine and other drugs. While he was not carrying a gun, they found a gun inside the pharmacy. The only fingerprints found on the gun were those of Edward di Cicco. Edward di Cicco claims that the pharmacist was dead when he entered the store and that he picked up the gun to move it away from the victim when he was attempting to find the keys. The ballistics report confirmed that this was the gun used to kill Vincent Morelli. The defendant should be found guilty.

The low-evidence version of this text contained the changes cited next. The first part of each item is what was in the original baseline text and the second part states the modified contents in the low-evidence text.

1) → There were no eyewitnesses to this crime. (New sentence added); 2) The defendant, Edward di Cicco, was looting Vince Morelli's pharmacy when he realized that the owner was present. → The defendant, Edward di Cicco, was one of several

men looting Vince Morelli's pharmacy when he realized that the owner was present; 3) The only fingerprints found on the gun were those of Edward di Cicco. → No fingerprints were found on this gun, however; 4) Edward di Cicco claims that the pharmacist was dead when he entered the store and that he picked up the gun to move it away from the victim when he was attempting to find the keys. → Edward di Cicco claims that the pharmacist was dead when he entered the store and that another looter killed him; 5) The ballistics report confirmed that this was the gun used to kill Vincent Morelli. → The ballistics report was inconclusive.

Changes 1, 3, and 5 added ambiguity to the account given by the prosecuting attorney. Changes 2 and 4 added alternative suspects.

To create the low-coherence–chronology narratives, we followed the procedure used in Voss et al. (1999), in which the order of sentences from the baseline narrative was randomized. The order of the sentences for the low-coherence version of the earthquake text was 6, 2, 15, 1, 7, 4, 5, 13, 16, 10, 14, 19, 17, 8, 11, 3, 12, 9, 18, 20. To preserve local coherence, minor sentence modifications were made such as replacing anaphors with the appropriate referent name.

These story manipulations were checked in a norming study with a group of 11 participants who were given all versions of all the narratives. The narratives were counterbalanced for condition and story order by using a Greco-Latin square. The participants were asked to judge the defendant's guilt, and the convincingness, quality of the evidence, and overall quality of the prosecutor's narrative. We used the narrative quality and evidence results to verify that our manipulations created the intended effects, those of lower guilt ratings and low-evidence quality with the low-evidence text and lower coherence–chronology ratings with the low-coherence–chronology text. Before conducting Experiment 1, some additional changes were made to the narratives as suggested by these results. We also examined mean ratings for each condition by story to ascertain whether the four stories were of comparable baseline quality and made changes to stories that appeared to deviate from the ratings obtained for the other three.

*Procedure.* Participants served in groups of 8. Each participant was given a packet containing the four different prosecutor's statements, each representing one of the four experimental conditions. Participants were instructed to assume the role of a juror. The four narratives and four experimental conditions were counterbalanced using a Greco-Latin square. The experimenter explained that each narrative represented the prosecuting attorney's closing argument in a court case and based on this argument, the participants were to make judgments about the guilt of the defendant.

*Measures.* After reading each narrative, each participant was asked to provide a rating of guilt on a scale from 1 to 11, annotated to maximize rating comparability between participants. For example, a rating of 9 was annotated as "I think X is guilty, but I have some doubt," whereas a rating of 10 was annotated "I am positive X is guilty, but I have a little doubt." The extreme ratings were 11 (*I am positive X is guilty*) and 1 (*I am positive X is not guilty*). Additionally, participants were asked three questions regarding the narrative itself. On an annotated scale of 1 (*lowest*) to 5 (*highest*), students were asked to judge convincingness of the prosecutor's argument, quality of the argument, and strength of the evidence. Annotations for these scales used language such as *not at all* or *rather* to indicate variation at the low end, and *very* and *extremely* to indicate variation at the high end.

## Results

Table 1 presents the means for all statistically significant judgment differences of Experiment 1 as well as means for a few nonsignificant differences.

*Guilt ratings.* Guilt judgments were higher in the strong evidence than in the weak evidence condition, $F(1, 224) = 96.84$, $p < .001$. However, the mean guilt rating did not vary significantly as a function of narrative condition, $F(1, 224) < 1$. Although there was little difference in mean guilt judgment for the two weak evidence conditions (6.09 vs. 6.19), the mean guilt judgment in the strong evidence and the baseline narrative compared to the mean of the strong evidence and disruptive narrative condition did not produce a significant Evidence × Narrative interaction, $F(1, 224) = 1.54$, $p < .21$. The failure of low-evidence conditions to

TABLE 1
Guilt and Goodness Ratings for the Evidence and Narrative and Selected Interactive Conditions of Experiment 1

| Condition | Guilt | Quality | Convincingness | Strength |
|---|---|---|---|---|
| Evidence (E) | | | | |
| Strong (S) | 8.93*** | 3.13*** | 2.97*** | 3.44*** |
| Weak (W) | 6.14 | 2.15 | 1.74 | 1.90 |
| Narrative (N) | | | | |
| Baseline (B) | 7.66 | 3.16*** | 2.62*** | 2.82*** |
| Disrupted (D) | 7.41 | 2.11 | 2.09 | 2.52 |
| Evidence × Narrative | | | | |
| SB | 9.23 | 3.89** | 3.38*** | 3.73*** |
| SD | 8.63 | 2.36 | 2.56 | 3.14 |
| WB | 6.09 | 2.44 | 1.86 | 1.91 |
| WD | 6.19 | 1.86 | 1.63 | 1.89 |
| Evidence × Gender | | | | |
| S Male | 9.33* | 3.27* | 3.20** | 3.53 |
| S Female | 8.53 | 2.98 | 2.73 | 3.34 |
| W Male | 5.94 | 2.03 | 1.66 | 1.78 |
| W Female | 6.34 | 2.27 | 1.83 | 2.02 |

*$p = .05$. **$p = .01$. ***$p = .001$.

yield higher guilt ratings in the coherent condition than in the disruptive condition does not support the idea that a more coherent narrative will compensate for weak evidence. The goodness ratings do suggest, however, that with strong evidence, a more coherent narrative may produce higher guilt ratings.

Gender did not significantly influence guilt judgments, with mean male and female judgments of 7.63 and 7.44, respectively ($F < 1$). However, the interaction of gender and evidence showed that men made more extreme evidence-based guilt judgments than women, $F(1, 224) = 4.51$, $p < .04$. In other words, compared to women, men made higher judgments of guilt when evidence was strong and lower judgments of guilt when evidence was weak, a result suggesting that men weighted evidence, or the lack thereof, to a greater extent than women. This result provides some support for the Meyers-Levy (1989) hypothesis that men focus more on a specific cue—in this case, evidence—than women.

A significant story effect was obtained, with the Story 2 mean guilt rating being significantly lower than the means of Stories 1 and 4. Table 2 presents the mean guilt ratings for each of the stories, $F(3, 224) = 6.81, p < .001$. The means of the Story × Evidence interaction, $F(3, 224) = 4.22, p < .01$, are presented in the columns for strong and weak evidence under guilt ratings. The high evidence ratings for the four stories varied only from 8.69 to 9.25, whereas the low evidence ratings varied from 4.50 to 7.53. This result suggests that the difference in guilt ratings as a function of story and evidence is due to the relative differences in the weak evidence condition, primarily in Story 2. A possible reason for the low guilt ratings in that story is that in the low-evidence condition it is explicitly stated that it was "difficult to see" the victim, increasing the likelihood that the shooting

TABLE 2
Mean Guilt and Goodness Ratings for the Story and the
Story × Evidence Conditions in Experiment 1

| Story | Guilt | | | Quality | | |
|---|---|---|---|---|---|---|
| | Baseline | Strong | Weak | Baseline | Strong | Weak |
| 1 | 8.00*** | 9.25*** | 6.75 | 2.89 | 3.41** | 2.38 |
| 2 | 6.64 | 8.78 | 4.50 | 2.52 | 3.34 | 1.69 |
| 3 | 7.23 | 8.69 | 5.78 | 2.55 | 2.94 | 2.16 |
| 4 | 8.27 | 9.00 | 7.53 | 2.59 | 2.81 | 2.38 |

| Story | Convincingness | | | Strength | | |
|---|---|---|---|---|---|---|
| | Baseline | Strong | Weak | Baseline | Strong | Weak |
| 1 | 2.70*** | 3.47** | 1.94 | 2.92** | 3.78* | 2.06 |
| 2 | 2.17 | 2.97 | 1.38 | 2.42 | 3.41 | 1.44 |
| 3 | 2.06 | 2.50 | 1.63 | 2.44 | 3.03 | 1.84 |
| 4 | 2.48 | 2.94 | 2.03 | 2.89 | 3.53 | 2.25 |

*$p = .06$. **$p = .01$. ***$p = .001$.

could be regarded as accidental. Furthermore, the possible motive of the victim having an affair with the defendant's wife was deleted in the low-evidence condition, whereas the original motive remained intact in the low-evidence condition for the other three stories. These two modifications in Story 2 likely combined to make the alternative of an accidental killing plausible, thereby producing a relatively low guilt rating compared with the evidence manipulation changes of Stories 1 and 4. Story 3 also had a substantial good and poor evidence difference, and this story appears to have a feasible alternative hypothesis in the weak condition, as the text suggests that someone other than the defendant may have killed the victim.

*Goodness judgments.* The quality judgment served as a check on the narrative manipulation. Narrative quality (see Table 1) was judged better in the coherent condition than the disruptive condition, $F(1, 224) = 61.36, p < .001$, and also better in the good evidence compared to the poor evidence condition, $F(1, 224) = 52.61, p < .001$. Also, although having a more coherent narrative produced higher quality ratings for both the strong and weak evidence conditions, the effect was substantially greater when the evidence was strong, $F(1, 224) = 12.53, p < .001$. This same set of results involving the evidence and narrative main effects and their significant Narrative × Evidence interactions held for judgments of convincingness, $F(1, 224) = 97.54, p < .001; F(1, 224) = 17.76, p < .001; F(1, 224) = 5.42, p < .02$; and strength, $F(1, 224) = 123.87, p < .001; F(1, 224) = 4.86, p < .03; F(1, 224) = 4.37, p < .04$, with $F$s presented for the evidence effect, narrative effect, and Evidence × Narrative interaction, respectively. These results indicate that the prosecutor's summary was judged better when it had both strong evidence and a more coherent narrative. Furthermore, the goodness rating interactions of evidence and narrative were also consistent with the guilt ratings in that a more coherent narrative was more effective in obtaining a guilty verdict when the evidence is strong compared to when it is weak. However, despite the narrative main effect and the Narrative × Evidence interaction obtained for the goodness ratings, the differences in narrative structure did not produce a significant effect of narrative or the Narrative × Evidence interaction in the guilt ratings. This difference suggests that goodness judgments are derived from narrative properties, but that judgments of guilt may be more restricted to evidential characteristics of the narrative.

None of the goodness ratings approached a significant gender effect, but the Gender × Evidence interaction was significant for convincingness, $F(1, 224) = 6.65, p < .01$, and was of borderline significance for quality, $F(1, 224) = 3.67, p < .06$. For argument strength, $F(1, 224) = 2.33, p < .13$. The means of the Gender × Evidence interactions, shown in Table 1, indicate that although significance varied for the three goodness ratings, the pattern of the goodness ratings was the same as the pattern of the guilt ratings; that is, men gave more extreme judgments than women in both the strong and weak evidence conditions.

Story effects were significant for two of the three goodness ratings: quality, $F(1, 224) = 1.64, p < .18$; convincingness, $F(1, 224) = 5.55, p < .001$, and strength, $F(1, 224) = 3.97, p < .01$. The means for these three ratings are presented in Table 2. As with the guilt ratings, all three goodness ratings for Story 2 were quite low, and the ratings for Stories 1 and 4 were highest. In the convincingness ratings, the mean of Story 1 differed from that of Stories 2 and 3. The Story × Evidence interaction was significant for the quality judgments, $F(3, 224) = 3.65, p < .01$; borderline for convincingness, $F(3, 224) = 2.45, p < .06$; and not significant for strength, $F(3, 224) = 1.77, p < .15$.

## Discussion

The first issue of Experiment 1, as mentioned earlier, concerns the relative role of evidence and narrative quality. These results indicate that if the evidence is poor, guilt and goodness judgments will be relatively low, regardless of the quality of the narrative. This finding does not support the hypothesis that a good narrative can compensate for poor evidence. With respect to narrative quality, Klettke and Graesser (2000) found that if a narrative contains contradictions, poor guilt ratings result. Although in this study the "jurors" gave higher goodness ratings for the coherent than for the disrupted narrative, narrative quality ratings did not influence guilt ratings. The findings of Voss et al. (1999), in which a disrupted narrative did produce significantly lower guilt and goodness ratings, taken with the present lack of an effect on guilt ratings suggest that the narrative quality may play a role when the evidence is neither good nor poor, but instead is somewhat uncertain. The other result regarding the interaction of evidence and narrative is that a good narrative does enhance goodness ratings when evidence is strong, with the guilt ratings showing the same tendency, although not significantly so.

Results involving the gender variable indicated that men made more extreme guilt and goodness judgments than women for both good evidence and poor evidence conditions. Men apparently gave stronger weight to evidence characteristics than women, or men focused primarily on the evidence information whereas women focused less on one aspect of the narrative (Meyers-Levy, 1989).

The results also show that although care was taken to verify similar ratings for each story on each of the relevant dimensions, story effects nevertheless occurred. As stated, the story effects seem due to more pronounced effects of the weak evidence conditions in Story 2 and to some extent in Story 3 with respect to the availability of alternative hypotheses regarding the defendant's guilt.

## EXPERIMENTS 2A AND 2B

Experiments 2A and 2B, as previously mentioned, focused on three issues. One was the extent to which guilt and goodness ratings are influenced by the relative certainty of the contents of the statement, with such information being crime-related or non-crime-related. The second issue was the extent to which emotional statements related either negatively to the defendant or crime or positively toward the victim influence guilt and goodness judgments, as compared to a narrative not containing emotional statements. The third issue was the extent to which participant gender influences guilt and goodness judgments and the extent to which interactive effects occur between the certainty and the emotional manipulations and the participant gender. Because there was a need for a within-subjects design, but for practical reasons a design with a limit of four conditions, two 2 × 2 experiments were simultaneously conducted.

## EXPERIMENT 2A

### Method

*Participants.* Ninety-six University of Pittsburgh undergraduates (48 men, 48 women) participated in Experiment 2A for partial course credit.

*Design and materials.* Experiment 2A had a 2 (certainty) × 2 (emotion) factorial design, crime-relevant uncertain information versus certain information (baseline) and defendant-related emotional expressions versus no emotional contents (baseline). Thus, there was a baseline condition (certain information and no emotional contents), no emotional contents and uncertain crime-related information, certain crime-related information and defendant-related emotional contents, and a condition with both uncertain crime-related information and defendant-related emotional contents.

The four baseline stories from Experiment 1 were used in Experiment 2A. Taking "The Earthquake," Story 1, presented earlier as a baseline, the following five changes were introduced to create the crime-relevant probability manipulations.

> The defendant, Edward di Cicco, was looting . . . → The defendant, Edward di Cicco, was probably looting . . . ; 2) Edward pointed his gun at Vince Morelli . . . → Edward most likely pointed his gun at Vince Morelli . . . ; 3) Edward di Cicco shot and killed him . . . → Edward di Cicco apparently shot and killed him . . . ; 4) The only fingerprints found on the gun were those of Edward di Cicco. → The only fingerprints found on the gun were probably those of Edward di Cicco; 5) The ballistics report confirmed that this was the gun used to kill Vincent Morelli. → The ballistics report confirmed that this could have been the gun used to kill Vincent Morelli.

The criminal-relevant emotion versions were created similarly.

> 1) He continued to loot the store anyway. → He was so obsessed that he continued to loot the store anyway; 2) Edward . . . → Gesturing wildly, Edward . . . ; 3) Edward

pointed his gun at Vince Morelli ... → Edward burst into the store, pointed his gun at Vince Morelli ... ; 4) Edward was stuffing the drugs into his bag ... → Edward was frantically stuffing the drugs into his bag; 5) Edward di Cicco shot and killed him ... → Edward di Cicco shot him ruthlessly.

Four text versions for each story were constructed such that there was one version for each condition of the experiment. By using the resulting four versions of each of the four stories, each individual participated once in each of the four experimental conditions and each condition for each participant involved a different narrative, as determined by a 4 × 4 Greco-Latin square.

A validity check for the manipulations was run using 16 additional participants (9 men and 7 women). Each rated all 16 stories of this study and an additional 12 used in Experiment 2B for argument strength, definiteness, and emotional impact. The stories were presented in blocks, so that the participants saw all the baseline stories first, followed by four additional blocks containing each of the remaining versions. Presentation order was counterbalanced with a Greco-Latin square for story and story version. The uncertainty manipulation resulted in lower ratings for definiteness across all stories except in one case, and lower ratings of story strength were obtained in all but three cases. The emotion manipulations resulted in increased ratings for emotional impact in all but four cases. Subsequently, adjustments were made to the stories in the conditions that did not produce the expected results. We also collected guilt ratings for all stories in the pilot study and made some changes to the baseline versions of individual stories so that the mean guilt rating was similar across all texts.

*Procedure and measures.* The same procedure described in Experiment 1 was followed here. Participants were asked to provide guilt ratings, followed by quality, convincingness, and—in place of strength ratings—quality of evidence ratings. The same scales described in Experiment 1 were used, with the exception of evidence strength ratings that ranged between 10 (*very strong*) and 1 (*not strong*).

## Results

*Guilt ratings.* Uncertain evidence produced lower guilt ratings at a borderline significance level compared to the baseline condition, $F(1, 352) = 3.51, p < .06$ (see Table 3). Defendant-related negative emotional content did not significantly affect guilt ratings ($F < 1$). Gender also did not influence guilt ratings ($F < 1$).

There was a significant story effect on guilt ratings, $F(3, 352) = 5.34, p < .001$. As suggested by the means in Table 3, guilt ratings on the four stories significantly differed from each other except for Stories 1 and 2. The only significant interaction obtained was that of Emotion × Story × Gender, $F(3, 352) = 2.88, p < .04$. The means of this interaction, shown in Table 4, indicate that for all stories,

TABLE 3
Mean Guilt and Goodness Ratings for the Main Effects of Experiment 2A

|  | Guilt | Quality | Convincingness | Evidence |
|---|---|---|---|---|
| Information certainty | | | | |
| Baseline | 8.26* | 3.67** | 3.31*** | 7.28*** |
| Uncertain | 7.75 | 3.01 | 2.60 | 6.35 |
| Emotion | | | | |
| Baseline | 8.03 | 3.19** | 2.80** | 6.54** |
| Emotional | 7.98 | 3.48 | 3.12 | 7.09 |
| Gender | | | | |
| Male | 7.88 | 3.37 | 3.00 | 6.67 |
| Female | 8.13 | 3.31 | 2.92 | 6.96 |
| Story | | | | |
| 1 (Burglary) | 8.01*** | 3.10*** | 2.76*** | 6.52*** |
| 2 (Hunting) | 8.01 | 3.43 | 3.07 | 6.77 |
| 3 (Mob attack) | 7.23 | 3.09 | 2.64 | 6.25 |
| 4 (Wife killing) | 8.77 | 3.72 | 3.37 | 7.72 |

*$p = .06$. **$p = .01$. ***$p = .001$.

TABLE 4
Mean Guilt Ratings of the Story × Emotion × Gender Interaction of Experiment 2A

| | Male | | Female | |
|---|---|---|---|---|
| Story | Baseline | Emotion | Baseline | Emotion |
| 1 | 8.38* | 7.13 | 8.08 | 8.46 |
| 2 | 8.00 | 7.63 | 8.13 | 8.29 |
| 3 | 6.42 | 8.25 | 7.42 | 6.83 |
| 4 | 9.08 | 8.17 | 8.71 | 9.13 |

*$p = .05$.

the direction of the difference of the baseline and emotion conditions was opposite for men and women. For men, the defendant-related emotion condition produced lower guilt ratings in Stories 1, 2, and 4 and higher guilt ratings in Story 3. For women, however, Stories 1, 2, and 4 produced higher guilt ratings and Story 3 produced lower guilt rating judgments in the defendant-related emotion condition. Examining the stories, men produced lower guilt ratings for stories in which the emotional statement was crime-related, whereas women's ratings were lower for the story in which the emotional expression was person-related.

In summary, the guilt rating data suggest that making evidence relatively uncertain produced marginally lower guilt ratings, and that neither emotional contents of the crime or gender significantly influenced guilt judgments. There was, however, an interaction of story, gender, and emotion, suggesting that men and women responded differently to the particular emotional contents of each story, with women responding to emotional statements related to the defendant and men responding to emotional statements pertaining to the crime and evidence.

*Goodness judgments.* For all three ratings, the pattern of main effects was identical. As presented in Table 3, the means showed that the prosecutor's statement was rated as poorer in the crime-related uncertain condition than in the baseline condition, $F(1, 352) = 7.42, p < .01$; $F(1, 352) = 40.71, p < .001$; and $F(1, 352) = 17.60, p < .001$, for the quality, convincingness, and evidence ratings, respectively. These results are consistent with the guilt rating findings, although the magnitude of the difference in guilt ratings is not as substantial.

As also shown in Table 3, the means of the three goodness judgments were higher in the baseline condition than in the defendant-related emotion condition, $F(1, 352) = 7.42, p < .01$; $F(1, 352) = 7.92, p < .01$; and $F(1, 352) = 6.43, p < .01$, for the quality, convincingness, and evidence ratings, respectively. These judgments indicated that the inclusion of the defendant-based emotion contents produced a judgment of poorer quality, but this effect did not carry over to the guilt judgments. Gender was not significantly related to goodness judgments.

Story had a significant effect on all three goodness judgments. Analyses indicated $F(3, 352) = 8.05, p < .001$; $F(3, 352) = 8.70, p < .001$; and $F(3, 352) = 8.45, p < 001$, for the quality, convincingness, and evidence judgments, respectively. For each rating, Story 4 was rated significantly higher than Stories 1 and 3. This result, moreover, is similar to the guilt ratings previously discussed, as Story 4 ratings were significantly greater than those of the other three conditions, whereas Story 3 yielded ratings lower than those of Stories 1 and 2.

One possibility for these results is that the stories varied with respect to the extent an alternative hypothesis for the crime became more apparent in the crime-related uncertain condition. Story 4, which received relatively high guilt and goodness ratings, did not provide a reasonable alternative to the guilt of the defendant. In both versions, Raymond tells Myrna that he will kill her and his gun was recovered with his fingerprints. The difference of "he presumably shot her" and "he shot her" seems small in the context of an explicit statement that he will kill her and the additional evidence against him. Furthermore, although the evidence against him becomes weak when the uncertain changes are added, there is nothing that would suggest another person may have committed the crime. In Story 3, although the evidence is against Matthew, there was a mob of boys and any one of them could have committed the crime. Hence, in this story, there are lower guilt ratings, possibly because of a more apparent alternative explanation for the events, even in the certainty condition. In Story 1, there is little support for an alternative scenario unless some other looter committed the crime.

A significant Emotion × Story × Gender interaction was found, $F(3, 224) = 2.63, p < .05$. This interaction appears to be due to the previously discussed characteristics of Story 3. In this story, men provided much higher evidence ratings in the emotion condition ($M = 7.25$) than in the baseline condition ($M = 5.50$). For women, the two respective means were 6.00 and 6.25. The men's baseline rating suggests that in the "Hunting Story" men did not consider the evidence for Paul's shooting of Rob strong, perhaps finding a credible alternative explanation of a hunting accident. Although the emotional contents were not related to evidence per se, they did pertain to the description of the crime itself and included statements such as, "Rob lying in the grass, dead, his blood splattered all over the woods," as compared to "Rob lying in the grass, dead," in the baseline condition. The fact that men are more affected by this manipulation than women fits with the Meyers-Levy (1989) selectivity hypothesis, provided it is assumed that the men interpreted the emotional conditions as related to the evidence in the story, an interpretation suggested by the increase in their evidence strength judgments.

With respect to the previously mentioned issues, although crime-related uncertainty produced substantially lower goodness judgments than the baseline, it produced lower guilt ratings only to borderline significance. Furthermore, although negative emotional expressions in the narrative produced higher goodness ratings than those found in the nonemotional condition, guilt ratings were not influenced. These two effects suggest that the prosecutor's narrative is judged as a narrative for its quality, convincing, and evidence contents, but that the guilt judgments are made according to a more restrictive set of criteria. It appears that by taking on the role of a juror, participants judge the narrative in relation to the prosecutor's goal. Consequently, their guilt judgments may reflect additional processing or interpretation based on the jurors' own perceptions of the case.

With respect to gender, the Emotion × Gender interaction has $F < 1$, but the results indicate that gender may play a role in relation to the particular stories and the particular emotional expressions used in those stories. Specifically, emotion produced higher guilt ratings than the baseline for women for three stories in which the emotional expressions involved the criminals. However, for men, the baseline guilt rating was relatively low, possibly because they thought that a hunting accident was a reasonable interpretation of the crime, but added emotional expressions, which may have affected the quality of the evidence, produced higher ratings.

## EXPERIMENT 2B

Experiment 2B, as with Experiment 2A, consisted of manipulations of the certainty of narrative statements and the inclusion of emotional statements. In Experiment 2B, however, the certainty manipulation consisted of the same baseline condition used in Experiment 2A and a second condition in which the textual changes added uncertainty to five aspects of the narrative; however, none of the points was related to the crime. Thus, the question was whether crime-irrelevant uncertainty would influence guilt and goodness judgments. The emotion condition employed the same baseline as in Experiment 2A, but the five emotional insertions related to the victimization in the crime. Here, the intent was to evoke a sense of empathy in the participants. Gender was again orthogonal to both variables.

## Method

*Participants.* Ninety-six University of Pittsburgh undergraduates (48 men, 48 women), not having participated in any of the previous studies described here, participated in the experiment for partial course credit.

*Design and materials.* This study followed the same design as described for Experiment 2A. As indicated, however, neither the uncertainty changes nor the emotion manipulations involved the crime itself. The five changes that produced the crime-irrelevant uncertainty were as follows.

> 1) ... the earthquake that happened on Tuesday ... → ... the earthquake that I believe happened on Tuesday ... ; 2) ... windows broken and this led to widespread looting. → ... windows broken and this most likely led to widespread looting; 3) Because they were concerned about losing their inventory ... → Probably because they were concerned about losing their inventory ... ; 4) ... many shopkeepers stayed in their stores until the police came ... → ... many shopkeepers stayed in their stores at least until the police came ... ; 5) Vince Morelli was one of these shopkeepers, staying in his pharmacy in order to protect his goods. → Vince Morelli was one of these shopkeepers, staying in his pharmacy, we assume to protect his goods.

The emotion condition consisted of these five victim-related changes:

> 1) Vince Morelli was one of these shopkeepers ... → Vince Morelli was one of these devoted shopkeepers ... ; 2) Edward pointed his gun at Vince Morelli → Edward pointed his gun at the shocked Vince Morelli ... ; 3) He was given the keys. → With trembling hands, he was given the keys; 4) Vince Morelli was not going to let this happen. → Mustering up his courage, Vince Morelli was not going to let this happen; 5) Vince Morelli reached under the cash register ... → Vince Morelli tried to control his shaking as he reached under the cash register.

As in Experiment 2A, a within-subjects design was achieved by using one condition from each of the four stories so that each participant read all four stories and all four conditions, counterbalanced appropriately. The measures and procedures used here were identical to those used in Experiment 2A.

## Results

*Guilt ratings.* The means presented in Table 5 indicate uncertain crime-irrelevant information had a borderline significance effect on the guilt ratings, $F(1, 352) = 3.72$, $p < .055$, producing lower guilt ratings than the baseline. This finding suggests that irrelevant uncertainty may have created a general perception for the reader that the entire prosecutor's statement was uncertain. As shown in Table 5, the baseline condition yielded a higher mean guilt rating than the emotion condition, $F(1, 352) = 4.21$, $p < .04$. Thus, although the emotional contents emphasized the victim's plight, lower judgments of guilt were obtained in the emotion conditions. Also, overall, women did provide significantly higher guilt ratings than men, $F(1, 352) = 12.15$, $p < .001$ (see Table 5).

Story also had a significant effect on guilt judgments, $F(3, 352) = 2.73$, $p < .04$. The mean of Story 3 differs significantly from the means of Stories 1 and 4. As with Experiment 2A, this effect appears to be driven by Story 3, with its baseline having a relatively salient alternative hypothesis. The only significant interaction of the guilt rating analysis is the Certainty × Emotion × Story interaction, $F(3, 352) = 3.67$, $p < .01$. For the uncertain baseline condition, ratings for the non-emotional baseline are higher than the emotion content condition for Stories 1, 2, and 3, with the reverse holding for Story 4. For the uncertain information condition, ratings are higher with emotional contents in Stories 1 and 2, with the reverse in Stories 3 and 4.

*Goodness judgments.* The results for the three goodness judgments were reasonably consistent. The baseline condition was rated as having significantly

TABLE 5
Means for the Main Effects of Experiment 2B

|  | Guilt | Quality | Convincingness | Evidence |
|---|---|---|---|---|
|  |  | *Goodness Measures* | | |
| Information certainty | | | | |
| Baseline | 8.74** | 3.63*** | 3.37*** | 7.00 |
| Uncertain | 8.25 | 3.34 | 3.07 | 6.89 |
| Emotion | | | | |
| Baseline | 8.76** | 3.58** | 3.34** | 7.26*** |
| Emotional | 8.23 | 3.39 | 3.09 | 6.62 |
| Gender | | | | |
| Male | 8.05**** | 3.44 | 3.11* | 6.73** |
| Female | 8.94 | 3.53 | 3.33 | 7.15 |
| Story | | | | |
| 1 (Burglary) | 8.67** | 3.62*** | 3.45**** | 7.32**** |
| 2 (Hunting) | 8.55 | 3.48 | 3.17 | 6.75 |
| 3 (Mob attack) | 7.90 | 3.18 | 2.84 | 6.18 |
| 4 (Wife killing) | 8.87 | 3.67 | 3.42 | 7.51 |

*$p = .06$. **$p = .05$. ***$p = .01$. ****$p = .001$.

better quality and convincingness than the narrative containing crime-irrelevant uncertain information, $F(1, 352) = 7.37, p < .01$, and $F(1, 352) = 6.14, p < .01$, respectively. However, quality of evidence ratings did not vary significantly ($F < 1$). This finding indicates that individuals separated evidence evaluation from the quality and convincingness judgments and also suggests why the guilt ratings of the baseline and uncertain conditions were of borderline significance. In fact, if evidence was the sole criterion for judgment for the guilt ratings, the difference in these conditions should not have approached significance because evidence was held constant.

The inclusion of victim-related emotional statements produced lower ratings than the baseline for all three goodness ratings, $F(1, 352) = 3.39, p < .07$ for quality; $F(1, 352) = 4.21, p < .04$ for convincingness; and $F(1, 352) = 8.65, p < .01$ for evidence. These findings are in agreement with the guilt rating results, indicating that participants were not convinced by the prosecutor's sympathetic statements about the victim. Instead, it appears that including these statements backfired, as guilt and goodness ratings were lower than they were when these statements were not included.

Gender of participant was not significant for the quality ratings ($F < 1$), but was of borderline significance for convincingness judgments, $F(1, 352) = 3.22, p < .07$, and evidence judgments, $F(1, 352) = 3.72, p < .05$. Women provided higher goodness ratings than did men, consistent with the guilt ratings.

Story was significant for all goodness ratings, $F(1, 352) = 7.37, p < .01$ for quality; $F(1, 352) = 5.27, p < .001$ for convincingness; and $F(1, 352) = 7.66, p < .001$ for evidence ratings. Furthermore, each of these goodness measures produced the same pattern of story differences as the guilt rating data. In all four cases, Story 3 yielded significantly lower ratings than Stories 1 and 4. No other difference was significant. The reasons for this finding are most likely the same as those suggested for the guilt rating findings.

The single significant interaction found in each of the three goodness measures was Uncertainty × Story × Gender, $F(3, 352) = 3.04, p < .03$ for quality; $F(3, 352) = 2.81, p < .04$ for convincingness; and $F(3, 352) = 3.68, p < .01$ for evidence. The pattern of means for this interaction is consistent for the convincingness and evidence ratings with one difference in the quality measure. For Stories 2, 3, and 4, the increased uncertainty condition caused ratings to decrease for both men and women, except for men's quality ratings of Story 2. For Story 1, adding uncertainty caused the men to decrease their guilt ratings, but caused women to increase their ratings for all three measures.

## GENERAL DISCUSSION

Although Voss et al. (1999) reported that narrative quality, defined in terms of coherence–chronology, influenced jurors' guilt ratings when evidence is held constant, the findings reported here indicate that the role of narrative quality was related to evidence conditions. These results show that poor evidence produces low guilt ratings, and Klettke and Graesser (2000) showed that contradiction in a narrative also produces low guilt ratings. However, when evidence is either overwhelmingly strong or weak, narrative quality is of relatively little importance. It tends to be of greater importance when evidence is inconclusive, as in the Voss et al. (1999) study. Experiment 1 also specifically showed that a good narrative does not compensate for bad evidence.

If it is assumed that a "juror" in this research constructed a scenario from the prosecutor's statement, the findings suggest that the juror had the ability to construct the scenario even in the disruptive narrative condition. Indeed, the relatively low goodness judgments for the disrupted narrative indicated that, at least for present conditions, the jurors were adept at separating evidential and narrative components. Furthermore, men focused more on the evidence, or at least weighed it more in their guilt judgments, than women. This finding would suggest that scenarios constructed by men may be more skeletal and heuristic and based on evidence, whereas female representations would include more scenario components. This suggestion is consistent with the Meyers-Levy (1989) selective hypothesis and with Kuhn's (in press) distinction of the "satisficing" jurors and the jurors who look at evidence more thoroughly. The view also is in agreement with information processing theories that embrace peripheral and central processing modes (Chaiken, 1980; Petty & Cacioppo, 1986).

There is another possibility regarding the nature of the processing. Schum (1993), following an earlier diagrammatic model by Wigmore (1937), noted that whereas some jurors construct scenarios, others may construct relational models, that is, models not temporal in nature but models that resemble diagrams of ill-structured problem solving (Voss, Greene, Post, & Penner, 1983). It is possible that some jurors, especially men, construct this type of model in their focus on evidence. A take-home lesson from Experiment 1 is that if you have reasonably good or quite good evidence, you should hire an attorney who is a fine narrator; if your evidence is poor, do not go to court.

Experiments 2A and 2B refined and added to the findings of Voss et al. (1999) concerning information uncertainty. Somewhat surprising is the finding that regardless of whether the information uncertainty is related to or irrelevant to the crime, the guilt ratings, compared to the baseline, are about 0.5 units lower and of borderline statistical significance. These findings, as previously noted, suggest that the narrative statements providing uncertainty produce an overall perception of the prosecuting attorney's narrative as indefinite. Intuitively, the crime-related statements should have produced a greater effect than the irrelevant statements because the crime-related statements should raise doubts about the defendant's guilt, whereas the irrelevant uncertainty should not.

The goodness ratings indicated that although having uncertainty in the crime-related narrative led to the narrative being judged as poor, the influence on the guilt ratings, which was not as strong, suggests the jurors regarded the narrative characteristics and evidence as separate, although related, narrative components. This notion is especially shown in the crime-irrelevant uncertainty condition, in which the goodness results were essentially the same as in the crime-related narrative, except that the evidence quality ratings were not different from the baseline. This finding indicates that the jurors in the uncertain crime-irrelevant condition quite readily separated the evidential and uncertain crime-irrelevant components. Again, the data do not tell us whether the jurors constructed a relational structure. A take-home lesson is that it is desirable to hire an attorney who is a clear and concise speaker, not given to qualifiers or hedges that may suggest doubt about the facts surrounding the crime.

The inclusion of crime- or defendant-related emotional statements in the prosecuting attorney's narrative yielded higher goodness ratings for the narrative than those found in the baseline condition, but there was no main effect of emotion on guilt ratings, despite the fact that evidence was rated as better than the baseline of the emotion condition. However, men did produce lower guilt ratings, compared to the baseline for Stories 1, 2, and 4, whereas women produced lower guilt ratings only on Story 3. Conversely, women produced higher guilt ratings on Stories 1, 2, and 4, whereas men produced higher ratings only on Story 3. A possible explanation for this interaction is that in most cases, as suggested by Meyers-Levy (1989), men relied more heavily on the evidence cue in making their judgments. They may have found the emotional statements distracting and reacted against them, thereby resulting in lower guilt ratings than those found in the baseline. Women, who are presumed to give more comprehensive consideration to the information in the stories, apparently took the emotional statements into account, producing higher ratings than the baseline in Stories 1, 2, and 4. As to the Story 3 results, whereas the negative emotional statements in Stories 1, 2, and 4 referred to personal characteristics of the defendant, the emotional statements in Story 3 were more pertinent to the situation surrounding the crime itself, including the evidence. Thus, men apparently were influenced by the emotional statements related to evidence; women seem to be more sensitive to criminal-related emotional statements. Thus, the data do indicate that the emotional information is incorporated into the narrative representation, but the extent to which it influences guilt ratings depends on the story, the nature of the emotion described in the story, and the gender of the juror.

When the narrative contains victim-related emotional expressions, guilt ratings are below the baseline, as are goodness ratings. Such emotion worked to oppose the idea that victim-related emotional statements would evoke empathy and produce higher guilt ratings than the baseline.

The incorporation of gender into these experiments produced the following tentative conclusions. Men responded more extremely to good or poor evidence than women. As previously mentioned, this finding supports hypotheses suggesting men do more heuristically focused processing than women, who do more comprehensive processing. Men and women also differentially respond to the specific emotional contents of particular stories. In general, men are influenced more if the emotional content can be related to evidence, whereas women are more influenced if the emotional content refers to the defendant. Although in Experiment 2B women, overall, provided higher guilt ratings than men, the failure to obtain particular significant interactions indicated there was no evidence that women were influenced by victim-related emotional statements.

Story effects occurred in all experiments despite attempts to equate the stories along characteristics related to the research. The fact that story effects were nevertheless different and that they interacted with the variables under study meant that we could only apply an a posteriori explanation regarding these effects. The results do suggest that guilt ratings may be a function of the extent to which an alternative hypothesis for the crime may be plausible. Also suggested is that gender interacts with the type of story and its emotional content. To study such inferences more thoroughly, simultaneous manipulation of the individual and story contents would be necessary.

In sum, narratives may be used in a courtroom to provide support for a claim about a defendant's guilt or innocence. Jurors do respond to the evidence as stated in the narrative, but factors such as uncertain statements and emotional expressions can influence the decision making of the jurors in these studies. We have seen here that individual differences of the jurors also play a role (Kuhn, in press), among them gender. This factor may produce differences in types of processing, with more specific heuristic processing or more comprehensive processing representing extremes of a range of many differences.

## ACKNOWLEDGMENT

We thank Deanna Kuhn, Jennifer Wiley, and Ronan Bernas for their helpful comments.

## REFERENCES

Chaiken, S. (1980). Heuristic versus systematic information processing and the use of source versus message cues in persuasion. *Journal of Personality and Social Psychology, 39,* 752–766.

Foucault, M. (1972). *The archeology of knowledge* (A. Sheridan Smith, Trans.). New York: Pantheon. (Original work published 1969)

Gernsbacher, M. A., Hallada, B. M., & Robertson, R. W. (1998). How automatically do readers infer fictional characters' emotional states? *Scientific Studies of Reading, 2,* 271–300.

Klettke, B., & Graesser, A. C. (2000, July). *Coherence and evidence in testimony evaluation in incest narratives.* Paper presented at the 10th annual meeting of the Society for Text and Discourse, Lyon, France.

Kuhn, D. (2001). How do people know? *Psychological Science, 12*(1), 1–8.

Leinhardt, G., Stainton, C., Virji, S. M., & Odoroff, E. (1994). Learning to reason in history: Mindlessness to mindfulness. In M. Carretero & J. F. Voss (Eds.), *Cognitive and instructional processes in history and the social sciences* (pp. 131–158). Hillsdale, NJ: Lawrence Erlbaum Associates, Inc.

Mandler, J. M., & Johnson, N. S. (1977). Remembrance of things parsed: Story structure and recall. *Cognitive Psychology, 9,* 111–151.

Meyers-Levy, J. (1989). Gender differences in information processing: A selectivity interpretation. In P. Cafferata & A. M. Tybout (Eds.), *Cognitive and affective responses to advertising* (pp. 219–260). Lexington, MA: Heath.

Pennington, N., & Hastie, R. (1993). The story model for juror decision making. In R. Hastie (Ed.), *Inside the juror: The psychology of juror decision making* (pp. 192–221). Cambridge, England: Cambridge University Press.

Petty, R. E., & Cacioppo, J. T. (1986). The elaboration likelihood model of persuasion. In L. Berkowitz (Ed.), *Advances in experimental social psychology* (Vol. 19, pp. 123–205). New York: Academic.

Schum, D. A. (1993). Argument structuring and evidence evaluation. In R. Hastie (Ed.), *Inside the juror: The psychology of juror decision making* (pp. 175–191). Cambridge, England: Cambridge University Press.

Trabasso, T., van den Broek, P., & Suh, S. (1989). Logical necessity and transitivity of causal relations in stories. *Discourse Processes, 12,* 1–25.

van Eemeren, F. H., Grootendorst, R., & Snoecle Henkemans, F. (1996). *Fundamentals of argumentation theory.* Mahwah, NJ: Lawrence Erlbaum Associates, Inc.

Voss, J. F., Greene, T. R., Post, T. A., & Penner, B. C. (1983). Problem solving skill in the social sciences. In G. H. Bower (Ed.), *The psychology of learning and motivation: Advances in research theory* (Vol. 17, pp. 165–213). New York: Academic Press.

Voss, J. F., Wiley, J., & Sandak, R. (1999). On the use of narrative as argument. In S. R. Goldman, A. C. Graesser, & P. van den Broek (Eds.), *Narrative, comprehension, causality, and coherence: Essays in honor of Tom Trabasso* (pp. 235–252). Mahwah, NJ: Lawrence Erlbaum Associates, Inc.

Wigmore, J. H. (1937). *The science of judicial proof as given by logic, psychology, and general experience, and illustrated in judicial trials* (3rd ed.). Boston: Little, Brown.

# APPENDIX A
# BASELINE, STORY 2

## Prosecutor's Statement

Paul Ryan and Rob Brown drove to DuBois together in Rob's truck. For years they had driven there on the first Saturday of deer season. They had packed the truck on Friday night so they could get an early start. Rob had looked forward to this hunt for the entire year. This time, however, Rob Brown was shot and killed by Paul Ryan. According to Paul, Rob was walking through the woods about 40 yards away when Paul saw the head and antlers of a deer to his right. He raised his gun, aiming at the deer, and fired. He claims that, being a poor shot, his shot missed the deer, but that he saw something else fall. He said he ran to see what he had hit, and found Rob lying in the grass, dead.

Paul says that he immediately went to a nearby cabin where he contacted the police. He claims that this was all a terrible accident. However, the police investigation concluded that, while there were deer tracks in the area where Paul and

Rob had been walking, the area had only a few trees and a little brush and thicket, and that Rob was quite likely fully visible to Paul. Furthermore, during the investigation, Paul's wife, Rachel, testified that she and Rob had been having an affair for over a year and a half. Mary Jacoby, a friend of Rachel Ryan's, testified that she, Mary, had thought there was an affair and had told Paul about her suspicions just prior to the hunting trip. Since Paul had just discovered that Rob had been having an affair with his wife, he had a motive. Furthermore, since the police have established that Paul was quite likely able to see Rob when he was shot, the death of Rob Brown was a premeditated murder and not a freak accident. Paul should be found guilty of first-degree murder.

### Experiment 1: Evidence Manipulations

1) ... (the area had only a few trees and a little brush ... Rob was quite likely fully visible to Paul → ... the area had a number of trees and quite a bit of brush ... making it difficult for Paul to see Rob; 2) Rachel testified that she and Rob had been having an affair for over a year → Rachel testified that before she and Paul were married, she and Rob went together for over a year; 3) Mary had thought there was an affair and had told Paul about her suspicions → Mary had known about Rachel and Rob going together before Rachel's marriage to Paul; 4) Since Paul had just discovered that Rob had been having an affair with his wife, he had a motive. → Since Rob had gone with Rachel some years ago, Paul had a motive to shoot Rob; 5) the police have established that Paul was quite likely able to see Rob → the police could not establish that Paul was able to see Rob.

### Experiment 2A: Uncertain Information Manipulations

1) ... and that Rob was quite likely fully visible to Paul. → ... and that Rob could have been fully visible to Paul; 2) ... Rob had been having an affair for over a year and a half. → ... Rob had been having sort of an affair for over a year and a half; 3) Since Paul had just discovered that Rob had been having an affair ... → Since Paul had just discovered that Rob probably had been having an affair ...; 4) ... he had a motive. → he also may have had a motive; 5) ... the police have established that Paul was quite likely able to see Rob when he was shot ... → ... the police have established that Paul might have seen Rob when he was shot. ...

### Experiment 2A: Emotion Manipulations

1) This time, however, Rob Brown was shot and killed ... → This time, however, Rob Brown was brutally and mercilessly shot and killed ...; 2) ... but that he saw something else fall. → ... but that he saw something else fall violently to the ground; 3) ... Rob lying in the grass, dead. → ... Rob lying in the grass, dead, his blood splattered all over the woods; 4) ... she and Rob had been having an affair

for over a year ... → ... she and Rob had been having a steamy, illicit love affair for over a year ... ; 5) ... the police have established that Paul was quite likely able to see Rob when he was shot ... → ... the police have established that Paul was able to see Rob, his innocent and unsuspecting target, when he was shot ...

### Experiment 2B: Uncertain Information Manipulations

1) Paul Ryan and Rob Brown drove to ... → Paul Ryan and Rob Brown usually drove to ... ; 2) ... drove to Dubois together ... → drove to Dubois or some other place together ... ; 3) ... together in Rob's truck. → together in Rob's truck or possibly Paul's car; 4) ... there on the first Saturday of deer season. → ... there on the first Saturday or at least sometime during deer season; 5) They had packed the truck on Friday ... → They had probably packed the truck on Friday. ...

### Experiment 2B: Emotion Manipulations

1) ... there on the first Saturday of deer season. → ... there on the first Saturday of deer season, always having a good time laughing at Rob's jokes; 2) They had packed the truck ... → Excited about the hunt, Rob suggested they pack the truck ... ; 3) Rob had looked forward to this hunt ... → Rob had enthusiastically looked forward to this hunt ... ; 4) ... to this hunt for the entire year. → ... to this hunt with his best friend for the entire year; 5) According to Paul, Rob was walking through the woods ... → According to Paul, alert and cautious, Rob was walking through the woods. ...

# APPENDIX B
## BASELINE, STORY 3

### Prosecutor's Statement

The victim, Roger Wilson, was hit by a baseball bat and died. This is how the crime took place. Roger Wilson had dropped off his co-worker, Susan Walker, at her home. He then drove down Crawford Road in order to get onto the freeway. As he was driving, he saw a small girl run out from behind a parked car. Before he could stop, his right fender hit her and she fell to the ground. Roger quickly got out of his car and checked to see if the girl was seriously hurt. She was not. Roger turned to call the police, but a group of teenagers began to push him around. Then one of the teenagers took a baseball bat and hit Roger with it. Roger fell over and died.

A few minutes later police arrived on the scene and interviewed those present. A person living across the street had witnessed the events, but she could not identify who struck Roger. Then the police discovered a blood-covered bat in the rear seat of a car parked nearby. The car belonged to Matthew Moran, the older brother of the girl that Roger had hit. Later analyses revealed that the blood was that of the victim and that the victim's hair was also on the bat. The bat also had fingerprints on it, but the fingerprints were smudged and could not be identified as those of Matthew Moran. Matthew claims someone else threw the bat into his car through the open window, but the police didn't mention an open window in their report. We have also learned that Matthew often became angry when he felt someone was mistreating his little sister. This served as the motive to hit the victim.

The evidence therefore indicates that Matthew Moran used the bat to kill Roger Wilson. He had the motive, the means, and the opportunity.

### Experiment 1: Evidence Manipulation

1) the blood was that of the victim ... → the blood could not be identified as that of the victim; 2) the victim's hair was also on the bat. → it was unclear whose hair was on the bat; 3) the police didn't mention an open window in their report. → police did mention in their report that the car windows were open; 4) Matthew often became angry ... → Matthew typically was a caring person and not temperamental; 5) This [his anger] served as the motive to hit the victim. → seeing his sister get hit by the car probably served as the motive to hit the victim.

### Experiment 2A: Uncertain Information Manipulation

1) Later analyses revealed that the blood was that of the victim ... → Later analyses revealed that the blood was probably that of the victim ... ; 2) ... and that the victim's hair was also on the bat. → ... and that what looked like the victim's hair was also on the bat; 3) ... fingerprints were smudged and could not be identified as those of ... → ... fingerprints were smudged and could not be identified completely as those of ... ; 4) We have also learned that Matthew often became angry ... → We have also learned that Matthew may have often became angry ... ; 5) This served as the motive to hit the victim. → ... and there is a chance this served as the motive to hit the victim.

### Experiment 2A: Emotion Manipulation

1) ... but a group of teenagers began to push him around. → ... but a mob of rowdy, yelling teenagers began to push him around; 2) ... took a baseball bat and hit Roger with it. → ... took a baseball bat and viciously struck Roger with it; 3) Roger fell over and died. → Roger fell over, his face getting covered with blood as he collapsed, and died; 4) A person living across the street had witnessed the events ... → A person living across the street had witnessed the brutal and disturbing events ... ; 5) ... Matthew often became angry when he felt someone was

... → ... Matthew often became angry, losing his temper and becoming violent when he felt someone was. . . .

### Experiment 2B: Uncertain Information Manipulations

1) Roger Wilson had dropped off his co-worker . . . → Roger Wilson had apparently dropped off his co-worker . . . ; 2) He then drove down Crawford Road in order to get onto the freeway. → He then drove down Crawford Road, probably to get onto the highway; 3) As he was driving, he saw a small girl . . . → As he was driving, he thought he saw a small girl . . . ; 4) A few minutes later police arrived . . . → Witnesses thought it was a few minutes later when police arrived . . . ; 5) A person living across the street . . . → A person who probably lives across the street. . . .

### Experiment 2B: Emotion Manipulations

1) He then drove down Crawford Road in order to get onto the freeway. → He then drove carefully down Crawford Road in order to get onto the freeway; 2) . . . he saw a small girl run out from behind a parked car. → . . . he saw a small girl run out from behind a parked car and it frightened him; 3) Roger quickly got out of his car . . . → Shaking and perspiring, Roger quickly got out of his car . . . ; 4) . . . checked to see if the girl was seriously hurt. → . . . gently but carefully checked to see if the girl was seriously hurt; 5) Roger turned to call the police . . . → Relieved, Roger turned to call the police. . . .

## APPENDIX C
## BASELINE, STORY 4

### Prosecutor's Statement

It all began when Raymond Hammond saw his ex-wife, Myrna Ramsey, walking along the jogging trails near Bridge Street. She had just moved from Castle City. Five years earlier, Raymond had swindled a large amount of money from her when she worked at an insurance company there. Now Raymond was afraid that she would tell his current wife about these shady dealings. When he saw Myrna stop to talk to two people who were walking their dogs, Raymond approached her. Raymond told Myrna that he would kill her if she talked with his current wife Connie. He then left in a rush, crossing through the busy traffic on Forward Street.

Three days later Myrna did call Connie and arranged to meet her. Raymond was home when Myrna called and he overheard the conversation from the bedroom. He had heard where Myrna and Connie were to meet, at the Midway Restaurant, and he drove to that destination a half-hour before the appointed time. He waited in a sheltered doorway across the street from the restaurant until he saw Myrna approaching. When he saw her, he grabbed her purse, took out his gun, and shot her. He then quickly got in his car and drove away. Later, two eyewitnesses were sure that his car was the one they saw driving away from the scene. Four hours later, the police picked him up at his home. During the intervening 4 hours, Raymond Hammond attempted to get rid of the murder weapon by driving his car to the river and throwing the gun in the water. Later, the gun was recovered and identified as his. Having been at the river bottom, the gun had no fingerprints on it. Raymond claims that he had lost that gun several months before and didn't know he should report it missing. In light of the evidence presented, Raymond Hammond should be found guilty.

### Experiment 1: Evidence Manipulation

1) Raymond was home when Myrna called . . . → Raymond was not home when Myrna called; 2) . . . he drove to that destination a half-hour before the appointed time. → . . . a man resembling Raymond Hammond was seen in the area a half-hour before the appointed time; 3) two eyewitnesses were sure that his car was the one they saw driving away → two eyewitnesses indicated they saw the car but could not identify the driver; 4) During the intervening 4 hours, Raymond Hammond attempted to get rid of the murder weapon by driving his car to the river . . . → During these 4 hours, Raymond Hammond said he was having lunch and watching a movie; 5) the gun was recovered and identified as his. → a gun was recovered but its owner is not identified.

### Experiment 2B: Uncertain Information Manipulation

1) . . . walking along the jogging trails near Bridge Street. → . . . walking along the jogging trails probably near Bridge Street; 2) She had just moved from Castle City. → She may have just moved from Castle City; 3) When he saw Myrna stop to talk to two people . . . → When he saw Myrna stop, possibly to talk to two people . . . ; 4) He then left in a rush, crossing through . . . → He then left in a rush, probably crossing through . . . ; 5) Three days later Myrna did call . . . → Around 3 days later Myrna did call. . . .

### Experiment 2B: Emotion Manipulation

1) . . . walking along the jogging trails near Bridge Street. → . . . walking peacefully along the jogging trails near Bridge Street; 2) She had just moved from Castle City. → Feeling like she was starting a new life, she had just moved from Castle City; 3) . . . when she worked at an insurance company there. → When she worked at an insurance company there and she felt that she had been manipulated; 4) When he saw Myrna stop to talk to two people . . . → When he saw Myrna stop

to cheerfully talk with two people . . . ; 5) Raymond told Myrna that he would kill her . . . → Raymond told Myrna, shocked to see him, that he would kill her. . . .

## Experiment 2A: Uncertain Information Manipulation

1) . . . when Myrna called and he overheard the conversation . . . → . . . when Myrna called and he might have overheard the conversation . . . ; 2) He waited in a sheltered doorway . . . → Apparently, he waited in a sheltered doorway . . . ; 3) When he saw her . . . he took out his gun, and shot her. → When he saw her, he presumably took out his gun, and shot her; 4) Later, two eyewitnesses were sure that his car . . . → Later, two eyewitnesses were fairly sure that his car . . . ; 5) Raymond Hammond attempted to get rid of the murder weapon . . . → . . . Raymond Hammond evidently attempted to get rid of the murder weapon. . . .

## Experiment 2A: Emotion Manipulation

1) . . . at the Midway restaurant, and he drove . . . → at the Midway restaurant, and with murder in his heart he drove . . . ; 2) When he saw her . . . he took out his gun . . . → Fuming with anger when he saw her, he took out his gun . . . ; 3) He then quickly got in his car and drove away. → As she sunk to the ground in a pool of blood, he then quickly returned to his car and drove away; 4) . . . the one they saw driving away from the scene. → . . . the one they saw driving in a reckless fury away from the scene. 5) . . . the police picked him up at his home. → . . . the police picked him up at his home after he threatened to attack the officers.

# Acknowledgment of Reviewers for Volumes 31 and 32

Anne Anderson
Elisabeth Armstrong
Steve Athanases
Tom Barney
Sue Brown
Wilma Bucci
Nancy Budwig
Catherine Ann Cameron
Herbert Colston
Scotty Craig
Colette Daiute
Christine Dollaghan
Stephen Dopkins
Richard Ely
Anders Ericsson
Rebecca Fincher-Kiefer
Michelle Foster
Sue Fussell
Ronald Gallimor
Barry Gholson
Rachel Giora
Art Glenberg
Judith Green
Douglas Hacker
Maya Hickman
Gregory Hume
Jukka Hyona
Sally Jacoby
Eilene Kintsch
Bianca Klettke
Celia Klin
Helga Kotthoff
Juliet Langman

James Lantoff
Carolyn Letts
Ivan Leudar
Kristen Link
Shulan Lu
Joe Magliano
Brenda Manning
Andrew Monk
Catherine Morocco
Katherine Nelson
Ageliki Nikolopoulou
Elleen Pace Nilsen
Angela O'Donnell
Brent Olde
Tony Pellegrini
Jamie Pennebaker
Natalie Person
Victoria Pomeroy
Janie Rees-Miller
Elizabeth Robinson
Sonya Rajan
Debbie Rowe
Ted Sanders
Murial Saville-Troike
Franz Schmalhofer
Diana Sharp
Cheryl Tomoeda
Connie Varnhagen
Johannes Wagner
Marcia Walton
Shannon Whitten
Jennifer Wiley
Kai Zimmerman